OXFORD WORLD'S CLASSICS

THE OXFORD SHAKESPEARE

General Editor · Stanley Wells

The Oxford Shakespeare offers new and authoritative editions of Shakespeare's plays in which the early printings have been scrupulously re-examined and interpreted. An introductory essay provides all relevant background information together with an appraisal of critical views and of the play's effects in performance. The detailed commentaries pay particular attention to language and staging. Reprints of sources, music for songs, genealogical tables, maps, etc. are included where necessary; many of the volumes are illustrated, and all contain an index.

ALAN BRISSENDEN, the editor of *As You Like It* in the Oxford Shakespeare, is Reader in English at the University of Adelaide.

THE OXFORD SHAKESPEARE

All's Well that Ends Well
Anthony and Cleopatra
As You Like It
The Comedy of Errors
The Complete Sonnets and Poems
Coriolanus
Cymbeline
Hamlet
Henry V
Henry IV, Part 1
Henry IV, Part 2
Henry VI, Part One
Henry VI, Part Two
Henry VI, Part Three
Julius Caesar
King Henry VIII
King John
King Lear
Love's Labour's Lost
Macbeth
Measure for Measure
The Merchant of Venice
The Merry Wives of Windsor
A Midsummer Night's Dream
Much Ado About Nothing
Othello
Pericles
Richard II
Richard III
Romeo and Juliet
The Taming of the Shrew
The Tempest
Timon of Athens
Titus Andronicus
Troilus and Cressida
Twelfth Night
The Two Gentlemen of Verona
The Two Noble Kinsmen
The Winter's Tale

OXFORD WORLD'S CLASSICS

WILLIAM SHAKESPEARE

As You Like It

Edited by

ALAN BRISSENDEN

OXFORD
UNIVERSITY PRESS

Great Clarendon Street, Oxford OX2 6DP

Oxford University Press is a department of the University of Oxford.
It furthers the University's objective of excellence in research, scholarship,
and education by publishing worldwide in

Oxford New York

Athens Auckland Bangkok Bogotá Buenos Aires Calcutta
Cape Town Chennai Dar es Salaam Delhi Florence Hong Kong Istanbul
Karachi Kuala Lumpur Madrid Melbourne Mexico City Mumbai
Nairobi Paris São Paulo Shanghai Singapore Taipei Tokyo Toronto Warsaw
with associated companies in Berlin Ibadan

Oxford is a registered trade mark of Oxford University Press
in the UK and in certain other countries

Published in the United States
by Oxford University Press Inc., New York

First published by the Clarendon Press 1993
First published as a World's Classics paperback 1994
Reissued as an Oxford World's Classics paperback 1998
Reissued 2008

British Library Cataloguing in Publication Data
Data available

Library of Congress Cataloging in Publication Data
Shakespeare, William, 1564–1616.
As you like it / edited by Alan Brissenden.
p. cm.—(Oxford world's classics)
Includes index.
I. Brissenden, Alan. II. Title. III. Series.
822.3'3—dc20 PR2803.A2B7 1994 93–25742

ISBN 978–0–19–953615–3

8

Printed in Great Britain by
Clays Ltd, St Ives plc

PREFACE

ALL editors of Shakespeare are indebted to their predecessors. An editor of *As You Like It* is above all indebted to Richard Knowles for his magisterial Variorum edition of 1977. My acknowledgements in the text are a small indication of the pervasive use I have made of his work. The officers of the several libraries in which I have worked have been invariably helpful, and I am particularly grateful to Liz Lee, Susan Woodburn and Cheryl Hoskin at the Barr Smith Library in the University of Adelaide, Valmai Hankel and Jenny Tonkin in the State Library of South Australia, the assistants in the Bodleian Library and the English Faculty in Oxford, Marian Pringle at the Shakespeare Centre Library, Stratford-upon-Avon, Niki Rathbone at the Birmingham Shakespeare Library, the staff of the Wolanski Library at the Sydney Opera House, and James Fowler of the Victoria and Albert Theatre Museum.

One of the many joys of working on a play is that it brings one into closer contact with the theatre itself. I learned much through conversation and correspondence with several people, especially John Bell, Tony Church, Leo McKern, Fiona Shaw and the late Dame Peggy Ashcroft. Ron Haddrick kindly lent me his prompt copy of the 1957 Stratford production, and John Burgess sent me reviews and a prompt copy of the National Theatre's in 1979. Colin Leslie of BBC Television provided essential information, and Wendy Humm arranged for me to see a videotape. Assisting with the Adelaide University Theatre Guild's production in 1988 helped me try out ideas and discover unsuspected nuances of meaning in the play.

It is always heartening to receive willing replies to queries by letter, particularly when those replying include Michael Billington, Adrian Colman, R. W. Dent, Ian Donaldson, Andrew Gurr, Michael Metcalf, F. W. Sternfeld, the late J. C. Trewin, Wendy Trewin, and David Wiles. Stephen Orgel not only wrote, but also very generously sent me the drafts of two essays.

My colleagues, students and friends have been forbearing and patient in allowing me to talk so persistently about the play (some were foolhardy enough to encourage conversation on the topic). For discussions and help of other kinds I am particularly grateful to Hugo and Mary Rose Brunner, Barbara Everett, Emrys Jones and Julian Roberts, in Oxford; to Robert Smallwood and Russell Jackson in Stratford; and in Adelaide to Penny Boumelha, Tom Burton, Charles Edelman, Martin Holt, Kevin Magarey, Paul Skrebels, Jeff Tomlinson, Michael Tyler and George Turner. Reg Foakes, on a visit, helped me refine my ideas at a critical time. Tim Mares read through my manuscript, made invaluable comments and saved me from folly on several occasions. Robin Eaden, who also read the manuscript, contributed indispensably by her research skills, good sense and advice, and prepared the index.

For deciphering foul papers and wrestling with my inept word processing, I thank and admire Shirley Bowbridge and particularly Marie Cominetti.

Research for this edition was begun during a period of study leave, spent mainly in Oxford, from the University of Adelaide, which also provided a grant-in-aid, which I thankfully acknowledge. I am grateful also to the Wolfson College, Oxford, for electing me a Visiting Fellow in 1987 and 1992, so making my time there more productive.

Stanley Wells is a model for all general editors. His patience, skill and knowledge are beyond praise. From Oxford University Press Frances Whistler sent photocopies, faxes, and support, and at Halesowen Christine Buckley, with experienced and expert judgement, helped the manuscript to its final shape.

Members of my family have all contributed, in differing ways, to this edition, Roger and Debbie, a helpful American link in Boston, and in Adelaide Piers and Kerry, Celia, who cast a critical student eye over its progress, and especially my wife Libby, sustainer, encourager and friend.

ALAN BRISSENDEN
Adelaide and Oxford

CONTENTS

LIST OF ILLUSTRATIONS

The editor and publisher have made all efforts to trace the owners of copyright in illustrations, and apologize where these efforts have not been successful.

INTRODUCTION

In the eighteenth century Samuel Johnson declared, 'Of this play the fable is wild and pleasing'. In the twentieth Helen Gardner proclaimed it 'the last play in the world to be solemn over'.[1] *As You Like It* is certainly the most light-hearted of Shakespeare's comedies, though it has its complexities. It also has in Rosalind the longest of all his female roles, and in the lines beginning 'All the world's a stage' one of his two best-known speeches.

The Play's Date

The play has been delighting audiences ever since its first known performance in 1740. Even though no record of any earlier production has yet been discovered, we can be sure that it was written 140 years earlier, by the middle of 1600; and we have this information because at that time English printers needed to enter the names of any books they wished to print in the Register of the Stationers' Company, which acted to protect the makers and sellers of books. Intriguingly, a preliminary leaf of Book C of the Register has a list of plays entered to the Lord Chamberlain's Men, the theatre company to which Shakespeare belonged:

4 Augusti
As yo^{w} like yt: / a booke
Henry the ffift: / a booke
Euery man in his Humo^{r}. / a booke } to be staied
The cōmedie of muche
A doo about nothinge. / a booke

This is clearly not a regular entry; not only is it written on a fly-leaf, but it does not include the name of the stationer and a record of the fee paid, as normal entries do, nor is it assigned a year. However, 1600 is universally accepted because an immediately preceding note includes the date '27 may 1600', and *Henry V* and *Every Man in His Humour* were formally entered in the body of the Register on 14 August 1600, with *Much Ado*

[1] Johnson (1989), p. 180; Gardner, '*As You Like It*' in *More Talking of Shakespeare*, ed. John Garrett (1959), p. 17.

About Nothing apparently added nine days later. But there was no formal entry for *As You Like It*.

The significance of 'to be staied'—that is, the registration or licensing for printing of these plays was to be delayed, or perhaps stopped—is puzzling, and has been much discussed. The two most popular explanations are first, that the players, or their patron the Lord Chamberlain, or even the playwright himself, wanted to forestall piracy—someone printing unauthorized versions of the plays; second, that the note, which is unusual, was a reminder that the formal entry on the Register proper was to be held over for a while, rather than publication prevented altogether. As Richard Knowles[2] points out, if the players wished to raise cash, they could sell some of their most popular plays and, to ensure their profits, give notice of their intention to sell them to a printer.

Henry V, *Every Man in His Humour* and *Much Ado About Nothing* were all in print within twelve months but *As You Like It* did not appear until 1623, in the first folio edition of Shakespeare's plays. Why the staying order was applied and why alone of the four *As You Like It* remained unprinted for so long are further mysteries still needing solution. E. K. Chambers suggests that the play was 'effectively suppressed'[3] by the Chamberlain's Men themselves, to prevent piracy. John Dover Wilson is among those who believe that they wanted to prevent publication because the play was a popular success[4]—a view difficult to sustain in the absence of any contemporary allusion to it.

The 'staying order' can also be viewed in the context of a decree issued by the Archbishop of Canterbury and the Bishop of London on 1 June 1599, to the Master and wardens of the Stationers' Company. This decree prohibited the printing of satires and epigrams, named some to be burnt and ordered that no new plays were to be printed 'except they be allowed by such as have authority'[5]—that is, men, mostly clerics, appointed by the Archbishop and other bishops as 'correctors'. The Chamberlain's Men might not have been given permission to print, even had they so wished.

[2] Knowles, p. 362.
[3] Chambers (1923), iii. 191.
[4] Wilson, p. 93.
[5] Chambers (1923), iii. 169n.

There is room for a little speculation on a possible reason. As well as being a sensitive time for satire, the years 1599–1600 were politically nervous with regard to the Earl of Essex, who had taken a force to Ireland in July 1599 to fight the Earl of Tyrone. One of Essex's captains of horse was John Harington, Queen Elizabeth's godson, who was in disfavour at court that year; he was, moreover, one of the fifty-nine new knights created by the Earl during the Irish campaign. When the newly-dubbed Sir John returned to court to report on the Irish situation, the Queen, furious, sent him packing. Harington had previously aroused the royal displeasure in 1596, with the publication of *The Metamorphosis of Ajax*, his satirical discourse on his recent invention, the water closet. This witty and practical pamphlet rapidly had three editions; it also earned him the nickname 'Ajax',[6] with the available pun on 'jakes', also spelt 'jaques',[7] an Elizabethan word for a lavatory. Among the books the bishops ordered to be burnt were two scatological satires by John Marston. Now whether or not Shakespeare intended his melancholy character Jaques in *As You Like It* to refer to Harington (who was not melancholy—the Queen called him 'the merry poet my godson'), an official, a 'corrector' acting under terms of the bishops' decree, could have considered that it did, and suppressed the play on four counts: first, the name Jaques itself, with its lavatorial/Harington associations; second, the fact that Harington was the Queen's godson; third, the satirical qualities of the role; fourth, the relationship of Harington with the Earl of Essex, who was out of favour with the Queen even before he went to Ireland. On his unexpected return in September Essex was taken into custody, and not released until the next August.[8] It is to be noted that when the Quarto of *Henry V*, which had been stayed, was printed

[6] Nashe, for example, makes pointed references (Nashe, iii. 177; v. 195), and John Chamberlain writes at least twice of 'Sir Ajax Harington' (*Letters of John Chamberlain*, ed. Norman E. McClure (Philadelphia, 1939), Memoirs of the American Philosophical Society, XII, Pt. I, pp. 84, 397).

[7] As it is in *The Historie of King Lear* (1608), sig. E1^v.

[8] That public figures were presented or alluded to in plays is clear from an impassioned letter of Essex to the Queen during this time (12 May 1600) in which he says, 'The prating tavern haunter speaks of me what he lists; the frantic libeller writes of me what he lists; they print me and make me speak to the world, and shortly they will play me upon the stage', *Calendar of State Papers, Domestic Series, Elizabeth, 1598–1601* (Nendeln, 1967), CCLXXIV, p. 435. Compare Cleopatra: 'I shall see | Some squeaking Cleopatra boy my greatness | I'th' posture of a whore' (*Antony* 5.2.215–17).

in 1600 it was without the choruses, which include lines referring favourably to Essex.[9] These could be omitted from the text without structural damage; to remove Jaques without injuring the fabric of *As You Like It* would be virtually impossible, and so, it can be argued, it remained unpublished at that time.

The play is not mentioned in Frances Meres's book of moral thoughts, *Palladis Tamia* (entered on the Stationers' Register 7 September 1598), which towards the end contains a list of current English authors including Shakespeare, 'the most excellent in both kinds for the stage', the 'kinds' being comedy and tragedy. The Shakespearian comedies listed by Meres are 'his *Gentlemen of Verona*, his *Errors*, his *Love Labour's Lost*, his *Love Labour's Won*, his *Midsummer Night's Dream*, and his *Merchant of Venice*'.[10] Because a play is not in Meres's list is no proof that it did not exist, but *Much Ado* is not there either, and it is usually held that that play was written late in 1598. The suggestion that *As You Like It* is the lost play *Love's Labour's Won* under another name has won little acceptance, nor has John Dover Wilson's theory that it is a revision of an earlier version of about 1593.[11]

Another clue to the date of composition is offered by the pages' song in 5.3, 'It was a lover and his lass', which was printed in Thomas Morley's *First Book of Airs* in 1600, with slightly different verse order and some verbal variation. It has been suggested that Morley prepared the *Book of Airs* in either 1600, or, more probably, 1599, as he says in his introduction that the songs were 'made this vacation time' (sig. A2^{r}), that is probably during the period June–September. As the book was not entered on the Stationers' Register, no precise date for it is available, and it is impossible to say whether song or play came first, or even whether Shakespeare wrote the words. Arguments vary between those suggesting that Shakespeare and Morley collaborated on the song and those suggesting it was by neither, but 'indebted

[9] This and other relevant issues are discussed by Janet Clare in '*Art made tongue-tied by authority*' (Manchester, 1990), Ch. 2. See also Gary Taylor's comments in his edition of *Henry V* (Oxford, 1982), esp. pp. 4–6, 20–1. In '"Like the old Robin Hood": *As You Like It* and the Enclosure Riots' (*SQ*, 43 (1992), pp. 1–19), Richard Wilson links the play with another sensitive issue, the protest of forest rioters against enclosures.

[10] *Palladis Tamia*, ed. D. C. Allen (New York, 1938), p. 282.

[11] Wilson, p. 103. In the 1948 reprint of his 1926 edition, Wilson somewhat withdraws his earlier claims.

to popular tradition'.[12] Whatever the case, the song is extraordinarily apt for the point in the play where it occurs, though admittedly the verse order of the *Book of Airs*, which has been accepted since Samuel Johnson used it in 1765, is more appropriate to that specific point than the verse order of the Folio itself.

As You Like It sits comfortably with a group of Shakespeare's comedies which explore the nature of love: *A Midsummer Night's Dream* (1595–6), *The Merchant of Venice* (1596–8), *Much Ado About Nothing* (1598) and *Twelfth Night* (1601–2). As well, pastoral stories, poems and plays were at a height of popularity in the late 1590s, and the Lord Chamberlain's Men would have only been financially sensible to have their chief dramatist provide them with a play to compete with those of other companies.[13] By 1599 they may already have had the greatly popular *Mucedorus* in their repertoire. With a hero and plot derived from Sidney's *Arcadia*, this fantastic romance had been first printed in 1598, and an edition of 1610, 'Amplified with new additions', names Shakespeare's company, since 1603 the King's Men, as its actors. *The Thracian Wonder*, which dramatizes Robert Greene's pastoral novel *Menaphon*, also dates from about 1600, and *The Maid's Metamorphosis*, acted by the boys' company of St Paul's, who were perhaps the 'little eyases' mentioned by Rosencrantz in *Hamlet* (2.2.340), was printed in that year.

The evidence suggests, then, 1599–1600 as the time of the play's completion.

The Source

In 1765 Johnson proposed, without naming it, that 'a little pamphlet' was the source for *As You Like It*; two years later Richard Farmer, without mentioning Johnson, declared that 'the old Bard' had used 'Lodge's *Rosalynd* or *Eupheus* [sic] *Golden Legacye*, 4to. 1590'.[14] *Rosalynde* is a pastoral romance written by Thomas Lodge during a sea voyage to the Canary Islands during 1586–7 and published in 1590. Its subtitle, *Euphues Golden Leg-*

[12] Ernest Brennecke, Jnr, 'Shakespeare's Musical Collaboration with Morley', *PMLA*, 54 (1939), 139–49; F. W. Sternfeld, in a private letter (8 Sept. 1990).

[13] Andrew Gurr has illuminated this issue with regard to other plays in 'Intertextuality at Windsor', *SQ*, 38 (1987), 189–200.

[14] *An Essay on the Learning of Shakespeare*, 3rd edn. (1789), pp. 23–4.

acy, indicates the kind of prose that readers could expect, since John Lyly's *Euphues: The Anatomy of Wit* (1578) had given the name 'euphuism' to the distinctively balanced, antithetical style in which it was composed, and which had considerable vogue in both writing and court conversation for over a decade. Lodge's style is less rigidly mannered than that of either his model Lyly or his friend Robert Greene, who wrote several euphuistic novels.[15] *Rosalynde* was popular. There were further editions in 1592, 1596, and 1598, and seven more from 1604 to 1642. There is no evidence to support Edmund Gosse's claim that this success was 'Probably on account of the use made of it by Shakespeare'.[16] Lodge dedicated his little book to the Lord Chamberlain, Lord Hunsdon, whose son, the second Lord Hunsdon, succeeded him in the post; as both were patrons of Shakespeare's company, it is pleasant to think, though unprovable, that either may have brought the book to Shakespeare's attention. But its popularity may have as easily recommended it to him. With *As You Like It*, as with *Romeo and Juliet*, he was dramatizing a well-known, well-liked piece of romantic fiction.

Lodge begins his story with the deathbed legacy of Sir John of Bordeaux, who bequeaths the greatest share of his estate to his third and youngest son, Rosader. This favouritism rankles so with the eldest, Saladyne, that he keeps Rosader in 'servile subjection, as if he had been the son of any country vassal' (5^r); he also decides that as their second brother, Fernandyne, 'is a scholar, and hath no mind but on Aristotle . . . if he have learning it is enough' (5^r). After enduring the situation for two or three years, Rosader, now a young man with a beard coming, rebels; Saladyne sets his men on him, but he drives them off with a rake and pursues Saladyne himself, who is able to persuade him to a reconciliation. The evil brother is merely biding his time, however, and when Torismond, who has usurped the throne of France from the king, Gerismond, holds a day of wrestling and tournament, Saladyne bribes a Norman wrestler to kill Rosader,

[15] The suggestion that Greene may have helped in revising *Rosalynde* and having it published was made by H. C. Hart in *Notes and Queries* (10 Sept., 5 (1906), pp. 202–3) and discussed by Paula Burnett in her Oxford B.Litt. dissertation, 'Thomas Lodge: *Rosalynde*. A critical edition' (1968), pp. v and clx.

[16] *The Complete Works of Thomas Lodge*, ed. Edmund Gosse, 4 vols. (New York, 1963; repr. of 1883 edn.), i. 'Bibliographical Index', p. 5. Folio numbers from vol. i of this edition are given for all subsequent quotations from *Rosalynde*.

whom he then incites to enter the contests by saying he can best uphold the family name. Inspired by the 'heavenly and divine' (12[r]) Rosalynde, the daughter of the exiled Gerismond and companion to Torismond's daughter, Alinda, Rosader kills the Norman; but Torismond is delighted to discover that the victor is the son of Sir John of Bordeaux. Rosalynde, 'whom the beauty and valour of Rosader had already touched' (9[r]), sends him a jewel from her neck and he replies with a quickly-penned ten-line sonnet in the best Petrarchan clichés. Returning home to discover that Saladyne has barred the door, he kicks it down and rushes in with drawn sword, only to find nobody but the old English servant, Adam Spencer, who soon effects another reconciliation between the brothers; Saladyne, however, is again only 'concealing a poisoned hate in a peaceable countenance'(10[r]).

Meanwhile, Torismond, fearful that the beautiful Rosalynde will marry and her husband seize the throne in her right, banishes her, telling her to find her father in the forest of Arden. When Alinda makes an impassioned plea for her friend, he banishes her too. She cheerfully comforts Rosalynde, saying she will be a 'faithful copartner of all [her] misfortunes' (13[v]) and that they can be 'fellow mates in poverty' (14[r]). They decide to flee in disguise, Alinda becoming Aliena, a woman 'homely in attire', and Rosalynde, being taller, her page, Ganymede. Arrived at the forest side, they find passionate verses carved in the bark of trees, and an old shepherd, Coridon, comforting a lovelorn young shepherd, Montanus. Aliena buys the cottage and flocks of Coridon's master, and she and Ganymede become happy shepherds.

Rosader is meanwhile escaping with Adam Spencer's help from the sadistic brutality of Saladyne, killing some of his brother's villainous friends on the way; he and Adam even break through the Sheriff and his men, brought in as reinforcements, and reach the forest of Arden, 'thinking . . . to get to Lyons' (23[v])—an indication of place which has significance for the idea of locality in *As You Like It*, which is discussed below (pp. 39–41). When both are nearly dead from hunger, Rosader goes in search of food and comes on the exiled King Gerismond celebrating his birthday with his 'lusty crew of outlaws' (24[v]); the fugitives are welcomed and their lives saved. Saladyne, on the other hand, is thrown in prison by Torismond, who seizes his lands; but this gives him opportunity to repent his wrongs against Rosader, and when

Torismond banishes him he determines to seek his brother, who by this time is wandering in Arden as a forester, carving on trees sonnets to Rosalynde, one of which is discovered by Aliena and Ganymede. When Rosader meets them he reads them another, and after he leaves, Aliena teases her friend, who then passionately examines her own heart and finds love there.

The next day, after Rosader has read out three more sonnets, Ganymede suggests the versifying swain should woo 'him' as if 'he' were Rosalynde (though there is no suggestion that this in any way should be a cure for lovesickness); their wooing, in the form of a verse dialogue, leads to a mock marriage suggested by Aliena, 'Rosader full little thinking he had wooed and won his Rosalynde' (37^r).

Now banished from Bordeaux, Saladyne wanders through Arden (also hoping to get to Lyons), where Rosader discovers him asleep, and about to be attacked by a lion. After struggling with his conscience, Rosader kills the beast, and the awakened Saladyne, not recognizing his rescuer, pours out his remorse. Rosader reveals himself, takes his repentant brother to Gerismond, and then spends a few days showing him around the forest, causing Ganymede much anxiety—though when he at last arrives again, it is Aliena who scolds him. And it is Aliena's beauty that leads to an attack on her and her page by a band of forest robbers, who hope to gain a pardon by presenting her to King Torismond, 'a great lecher' (42^v) (and, unknown to them, her father). The attack is defeated by Rosader with the help of Saladyne, who happens to be passing, and who falls in love with Aliena on the spot.

The next day Coridon brings Ganymede and Aliena to where the disdainful Phoebe is being wooed (in English and French) by Montanus; Ganymede berates the hard-hearted shepherdess, who then promptly falls in love with the page; when Phoebe returns home she becomes sick, takes to her bed and sends a letter with a sonnetto (based on Petrarch's *Rime* 189) to Ganymede, who comes and tells her she should 'with the love of Montanus quench the remembrance of Ganymede' (58^r). The infatuated shepherdess agrees she will love her suitor if reason can end her love for the page. Saladyne and Aliena meanwhile are planning to marry in a few days, and Ganymede promises the downcast Rosader that he will be able to marry Rosalynde, who will be made to appear through the mystical art of a friend of Ganymede's who is 'deeply experienced in necromancy and magic' (59[r]).

Preparations are made for the weddings, to which come the forest shepherds, the exiled lords and Gerismond, who is reminded of his daughter Rosalynde by Ganymede's features; the page then goes off and returns as Rosalynde indeed. She gives herself to her amazed father, who joyfully hands her in marriage to Rosader; Phoebe is now happy enough to accept Montanus and only Saladyne is downcast, until Aliena tells him she is in fact the princess Alinda. The three marriages are solemnized in a conveniently nearby church and at the feast which follows Coridon entertains the company with a song (which imitates Perigot's in the August Eclogue of Spenser's *Shepheardes Calender*). Suddenly Fernandyne, the second son of Sir John of Bordeaux, appears with news that the twelve peers of France are about to fight in Gerismond's defence against Torismond. The King and the three brothers arm themselves, join the peers and defeat Torismond, who is slain, and then continue on to Paris, where Gerismond resumes his throne and all ends happily.

A final paragraph points the moral lessons which are the 'golden legacy' that Euphues, the teller of the tale, leaves to the children of his friend Philautus: the need for filial obedience, brotherly concord and virtuous action, and the recognition that younger brothers may be superior in integrity to their seniors. The second and subsequent editions of the novel contain 'The Schedule annexed to Euphues' Testament', in which the writer says the sons of Philautus will find not only moral lessons, but 'love anatomized' [A4[r]]. Shakespeare concentrates the moralizing into one character, and makes the anatomy of love a main subject of his play.

Lodge based the story of the sons of Sir John of Bordeaux on the more boisterous *Tale of Gamelyn*, a mid fourteenth-century narrative poem found in twenty-five manuscripts of Chaucer's *Canterbury Tales*. It was not printed in any early editions of Chaucer, and since Thomas Tyrwhitt's edition of the *Tales* (1775–89), it has not been considered as being by Chaucer. In one extant manuscript only (Cambridge MS Ii.3.26) is the father of the three sons called Sir John of Bordeaux. Among the narrative elements that Lodge found in the *Tale* are the subjection of the youngest brother by the eldest, the wrestling match, the violence of the fraternal conflict, the faithful servant Adam, and the flight to the forest. To these he added the French setting, the story of the usurper and the banished king, the pastoral ethos and the love stories, which proceed by a series of prose meditations and dialogues, eclogues, sonnets, and other verses.

Shakespeare takes the basic story, discards most of the physical violence, and introduces more family relationships and extra characters, including another pair of lovers, Touchstone the clown and the country wench Audrey. Lodge's pastoral discourse of love becomes Shakespeare's anatomy of love and material for high comedy; its conventional moralizing is transmuted and satirized in the introduced character Jaques. The violence which Lodge softened from the *Tale of Gamelyn* is reduced further by Shakespeare—there are no deaths in *As You Like It*—and bloody conflict is replaced with benign, spiritual transformations. By rearranging incidents, Shakespeare tightens movement, gives more plausibility, and strengthens elements of character and action. The encounter between Silvius and Phoebe observed by Corin, Rosalind, and Celia (3.5) provides an example. In *Rosalynde* this occurs after Saladyne has arrived in the forest, saved Rosader and the women from the robbers, and fallen in love with Aliena. Shakespeare's rearrangement places the incident in the centre of the play to form a core of love scenes. In 3.2 Orlando's verses are discovered, he appears, and Rosalind begins her 'cure' of his love-sickness. In 3.3 Touchstone and Audrey are almost married by Sir Oliver Martext. Rosalind bewails Orlando's tardiness in 3.4 and then defends him when Celia teases her. Phoebe's rejection of Silvius, Rosalind's advice to them and Phoebe's sudden infatuation follow, in 3.5, and in the next scene, 4.1, Rosalind's manipulation of people and events reaches a height with the apparent mock marriage between Ganymede and Orlando. These five scenes, all concerned with love, and the heart of the comedy, are framed by the two shortest, the banishment of Oliver (3.1) and the hunting-chorus (4.2).

Within this group, in 3.5 Shakespeare takes his treatment of love to an extreme dimension of artificiality. Lodge's characters, setting and dialogue are all expressed through the conventional mannerisms of pastoral and the patterned rhythms, far-fetched images and classical allusions of euphuism. Rosader and Rosalynde discuss each other in just the same terms as Montanus and

Phoebe: 'I have with Apollo enamoured myself of a Daphne, not (as she) disdainful, but far more chaste than Daphne,' says Rosader (28^r); Phoebe refusing Montanus tells him 'Wert thou, Montanus, as fair as Paris, as hardy as Hector, as constant as Troilus, as loving as Leander, Phoebe could not love . . . and therefore if thou pursue me with Phoebus, I must fly with Daphne' (49^r). Orlando's classical comparisons, however, are ridiculed (3.2), and when Rosalind talks of Troilus and Leander it is to use them to mock the romantic ideal of dying for love (4.1.89–97). Rosalind and Orlando speak in prose—albeit Rosalind's is at times highly patterned prose, as Brian Vickers has shown[17]—but the exchange between Phoebe and Silvius, in which Rosalind joins, is not only itself in verse, but is introduced by a thirteen-line verse passage which ends with two rhyming couplets. The pastoral lovers are thus placed at a further remove from reality, their artificiality emphasized, and the pastoral mode they represent mocked.

They are distanced in a different way by becoming an illustration of the third of the seven ages on the stage of Jaques's world (2.7). When Corin invites Rosalind and Celia to view Silvius and Phoebe as presenting 'a pageant truly played | Between . . . true love | And . . . proud disdain' (3.4.47–9), Rosalind sees herself becoming 'a busy actor in their play' (3.4.54). She becomes, of course, not merely actor, but director as well, telling the others how to play their parts, directions which fail so far as Phoebe is concerned because the scornful shepherdess becomes as infatuated with the didactic pageboy as Silvius is with Phoebe herself. The comedy is multilayered, energized by irony: just after telling Silvius she is 'sure there is no force in eyes | That can do hurt' (3.5.26–7), Phoebe falls in love at first sight with Ganymede, who has decided to teach her a lesson.

Shakespeare again concentrates the action of his source here. In Lodge, Rosalynde's realization of Phoebe's infatuation comes only at the end of the interview, so there is no opportunity for the further rebuke and warning that Shakespeare's Rosalind gives the shepherdess; in the play the scene concludes with Phoebe's catalogue of Ganymede's attractions and her decision to send 'him' a taunting letter. This incident takes place some time later in Lodge; Phoebe is so overcome by 'the form of Ganymede in

[17] Vickers, pp. 209–11.

her mind' (54[r]) that she takes to her bed, where she recalls a similar list of his beauties and decides to write to him. As in Shakespeare, her suitor is the bearer of the letter, but in Lodge Montanus 'did perceive what passion pinched her: yet . . . became a willing messenger of his own martyrdom' (55[r]), whereas Silvius is made even more ridiculous by believing that he is carrying a letter of scorn. Montanus, learning the truth, is prepared to be love's martyr and pleads for Ganymede to accept Phoebe's love; Silvius, though Celia sympathizes with him, is berated by Rosalind for being 'a tame snake' (4.3.71) and not given a chance to say anything.

Such compression of incident and enrichment of character typify Shakespeare's treatment of Lodge's tale. By turning the unrelated Torismond and Gerismond (names borrowed by Lodge from *Il Re Torismondo* (1587), a play by Tasso) into the brother dukes, Frederick and Senior, he provides for parallel reinforcement of the Oliver–Orlando plot; he thus also makes the women cousins and so more plausibly brother and sister, as they become when disguised. In Lodge, Aliena and Ganymede are mistress and page, and throughout the story Alinda/Aliena is as much, if not more, in control of events, and has as much to say, as Rosalynde/Ganymede. Shakespeare's development of their relationship is characteristically subtle. Celia is at first dominant, and she chooses to go into exile with Rosalind at her own insistence, not, as in Lodge, because she is banished also. By making Celia defy her father in this way he makes her a strong, brave character; but once away from the court, she becomes more dependent, and subordinate to Rosalind, now Ganymede, since 'doublet and hose ought to show itself courageous to petticoat' (2.4.6–7). As the play progresses and Rosalind becomes more and more engrossed in Orlando, Celia becomes increasingly less important to her—indeed, as soon as he appears, in 3.2, Celia is left with nothing to say for the rest of the scene. When, at their next meeting, she does get the chance to speak, it is a brief comment, tart with jealousy (4.1.60–1), and she has not only to stand by and watch and listen while her cousin entices the lovesick Orlando into wooing her under false pretences, but she must succumb to Rosalind's demand that she say the vital words of the marriage ceremony over them. Celia's exasperation erupts as soon as Orlando leaves, and she accuses Rosalind, with an image drawn from a different context in Lodge, 'You have simply misused our sex in your love-prate. We must have your doublet and hose plucked over your head, and show the world what the bird hath done to her own nest' (4.1.184–7). In Lodge, the phrase occurs when Rosalynde and Alinda have just arrived in the forest and found Montanus's sonnets to Phoebe; Rosalynde as Ganymede decries the hypocrisy of women who, when 'they delight to be courted . . . freeze with disdain' and Aliena replies, 'And I pray you . . . if your robes were off, what metal are you made of that you are so satirical against women? Is it not a foul bird defiles the [*sic*] own nest?' (15^r). Shakespeare's transference of this image to its place after the intense emotionalism of the wooing and 'wedding' gives it a force which enlivens Celia's character when she has so very few lines. She is still disgruntled when she next appears, in 4.3; Rosalind, concerned only with Orlando's lateness, is completely lost to her, so that when Oliver arrives with the news of his brother's injury and his own conversion, Celia is open and available for the entry of love.[18]

As Rosalind later tells Orlando, Celia and Oliver 'no sooner met but they looked; no sooner looked but they loved' (5.2.31–3). Lodge's Alinda and Saladyne fall in love much less precipitately, after Saladyne has helped Rosader drive off the robbers. When the brothers depart, Alinda has a meditation and Rosalynde quotes Horace to her. Coridon then brings them to observe Montanus's unsuccessful courtship of the disdainful Phoebe, who is sternly spoken to by Rosalynde, and it is not until then that Saladyne appears with a sonnet he has composed during 'the previous sleepless' night. After lengthy confessions of mutual love, Alinda accepts his proposal of marriage. These events occupy twenty-two pages of Lodge's novel; the dazzling way in which Shakespeare transforms them exemplifies his whole treatment of the principal source material for *As You Like It*.

Love

Love is associated with Rosalind from the beginning, when she suggests falling in love as a game that might make her merry

[18] Some of the ideas in this section derive from a helpful conversation with Fiona Shaw, who played Celia in Adrian Noble's RSC production of *As You Like It* in 1985. A detailed interpretation of the relationship of the cousins is found in Fiona Shaw and Juliet Stevenson, 'Celia and Rosalind in *As You Like It*', in Russell Jackson and Robert Smallwood, eds., *Players of Shakespeare 2* (Cambridge, 1988), pp. 55–71.

(1.2.23), and Celia warns that she must be careful to 'love no man in good earnest', nor go so far that she cannot escape the situation without losing her honour. But, grieving for her father, Rosalind is in an emotionally receptive state when Orlando arrives to wrestle with Charles, and whereas in the first part of the scene Celia has been the initiator of dialogue, it is Rosalind who takes charge of the conversation when Orlando appears. Before and throughout the wrestling match, she makes the leading comments, and, ignoring her cousin's earlier warning, or rather, helpless against it, she begins to fall in love 'in good earnest', finally ensnaring Orlando symbolically within the circle of a necklace. The playfulness and frankness which are among the most attractive aspects of Rosalind's love are quickly apparent; she soon begins to think of Orlando as the father of her child (1.3.11), and when Celia advises her to 'hem', or cough, away the irritations in her heart, like a tickle in the chest, she punningly replies, 'I would try, if I could cry "hem" and have him' (1.3.19). But these are words of slight intensity compared with the torrent which rushes from her when Celia brings news of Orlando's arrival in the forest (3.2.211–42); when he appears, from being comically aghast at what she can do with her doublet and hose she discovers an excellent use for them as a cover for the baiting of her unawares lover. Within half a dozen lines the sly teasing has turned into a joyous sham mockery of love, lovers, and women. Under this satirical guise, Rosalind extracts from Orlando more declarations of his love for her, in a shorter time, than if he had known who she was.

To continue this wonderfully self-gratifying situation she devises the love cure. While this is Shakespeare's invention, the dialogue introducing it has several links in thought and word with Lodge. When Rosalynde and Alinda first enter the forest and discover Montanus's verse to the disdainful Phoebe, for example, Rosalynde as Ganymede says, 'You may see . . . what mad cattle you women be, whose hearts sometimes are made of adamant . . . and sometime of wax . . . they delight to be courted, and then they glory to seem coy; and when they are most desired then they freeze with disdain: and this fault is so common to the sex, that you see it painted out in the shepherd's passions, who found his mistress as froward as he was enamoured' (15^r^). After claiming that love is 'a madness', Shakespeare's Ganymede describes how 'he' cured another lovesick youth:

I set him every day to woo me. At which time would I, being but a moonish youth, grieve, be effeminate, changeable, longing and liking, proud, fantastical, apish, shallow, inconstant, full of tears, full of smiles; for every passion something, and for no passion truly anything, as boys and women are for the most part cattle of this colour . . . (3.2.388–94)

Shakespeare takes the idea of a misogynist catalogue from Lodge, adds a sly reference to the fickleness of boys,[19] and moves the whole idea into a further dimension by transferring it to the love cure. Lodge's Ganymede quickly reverts to being Rosalynde, saying to Alinda, 'put me but into a petticoat, and I will stand in defiance to the uttermost that women are courteous, constant, virtuous and what not' (15[r]); Shakespeare saves this change, transforming it to Rosalind's ecstatic outburst after Orlando has left following the mock marriage in 4.1. In Lodge, it is not till some time later, after Rosader has read out three love sonnets, that Ganymede says, 'let me see how thou canst woo: I will represent Rosalynde, and thou shalt be as thou art Rosader' (35[r]); there follows a three-page 'wooing eclogue' between the two, and the mock marriage. Lodge's heroine merely wants her man to go on confessing his love for her; Shakespeare's wants this too, but she is also testing him, challenging his wit, and, eventually, in a state of high excitement, marrying him, though he is unaware of it (4.1.112–26). Her insistence on his using the present tense—'I will' is not good enough: he 'must say, "I take thee, Rosalind, for wife"' (4.1.122–3)—indicates the steel-strong resolve beneath the bubbling disguise of the 'saucy lackey'; but the sensitive woman in love is less completely suppressed than Rosalind thinks. When Orlando says he must leave her for two hours, her 'Alas, dear love, I cannot lack thee two hours' (4.1.163) has a suddenness, a brevity and a spontaneity which contrast so markedly with the rest of her speeches in the immediate context

[19] Among the classical sources for the boy as capricious object of male desire is Virgil's second Eclogue, which was the basis for Richard Barnfield's 'The Affectionate Shepherd. Containing the Complaint of Daphnis for the Love of Ganymede' (1594). Its eroticism apparently led to gossip about Barnfield, who protested in his second book, *Cynthia* (1595), 'Some there were, that did interpret *The Affectionate Shepherd*, otherwise than (in truth) I meant, touching the subject thereof, to wit, the love of a shepherd to a boy; a fault, the which I will not excuse, because I never made' (A. H. Bullen, ed., *Some Longer Elizabethan Poems* (1903), p. 190).

that it is clear she is taken off guard, just as later when she faints on hearing from Oliver how Orlando has been wounded by the lioness (4.3.157.1). These chinks in her armour of disguise give a comical aspect to Rosalind's character which invites us to laugh at her, rather than laugh at what she is saying, or laugh with her at what she is doing; they are signals to us that even this most supremely self-aware of Shakespeare's comic heroines can momentarily lose her self-control.

Rosalind embodies Shakespeare's anatomy of love in the play. Falling in love at first sight may be foolish where Phoebe is concerned, but it is perfectly acceptable for the quartet of courtly lovers, and Rosalind is the first to fall. Sentimentalism is matter for mockery, but the ravings of Silvius nevertheless lead to Rosalind's contemplating the arrow in her own heart. She can scold the lovesick shepherd for being made a 'tame snake' by love, but she is ready enough to weep when Orlando does not come on time. She is scornful of Orlando's being late and reads him a lesson in how a lover should behave, but she herself has to learn a lesson in patience and discover, arch-manipulator though she is, that time and events, as well as her own emotions, are beyond her control. Rosalind's love also has some of the fleshly sensuality of Touchstone's, seen in her thinking of Orlando as the father of her child, and in her sexual repartee. The consummate glory of love, in Shakespeare always marriage, is Rosalind's final triumph, as, claiming magic powers, she organizes the wedding ceremony which ends the play.

To reach that end, to be a satisfying, as well as a satisfied, partner of Rosalind, Orlando needs to undergo an education—not the kind that he feels Oliver has deprived him of, for, after his unmannerly intrusion on Duke Senior and the exiled lords in 2.7, he quickly shows them he is 'inland bred', that he is gentle by nature as well as by birth. His education is to be, like that of Silvius, Phoebe, Touchstone, Audrey, and Rosalind herself, concerned with love. His desire to carve Rosalind's name on every tree is in fine romantic epic and pastoral style—the carving of their names by Medoro and Angelica in Ariosto's *Orlando Furioso* remained a well-known subject for artists for two centuries[20]—but his verses are ridiculed with bawdy parody by Touch-

[20] See Rensselaer W. Lee, *Names on Trees, Ariosto into Art* (Princeton, 1977), Chs. 4–8 (*passim*).

stone, his romantic description of his beloved gets a lewd response from Jaques, and Ganymede makes rude puns to him about cuckoldry; he is unaware of the first, his romantic idealism is proof against the second, but he is able to respond to the third, even if he loses the wit-combat. He takes on Ganymede's offer of being cured not because he wants to be cured of his love for Rosalind, but because he 'would be talking of her' (4.1.82–3). His romantic attitude is tempered only a little by his banter with Ganymede; his idea of marriage is for its lasting 'for ever and a day', and he finds Ganymede's description of wifely behaviour unlikely to apply to Rosalind. Extreme though this description is, it contains genuine warning that reality differs from the romantic ideal. What finally brings Orlando to a realistic view, however, is the maturity he gains through his decision to save Oliver, and then Oliver's falling in love, and imminent marriage. 'I can no longer live by thinking', he tells the bawdily jesting Ganymede, who then drops the banter and begins the serious business of arranging the marriages, and rebecoming Rosalind.

That Rosalind and Orlando's love, full of comic complexities, lies between the pastoral extravagances of Silvius and the earthy pragmatism of Touchstone is neatly indicated in 2.4 when the besotted shepherd goes off crying 'O Phoebe, Phoebe, Phoebe!'; Rosalind is reminded of her love, and Touchstone recalls, with a ribald innuendo, his love for the milkmaid Jane Smile. Silvius and Phoebe are an example of any number of pastoral lovers and disdainful mistresses, like Spenser's Colin Clout and his Rosalind, who 'deigns not [his] good will, but doth reprove' (*Shepheardes Calender*, 1, 63); the artificiality of their relationship is expressed not only through their language, but by the way in which Shakespeare distances them, making them actors in a pageant,[21] and Silvius the exemplar of Jaques's lover 'sighing like furnace'. Rosalind's realistic, rattling speech contrasts roughly with theirs, tumbling over the edge of verse into prose, her scolding a turbulent comic centre to the anguished pleas of Silvius and the balanced casuistries of Phoebe. In 5.2 Rosalind takes part in the litany by which Silvius explains his idea of love—a version still as extreme, idealistic, and romantic as at first—but sensible

[21] Peter Stein emphasized this aspect still further in his 1977 Berlin production by presenting the scene (3.5) as a play within the play (Schaubühne am Halleschen Ufer company).

realism takes over and she dismisses it in annoyance as 'like the howling of Irish wolves against the moon' (ll. 104–5) so that she can get on with the main business, the weddings. At the last Silvius has nothing to say, only Phoebe, who surrenders her love for Ganymede in a couplet when Rosalind appears as herself. The hieratic quality which the dialogue has now taken on can accommodate such formal artificiality, but the reality beneath the artificial expression of Silvius and Phoebe during the play is characteristically defined by Jaques when in handing out his bequests at the end he leaves to Silvius 'a long and well-deservèd bed': Silvius's pale-faced languishings have the same essential sexual basis as Rosalind's love and Touchstone's desires. The shepherd's sighing upon a midnight pillow, his holy and perfect love, are simply at the opposite end of the same scale as Touchstone's fear of cuckoldry and the fleshly need which drives him 'to take that that no man else will' (5.4.58). All the lovers are brought to marriage like 'couples . . . coming to the ark' (5.4.36), as Jaques says, an image which Alexander Leggatt pertinently remarks 'suggests both animal coupling and the working of a divine plan'.[22]

The suddenness of Celia and Oliver's mutual love has been felt by Swinburne and others to be disconcerting,[23] and both Charles Johnson in his version of the play, *Love in a Forest* (1723), and George Sand in her adaptation, *Comme il vous plaira* (1856), deprive Oliver of happiness; instead they enlarge and transform Jaques's part and reward him with Celia. But their love at first sight is in keeping with the suddenness of Oliver's 'instantaneous Pauline reversal', as Marjorie Garber calls it,[24] on being saved by Orlando, and, as has already been noticed, Celia is in a receptive state when he arrives. A good pair of actors can create an entirely believable and serious love situation which even Rosalind's comical fainting does not undermine.

Metamorphosis

Oliver's repentance is one of the play's later examples of change, of metamorphosis—that concept which is basic to theatre, which

[22] *Shakespeare's Comedy of Love* (1974), p. 214.

[23] *A Study of Shakespeare* (1880), p. 152.

[24] 'The Education of Orlando', in *Comedy from Shakespeare to Sheridan*, eds. A. R. Braunmuller and J. C. Bulman (Newark, 1986), p. 109.

fascinated Shakespeare and many of his fellow-dramatists, and which especially informs the ethos of *As You Like It*. It is obvious in the taking on of disguise by Rosalind and Celia and the sudden conversion of Duke Frederick at the edge of the forest, for instance. But it permeates the play's texture in various ways. When Duke Senior, searching for Jaques in the forest, says, 'I think he be transformed into a beast, | For I can nowhere find him like a man' (2.7.1–2), he is introducing a line of imagery continued when Orlando bursts in upon the exiles and Jaques queries, 'Of what kind should this cock come of?' (l. 90), and when Orlando, going to find Adam, sees himself as a doe seeking her faun (l. 128). Transformation of people into beasts, plants, and other things of nature was the stuff of Ovid's *Metamorphoses*, which Shakespeare knew well and drew on frequently. Touchstone refers to Ovid himself in 3.3, making a pun on 'goats' and 'Goths'—and all puns depend on transformation of meaning—while the transformation of humans into beasts through Pythagoras' theory of the transmigration of souls is matter for a witticism by Rosalind (3.2.171). In the wider world of the play, Arden is the place where Nature works its change on those who come there—some, like the exiled Duke and lords, Rosalind, Celia, and Orlando, seeking refuge, others, like Oliver and Duke Frederick, intent on evil.

These changes are not wrought simply by the forest's being the green world that Northrop Frye and C. L. Barber[25] discuss so eloquently; Rosalind insists on the element of magic. Perhaps, as Garber ingeniously suggests,[26] the magician Rosalind has conversed with since the age of three is herself, but whether that is the case or not, Hymen, god of marriage, arrives to celebrate the wedding rites, and the text does nothing to suggest that he is anything other than a god: not Amiens, or another lord, or William, or anyone else, dressed up. (If it has to be another character, then Corin would be closest to the source, as Lodge's Coridon dresses up and sings a song.) There is no reason why this should not be an early theophany, a precursor of the appearances of Jupiter in *Cymbeline* and Diana in *Pericles*. Like Paulina in *The Winter's Tale*, Rosalind emphasizes the lawfulness of her

[25] Northrop Frye, *A Natural Perspective* (1965); C. L. Barber, *Shakespeare's Festive Comedy* (Princeton, 1959).

[26] Garber, p. 111.

actions. Again like Paulina, she restores a daughter to a parent, but where Paulina's 'magic' is revealed as a benign deception, since Hermione's 'statue' which seems to come to life is in fact Hermione herself, and where even Prospero explains that the characters in his betrothal masque are 'all spirits' that melt 'into air, into thin air' (*Tempest* 4.1.149–50), there is no such explanation for Hymen.

The appearance of Hymen, Rosalind, and Celia, the marriage ritual with its rhymed verse, music and song—all contrast strongly with the comic realism of Touchstone's discourse on the lie which precedes them and the more formal, but still realistic, report of Jaques de Boys which follows. Hymen presides over the grand transformation of single men and women into husbands and wives. There are two transformations to come: one, Frederick's conversion, reported by Jaques de Boys, is within the narrative; the other, outside it, is the admission in the Epilogue that Rosalind has been played by a male actor, who modulates from his character by recalling her claim to have magic powers, saying he will 'conjure' the audience. He also uses the last 'if' in a play with more 'if's than any other play by Shakespeare.[27]

The lines beginning 'If I were a woman I would kiss as many of you as had beards that pleased me' uniquely draw attention to the fact that the part of Rosalind, like all female roles in the English theatre until 1660, was played by a male. This is the only time that Shakespeare focuses attention so explicitly on this fact, the only time he gives an actor playing a woman lines which proclaim the male beneath the female dress. Significantly, they occur in the Epilogue, that transitional passage which eases the audience back from the imaginary world of the play into everyday existence. Cleopatra's expression of fear that if taken captive to Rome she will see 'Some squeaking Cleopatra boy [her] greatness | I'th' posture of a whore' (*Antony* 5.2.216–17), may have a certain grim ironic humour, but it lacks the explicitness of Rosalind's words in the Epilogue, which direct attention to the whole comedy of sexual ambiguity which has gone before.

Like Julia in *The Two Gentleman of Verona*, Viola in *Twelfth Night* and Innogen in *Cymbeline*, Rosalind takes on male dress for protection. When Celia suggests that disguise is needed to avoid

[27] See Maura Slattery Kuhn, 'Much Virtue in *If*', *SQ*, 28 (1977), p. 44.

assault on their way to the forest of Arden, Rosalind's response is based on physique—the shorter Celia can stay as a woman, but Rosalind, being 'more than common tall', says she will have a 'gallant curtal-axe' upon her thigh, a boar-spear in her hand and a 'swashing and a martial outside', even if her heart may harbour womanish fears (1.3.113–21); that the need for male protection would possibly be supplied by Touchstone is not considered by Rosalind when she suggests that he accompany them. (In any case, his weapons would at best be words, not swords.)

There is no way of knowing the attitude of the Elizabethan audience, and particularly the men in that audience, to the boy actor playing a girl or woman, or to the more complicated situation of the female page disguise. Robert Kimbrough claims that 'from the standpoint of legitimate theatre, to maintain that there has ever been a comic device based on the actual sex of the actors is to fly in the face of a generic essential . . . An actor in role is whatever sex, age, and cultural origin the playwright asserts . . . We do Shakespeare a disservice not to accept his women as women.'[28] This may do well enough for a Portia or a Jessica, a Juliet or a Cressida. It does less well for a female character who takes on with her male disguise the name of Ganymede, 'Jove's own page', even when this is merely using the name in the source, in this case *Rosalynde*. The relationship of Jupiter and his cupbearer was well enough known for the word 'ganymede' to be current for a homosexual youth (*OED* 2), the word 'catamite' is closely derived, through corruption, from the name, and in the opening scene of Marlowe's *Dido Queen of Carthage* (*c.*1587), for example, Ganymede is described as 'that female wanton boy' (l. 51). Lorenzo's remark that the escaping Jessica will come to him in 'the lovely garnish of a boy' (*Merchant of Venice* 2.6.45) may contain a misprint for 'lowly', but alternatively it may be a nod in the direction of a suppressed homosexual element in Antonio's feeling for Bassanio, or even in Lorenzo's for Jessica. But when Viola remains in her boy's clothes at the end of *Twelfth Night* there is no indication of doubt in Orsino's mind that he wants to see her in her 'woman's weeds', so that she will be 'Orsino's mistress and his fancy's queen'. With Rosalind, the extra complication, the extra layer, is the female

[28] Robert Kimbrough, 'Androgyny Seen Through Shakespeare's Disguise', *SQ*, 33 (1982), p. 17.

role she adds to her male disguise; paradoxically, this is at the same time an additional mask and a reversion to her true role of woman.[29] The addition had the potential in the Elizabethan theatre to draw attention not only to the Ganymede persona Rosalind takes on, but to the boy actor three layers beneath. The audience's attention could also be drawn to the boy actor when Rosalind in her description of how she cured the lovesick youth says that, in pretending to be a woman, she was 'for every passion something, and for no passion truly anything, as boys and women are for the most part cattle of this colour' (3.2.392–4), a linking which is given painful distortion in a different context when Lear's fool declares, 'He's mad that trusts in the tameness of a wolf, a horse's health, a boy's love, or a whore's oath' (*The History of King Lear*, 13.14–15). Rosalind's lines are developed from a passage in Lodge, already referred to, in which Rosalynde/Ganymede says to Alinda/Aliena, 'You may see what mad cattle you women be', but Rosalynde makes no mention of boys. The addition is significant when it is made for a stage adaptation when female parts were played by boys. Later in the play, when Rosalind/Ganymede/Rosalind invites Orlando to woo her, and asks 'What would you say to me now an I were your very, very Rosalind?' and he replies 'I would kiss before I spoke' (4.1.63–6), if Orlando makes as if to suit action to word and kiss her, the opportunity for comedy is doubly enriched because Ganymede must dodge the kiss and the audience is reminded that beneath the sham Rosalind is a boy, Ganymede, beneath Ganymede the 'very' Rosalind of the play, but beneath this last, a 'very' boy, the actor. (This leaves aside the question of audience response to an Orlando who thinks it might be interesting to kiss a boy.)

Since the 1960s the subject of Renaissance attitudes to cross-dressing, transvestism, homosexuality, and boy actors has been given increasing attention, along with the reappraisal of historical

[29] These ambiguities of gender are explored and exploited in Théophile Gautier's *Mademoiselle de Maupin*, which had for a subtitle 'A Double Love' when it was first published in 1835. The novel culminates in a performance of *As You Like It* with the heroine/hero, Madeleine/Théodore playing Rosalind/Ganymede. Relationships between the novel and the play are discussed by Rosemary Lloyd, 'Rereading *Mademoiselle de Maupin*', *Orbis Litterarum*, 41 (1986), 19–32, and 'Speculum Amantis, Speculum Artis: The Seduction of Mademoiselle de Maupin', *Nineteenth Century French Studies*, 15 (1986–7), 77–86.

interpretation and development of literary critical theory.[30] At the same time feminist criticism has illuminated the significance of gender in Shakespeare's plays and likely attitudes of his audiences towards his heroines as women.[31] The National Theatre's 1967 production discussed below (pp. 66–7) showed that a modern adult all-male interpretation of the play can be successful, provided that a homosexual element is not blatantly emphasized, as it was in the same production's much-criticized 1974 revival.

Doubleness

In so far as theatre can exist only when there is at the minimum an actor and an audience, even an audience of one, and that an actor is a person who assumes a role, doubleness is an essential of theatre. In *As You Like It* doubleness informs many aspects of the play itself. In Rosalind it is taken to an extreme with a double layer of masks. Celia's disguise as Aliena is the other most obvious example, but nothing more is made of it—it remains a simple disguise. But as an informing idea, doubleness is introduced at the play's beginning, with two brothers in conflict: Orlando bitter at the way in which his elder brother Oliver has not discharged the will of their late father Sir Rowland de Boys and given him an education fitting a gentleman, Oliver plotting to have Orlando killed, acknowledging to himself that he does not know why he hates him, while suggesting that it could be plain envy. Like

[30] See, for example, Alan Bray, *Homosexuality in Renaissance England* (1982); Steve Brown, 'The Boyhood of Shakespeare's Heroines: Notes on Gender Ambiguity in the Sixteenth Century', *SEL*, 30 (1990), 243–63; Stephen Greenblatt, *Shakespearean Negotiations* (Berkeley, 1988); Carolyn G. Heilbrun, *Toward a Recognition of Androgyny* (New York, 1973); Michael Jamieson, 'Shakespeare's Celibate Stage' in *Papers, Mainly Shakespearian*, ed. George Ian Duthie (Edinburgh, 1964), pp. 21–39; Stephen Orgel, 'Nobody's Perfect: Or Why Did the English Stage Take Boys for Women?', *The South Atlantic Quarterly*, 88 (1989), 7–29; P. H. Parry, 'The Boyhood of Shakespeare's Heroines', *Shakespeare Survey* 42 (1990), 99–109; James M. Saslow, *Ganymede in the Renaissance* (New Haven, 1986).

[31] For example, Linda Bamber, *Comic Women, Tragic Men: A Study of Gender and Genre in Shakespeare* (Stanford, 1982); Juliet Dusinberre, *Shakespeare and the Nature of Women* (1975); Peter Erickson, *Patriarchal Structures in Shakespearian Drama* (Berkeley, 1985); Lisa Jardine, *Still Harping on Daughters* (Brighton, 1983); Madelon Sprengnether, 'The Boy Actor and Femininity in *Antony and Cleopatra*', in Norman N. Holland *et al.*, eds., *Shakespeare's Personality* (Berkeley, 1989), pp. 191–205; Carolyn Ruth Swift Lenz *et al.*, eds., *The Woman's Part: Feminist Criticism of Shakespeare* (Urbana, 1980).

other pairs in the play, Oliver and Orlando are in some respects reverse images of each other. Oliver is envious, murderous, deceitful, a brother 'the most unnatural | That lived amongst men' (4.3.123–4), Orlando, by Oliver's own admission, 'gentle; never schooled, and yet learned; full of noble device; of all sorts enchantingly beloved' (1.1.155–7). Where Oliver is devious and calculating, Orlando is hotheaded and passionate—it is he who lays hands on his elder brother, and who rushes in with drawn sword on the exiled Duke Senior and his lords. His sudden falling in love with Rosalind is not a particularly distinguishing characteristic in this play, as it happens to so many others: to Rosalind, to Phoebe, who self-justifyingly quotes Marlowe's '"Who ever loved that loved not at first sight?"' (3.5.83), to Celia and to Oliver, though only after his conversion to goodness which results from Orlando's saving him from certain death.

That encounter, which occurs off-stage and is described by Oliver himself, signals the joining of the opposite images which the brothers have represented throughout the play, even though they are not on stage together between 1.1 and 5.1. For all his excellences, Orlando needs to change as well as Oliver. Coming upon his brother asleep in the forest, the impending prey of a snake which glides away at his approach and of a hungry lioness, Orlando makes a decision, as Prospero does, that 'The rarer action is | In virtue than in vengeance' (*Tempest* 5.1.27–8); 'nature, stronger than his just occasion' (4.3.130), leads him to kill the lioness. This change in Orlando, the new ability to conquer a passion (in this case his justifiable anger at Oliver), brings about the change in Oliver which allows him to fall in love with Celia and to be deserving of her love.

These two sons of Sir Rowland de Boys are matched by the ducal brothers, the tyrannical, moody Frederick and the cordial, philosophical Duke Senior. Just as Oliver cannot easily find a reason for hating Orlando, so no reasons are given for Frederick's banishing his brother. The violence of Oliver's house, which the old servant Adam describes as 'but a butchery' (2.3.28), is paralleled by the physical violence of the court, where breaking of ribs is sport for ladies to watch, honour is of little account, and the Duke is given to unpredictable rages. Duke Senior's geniality, which helps inspire loyalty in his lords, is a mellower version of the gentle nobility which makes Orlando 'of all sorts enchantingly beloved' (1.1.156–7); his flash of anger at Jaques (2.7.64–9) is a mature, controlled expression of the same emotion that incites Orlando to attack Oliver in the first scene of the play. Duke Senior has gained (or perhaps completed) an education in the forest, where adversity has schooled him to read nature, to turn the chilly winds of winter into moral tutors, and to enjoy the lack of responsibility which forest life brings and the time it allows for contemplation and disputation. Orlando's entry into Arden signals the beginning of his education; expecting to have to use force to gain food, he learns that gentleness is sufficient; when he takes up Ganymede's offer to be cured of lovesickness, he unknowingly sets himself on an educative course which sharpens his mind, brings him self-awareness, and makes him a worthy partner for Rosalind. Orlando's journey is laid out before us for our enjoyment; Duke Senior has already made his; Oliver's education is sudden and complete, occurring off-stage, the circumstances told by Oliver himself in a context which mingles humour and seriousness; Duke Frederick's repentance is as precipitate as his earlier changes of mood, and placed at a further remove through being reported in the last scene of the play by Jaques de Boys. Johnson lamented that 'By hastening the end of this work Shakespeare suppressed the dialogue between the usurper and the hermit, and lost an opportunity of exhibiting a moral lesson in which he might have found matter worthy of his pen' (Joseph Moser helpfully made good the omission in 1809[32]); the inclusion of such a scene, however, would have led to the play's ending being slowed, the festivity towards which, as Northrop Frye tells us, comedy moves from irrational law would have been dimmed and the graded presentation of the educative processes described above would have been lost. As well, there was probably the practical reason that Duke Frederick's part was doubled; on the modern stage it is sometimes doubled by the actor playing Duke Senior, which makes, at the very least, for a good family resemblance.

Touchstone and Jaques, two of the characters Shakespeare introduced, form another pair. Touchstone may be a courtier who has trod a measure, flattered a lady and undone three tailors,

[32] Johnson (1989), p. 180; Joseph Moser, 'Additional Scene to Shakespeare's *As You Like It*', *European Magazine*, 55 (1809), 345–52.

but he is anything but 'the daintiest fool of the comedies', as S. E. Winbolt described him in 1895.[33] He is a sensualist, a master of bawdy, whose earthy sensibilities provide a contrast to the romanticism of the other lovers in the play, whom he slyly calls 'the rest of the country copulatives' (5.4.54–5), reducing them to the same level as the ill-favoured but honest Audrey and himself. Touchstone is a new kind of character in Shakespeare. He is not a serving-man clown, like Lance in *The Two Gentlemen of Verona* or Lancelot Gobbo in *The Merchant of Venice*, but a witty court jester. He is the first of Shakespeare's wise fools who are allowed to say what they like, who are intended to tell home truths, to cut people down to size, but who at the same time are liable for a whipping if they go too far. Where Lance has 222 lines to speak and Lancelot 178, Touchstone has 299—among Shakespeare's clowns only Feste in *Twelfth Night* has more, with 318.[34] There has been strong argument that the role of Touchstone was shaped for, and perhaps by, the actor Robert Armin, who joined the Chamberlain's Men some time after their chief clown, William Kempe, left the company early in 1599. It is not, however, established fact that Armin even played Feste. The coincidence of the name 'Touchstone' with Armin's training as a goldsmith and the name of the clown Tutch, in his own play *Two Maids of More-clack* (1598?), is attractively suggestive, but it is not known precisely when he joined the company, any more than it is known precisely when *As You Like It* was completed.[35]

On his first entrance Rosalind and Celia both refer to Touchstone as a 'natural', that is a person of little intellect, a born fool—it is immediately clear that the opposite is true, as they well know—and he may have worn for this scene at court the long coat of the idiot (Fig. 1).[36] In the forest he wears motley,

[33] *As You Like It*, London [1895], p. xx.

[34] The figures are from the tables in Spevack, vol. i.

[35] Discussion to 1976 is summarized in Knowles, pp. 373–7.

[36] Sniping at his enemy, Gabriel Harvey, Thomas Nashe writes, 'fools, ye know, always for the most part (especially if they be natural fools) are suited in long coats; whereupon I set up my rest to shape his garments of the same size, that I might be sure to sit on his skirts' (Nashe, iii. 17). The fool's long-skirted suit and the meaning of 'motley', particularly in relation to a portrait of the fool Tom Skelton, are discussed by E. W. Ives in 'Tom Skelton—A Seventeenth-Century Jester' (*Shakespeare Survey* 13 (1960), pp. 90–105). Versions of the portrait are held by the Shakespeare Institute, University of Birmingham, and at Muncaster Castle, Ravenglass, Cumbria. See Fig. 2.

1. A changeling (a natural idiot) represented on the stage. He has a handkerchief for his dribbling, and a hornbook to indicate that his education is still at a childish level. From the frontispiece of *The Wits, or, Sport upon Sport* (1673). (1.2.47)
2. Tom Skelton, the fool of the Bradshaigh family, Haigh Hall, Lancashire, *c.* 1659. The checks on his long-skirted motley costume are blue and yellow. (2.7.13)

the parti-coloured costume of the professional fool, but whether it is a long coat or a short tunic is not certain (Fig. 2). Touchstone is a commentator, not least on the morals of the world he inhabits; his first joke reflects on the lack of honour in Frederick's court, and his question to Le Beau a little later again shrewdly comments on court values. He mocks Silvius, Rosalind, and the very idea of romantic love with a bawdy reminiscence (2.4.43–51); he satirizes Orlando and the Petrarchan tradition with a shockingly lewd parody which insults both love poetry and Rosalind herself (who, however, disposes of him with smut wittier than his own (3.2.113–16)), and he is a conscious performer, even getting (5.4.84–5), in Vickers's felicitous phrase, 'the only encore in Shakespeare' (p. 219). He relishes words, and argument, though his sophistication is no true match for the simple good sense of Corin in their debate over the relative qualities of court and country life. But Touchstone is genuinely concerned with and for people; we have Celia's word that he is devoted to her, and, despite his remarks on being married by means of an improper ceremony so that he will be able more easily to leave his wife, and Jaques's smart comment that Touchstone and Audrey's marriage will last only a couple of months, it is Hymen's prophecy to which we should listen: 'You and you are sure together | As the winter to foul weather' (5.4.130–1). Rough though they may be, winter and foul weather are inseparable. In this, his last comment about other people, Jaques is wrong again, as so often he is, whereas Touchstone is usually right in his remarks about the world and the people in it.

Like Orlando and Oliver, Duke Frederick and Duke Senior, Touchstone and Jaques are, as it were, of the same family, but opposites. Jaques is neither a natural nor a licensed fool, but as the licensed fool mocks under the mask of the simpleton, Jaques comments satirically under the cloak (or should it be 'the hat'?) of the melancholic. Aristotle, according to Robert Burton in his *Anatomy of Melancholy* (1621), considered 'Melancholy men of all others [the] most witty', subject to 'a kind of *enthusiasmus* . . . which stirreth them up to be excellent philosophers, poets, prophets &c.'[37] Just as Touchstone's 'cover' is described before we meet him, so Jaques's assumed role is depicted, and at much greater length (2.1.25–43). Amiens and the First Lord espy him stretched out beneath an oak, beside a stream, in precisely the pose of Edward, 1st Lord Herbert of Cherbury, painted by Isaac Oliver about 1610–14 (Fig. 3). The tree in the left foreground of this picture is an oak, and the Earl's resting his head on his hand in the conventional posture of the melancholy philosopher represents his intellectual pursuits, just as the shield and his armour, being hung up in the background, indicate his knightly concerns. Roy Strong relates this to Nicholas Hilliard's miniature of the 9th Earl of Northumberland as a melancholy philosopher, painted *c.*1590–5, in which the Earl, dressed in black, his shirt

[37] Burton, i. 401 (Pt. I. Sec. 3. Mem. 1. Subs. 3).

3. Edward Herbert, 1st Baron Herbert of Cherbury, depicted as a knightly melancholic in a miniature by Isaac Oliver (1610–14). (2.1.30–2)

and doublet unfastened, a book beside him and his hat and gloves cast by, reclines with his head on his hand beneath a tree.[38] Northumberland, known as 'the wizard earl', was interested in philosophy, alchemy, and scientific experiment. The sylvan solitude sought by the melancholic is also a quality of pastoral, however, and the reclining posture is found in illustrations of pastoral prose and verse.

Jaques's weeping over the sobbing deer, which became a subject for nineteenth-century artists including Blake (Fig. 4) and Constable, would have been regarded as eccentric; Duke Senior himself is troubled by the fact that the deer are not safe from the huntsmen's arrows in their own forest confines, but not seriously enough to interfere with hunting them for food, and the Lord's account leads him to find Jaques to get some entertainment by teasing him in disputation, a sport Jaques is familiar with, and

[38] Roy Strong, *Artists of the Tudor Court* (1983), pp. 158–9, and 'The Elizabethan Malady: Melancholy in Elizabethan and Jacobean Portraiture', *Apollo*, 79 (1964), 264–9.

4. William Blake, 'Jaques and the Wounded Stag' (1806). Pen and watercolour drawing, one of six by Blake inserted in an extra-illustrated copy of the Second Folio (1632). (2.1)

only too anxious to avoid. Where the Duke has just been extolling the advantages to be got from the adversities of exile, Jaques has been 'invectively' decrying the forest life, claiming that the exiles are themselves usurpers, tyrants, and even worse, in the forest world which both he and the Duke liken to a city state.

This negativity characterizes Jaques throughout the play, but he fails to persuade anybody to his point of view. In his parody of Amiens's cheerful song he calls everyone else 'gross fools' without challenge, but the pessimism of his platitudinous speech on the seven ages of man is exploded by Orlando's entry with Adam in his arms. When he derides Orlando's love-carvings on trees he is dismissed with unsuspected wit by the lover, and his egotistical description of his own particular kind of melancholy is given short, patriotic shrift by Rosalind. His two positive actions both relate to Touchstone, whose marriage to Audrey by the hedge-priest Sir Oliver Martext he prevents, and whom he introduces into the exiled court, as if realizing that he himself is no longer able to act as the court wit when there is a professional fool in the forest. His delight in discovering Touchstone produces unwonted merriment in Jaques, who begs the Duke for a suit of motley to wear so that he too will be licensed to speak his mind and so 'Cleanse the foul body of th'infected world' (2.7.60). The Duke's burst of anger at his presuming to castigate others when he has been a sinner himself produces the standard response of the satirist: that he attacks vice in general, not particular people, that those who have done wrong will benefit from his attack, and those who have not will be unharmed. Jaques's defence rather runs out of puff, however, and Shakespeare is clearly satirizing the satiric vogue of the late 1590s which, taken up so zealously by such writers as Nashe, Hall, Jonson, and Marston, led to the bishops' bonfire in June 1599 (see above, p. 2). Attempts have been made to identify Jaques as a satiric portrait, particularly of John Marston, owing to the scatological aspect of Jaques's thought and speech, and Jonson, to whom Shakespeare was supposed to have administered a purge, but just as he satirizes the fashionable pose of melancholy, in life, literature, and art, so Shakespeare satirizes the satiric mode rather than any individual. He may, however, lay teasing invitations for the audience to make such identifications: Duke Senior's entreaty, 'Stay, Jaques, stay', for example, is exactly Maximilian's line (5.7.99) to the steward Melun disguised as a beggar, Jaques de Prie, in Jonson's comedy *The Case is Altered*, acted probably in 1598; but apart from the names, there is nothing in common between the two characters.

Hazlitt considered Jaques 'the only purely contemplative character in Shakespeare . . . his only passion is thought', he wrote.[39] This is not entirely true. Jaques has ambitions to change the world, which his skewed vision sees as being full of fools and filth, to be sneered and railed at. The only person whose company he enjoys is Touchstone, who he believes confirms him in his belief, but whom he misreads. Jaques's speech on the seven ages of man, with Hamlet's 'To be or not to be' the most famous in Shakespeare, is a restatement in good set negative terms of a topos known to every educated person. It was wildly misinterpreted in

[39] *Characters of Shakespeare's Plays* (1817; repr. 1962), pp. 240–1.

5. The sentimentalization of Jaques. Robert Smirke's painting of the first of the seven ages, engraved by P. W. Tomkins for the Boydell *Collection of Prints . . . Illustrating . . . Shakespeare* (2 vols. (1803 [1805]), i. Pl. XL). (2.7.143–4)

the eighteenth and nineteenth centuries. It was, for example, parodied as an afterpiece given by the actor playing Touchstone, set to music and performed as a character song, made the subject of paintings, engravings, and postcards, and even depicted on ladies' fans.[40] Parts became sentimentalized beyond recognition, particularly in illustrations. The infant, for instance, rather than 'mewling and puking in the nurse's arms' was shown gurgling and smiling on the nurse's lap (Fig. 5). The play, however, sets against the cynicism of the speech not sentimentalism but practical caring love, as Orlando brings in his old servant Adam to the food and friendship of Duke Senior and his lords.

Jaques is 'compact of jars', discordant: his being 'merry hearing of a song' is extraordinary. Melancholy and harmony do not

[40] The parody ('an Irregular, Poetic, Prosaic, Serio comic Paraphrase') is on a playbill for the Theatre Royal, York, 14 May 1789 (Birmingham Shakespeare Library, Playbills, *As You Like It*, vol. 2, p. 157); the character song is on a playbill for 25 April 1864, and the fan illustration in an advertisement for 1 January 1796, listed in F. Madan, *Catalogue of Shakespeariana* (1927), pp. 218, 241 respectively (Bodleian Library, John Johnson Coll., Sh. Box F). There are numerous paintings and engravings, some comprising complete books.

agree. Marston's play *The Malcontent* (*c.*1600) even begins with 'a sound of loud discordant music being heard', signalling the ruling humour of its chief character, Malevole. The melancholic is out of tune with society, and Jaques has no place in the play's concluding dance which symbolizes the concord of marriage and the continuation of the race.

Touchstone, on the other hand, is sensitive to discord; he tells the pages that he finds their singing of 'It was a lover and his lass' 'very untunable', which they perhaps deliberately mishear so that they can claim they 'kept time' (5.3.40–3). Touchstone's liking for harmony is just part of his general sociableness. He may have had four quarrels, but he was ever only 'like to have fought one', and his explanation of how the combat was avoided is not only a joke against manuals of swordplay but, in its description of the seven degrees of the lie, it glances impishly at Jaques's sardonic description of the seven ages of man.

Where Jaques avoids the Duke because he is too 'disputable', Touchstone enjoys debate, especially if he considers he is winning, as he thinks he is in his discussion with Corin on court and country life. And where Jaques likes to think himself cerebral, Touchstone is the self-acknowledged physical sensualist who recognizes desire as a handicap, one of the 'dulcet diseases'. But it can be cured, although the cure is marriage. 'Wedlock would be nibbling', he tells Jaques (3.3.74). When asked by the Countess in *All's Well That Ends Well* why he wants to marry, Lavatch the clown explains, 'My poor body, madam, requires it. I am driven on by the flesh' (1.3.28–9). Not much more could be expected of Touchstone and Lavatch, however, for fools were not troubled with passion, they were considered to be simply lecherous, and fickle.[41]

Lavatch proves to be so when he goes to court and discovers beauties different from those of his Isbel at Roussillon, and Jaques draws on the same commonly held belief when he prophesies so short a life for Touchstone's marriage. Touchstone may make jokes about whores, and invent a scurrilous parody impugning Rosalind's purity, but he is properly moral when it comes to the

[41] Burton, quoting Erasmus, says 'they are neither troubled in conscience, nor macerated with cares' (i. 172 (Pt. I. Sec. 1. Mem. 3. Subs. 3)). In Richard Brome's *The Queen's Exchange*, the fool Jeffrey expects to have 'at least half | A score of my wholesome country lasses with child' (*Dramatic Works*, 3 vols. (1873), iii. 530).

satisfaction of his own flesh; productions of the play which depict or even suggest pre-marital copulation between Touchstone and Audrey, as John Dexter's National Theatre production of 1979 did, are in defiance of the text.

It is implied that Jaques's licentiousness had its full rein while he was on his travels, which Rosalind assumes included Venice, for Elizabethans a place as infamous for its courtesans and their lubricity as it was famous for its art, wealth, and legal institutions, which Shakespeare exploited in *The Merchant of Venice*. Jaques's sexual experience has been of the city, and associated with disease, according to Duke Senior; Touchstone's adventuring is of the natural countryside, associated with Jane Smile the milkmaid and Audrey the goatherd. Paradoxically, Jaques despises the court, preferring to stay in the forest rather than returning with the other exiles (who thereby confirm his cynical view: Duke Senior who praised the forest life for what it taught him, the Lord who said he would not change such a life, and the other lords, are presumably all eager enough to return to court when the opportunity arrives). Touchstone has never made a secret of his preference. A fool at court, he is 'more fool' still to come to Arden, and while his comparisons of court and country to Corin may seem even-handed, there can be little doubt that he finds country life, 'in respect it is not in the court, . . . tedious' (3.2.18).

While Jaques and Touchstone differ in so many ways, they are also alike. Both criticize society, both ridicule romantic love, putting themselves outside it. Jaques derides it from his assumed intellectual loftiness, Touchstone from the lower regions of the flesh. Both are related to bad smells. Idiots—natural fools—were infamous for incontinence, and lack of restraint generally; Rosalind makes Touchstone the butt of a joke about this at 1.2.98. As already noted, Jaques's name is a pun on a current word for a lavatory, but as well, the disease of melancholy was closely related to evil odours: it was believed to cause unpleasant gases to build up in the body, leading to bad breath and farting; a recommended remedy was purging of the bowels. Gerard's *Herball*, for instance, advises that 'Pennyroyal . . . taken with honey and aloes, purgeth by stool melancholy humours.'[42] A century later, Tom D'Urfey's *Pills to Purge Melancholy* (1719)

[42] Enlarged edn., 1633; repr. 1636, p. 672.

offered a more pleasant cure, a book of songs, the title referring to the belief that music lightened the spirits of the afflicted.

The pun in Jaques's name was not unusual but it is more obvious than the puns in Touchstone's, whose name contains a sexual allusion, in so far as 'stone' = 'testicle'; more speculatively, the name may also allude to a well-known tavern fool, John Stone, as well as, perhaps, to the clown Tutch in Robert Armin's *Two Maids of More-clack*,[43] but the larger, more generally implied meaning is of 'touchstone' as a substance against which precious metals are tested, and this sense applies throughout the play. Orlando's verses, for example, are shown up as ridiculously extravagant when Touchstone extemporizes a bawdy parody; Jaques's pessimistic wit and his place as entertaining gall to the exiled court are diminished in the face of Touchstone's fresher humour; and the idealistic romanticism of the three other pairs of lovers is reduced to a more realistic level by Touchstone's reminder that fleshly desires are significant in the satisfaction of love.

These punning names are aspects of the play's doubleness of language, which begins with Orlando's cry, 'I am no villein', when Oliver calls him a 'villain' (1.1.52–3); the play on words is intensified in the old spelling form 'villaine', which is used for both words in the Folio. But much of the wordplay is bawdy, and given mainly to Touchstone, Jaques, and Rosalind. What amuses Jaques so much about Touchstone's moralizing on time, for example, is I suspect not so much the philosophic content as the bawdy implications of the language (2.7.12–43). Punning, like so much else, develops in the forest of Arden, Rosalind's page disguise liberating her into a male freedom of speech, though Shakespeare prepares the ground by making her first pun on Touchstone's smell (1.2.98), and then giving her a delightful little wordplay on 'father' and 'child' (1.3.11—of which prudery deprived her for more than a century).

The more that is learned about the meanings of words the clearer it becomes that Elizabethans found bawdy punning publicly acceptable and entertaining in a way lost by the nineteenth century but rediscovered in the twentieth.[44] That there were

[43] Wiles, p. 146.

[44] The pioneering work in this area by Eric Partridge with *Shakespeare's Bawdy* (1947) has been further developed by E. A. M. Colman in *The Dramatic Use of Bawdy in Shakespeare* (1974) and Frankie Rubinstein with *A Dictionary of Shakespeare's Sexual Puns and Their Significance* (2nd edn., 1989).

limits even for Elizabethans, however, is indicated by a passage in *Love's Labour's Lost* (4.1.110–48) in which Rosaline, Boyet, Maria, and Costard exchange *doubles entendres* based on hunting and cuckoldry (a common coupling that turns up again in the hunting chorus in 4.2 of *As You Like It*), and archery and intercourse. Maria protests to Costard, 'Come, come, you talk greasily, your lips grow foul' (l. 136); but Costard and Boyet continue for another two lines. Similarly, the brilliant extended exchange between Romeo and Mercutio (*Romeo* 2.3.35–92) is not halted by Benvolio's 'Stop there, stop there' (l. 86), rather it leads on to further verbal dexterities. A key word in that passage is 'wit' in its sense of 'sexual organ' (see Appendix A), a meaning central to an exchange between Rosalind and Orlando in 4.1 (154–61), which comes after the 'mock' marriage, and which plays with the conventional belief in the inevitability of cuckoldry. When this fear provokes Touchstone's concern in 3.3 he decides to find 'the forehead of a married man more honourable than the bare brow of a bachelor' (ll. 54–5), just as Benedick declares 'There is no staff more reverend than one tipped with horn' (*Much Ado*, 5.4.122–3). The Rosalind–Orlando banter is, in small, of the same kind as the exchange between the three gentlemen of Verona, and Rosalind's punning on 'wit' in this way is possible probably because she is in male disguise. This is Rosalind increasing the intensity of the double role she plays, making the most of the two genders she is presenting to Orlando.

Rosalind differs from all the other cross-dressed heroines of Shakespeare in the way she uses her disguise to educate her lover, and to secure him as a husband, by pretending to be what she is, a woman. This allows her both the freedom to speak and act as a man of the period, and the privileges of speaking and acting as a woman—'Do you not know I am a woman? When I think, I must speak,' she says when Celia protests at her interruptions (3.2.241–2). This loquacity is matter for a witticism by Anthony Trollope in *The Eustace Diamonds* (1872): 'Let a girl be upset with you in a railway train, and she will talk like a Rosalind', and it is a characteristic which caused Peggy Ashcroft, rehearsing the part in 1957, to write to George Rylands, 'Rosalind is a wonderful girl but I wish she didn't talk *quite* so much.'[45]

[45] *The Eustace Diamonds*', 2 vols. ([1872]; repr. 1950), ii. 2; Michael Billington, *Peggy Ashcroft* (1988), p. 170.

Rosalind's womanliness was the quality that in the nineteenth century particularly attracted audiences and was emphasized by English actresses between about 1840 and 1920, several of whom are discussed below under 'The Play in Performance' (pp. 50–81). The most famous, Helen Faucit, who acted the role first in 1839 and for the last time in 1879, blushed, trembled, wept, sparkled, and brought a great sense of playfulness to the part; but she had difficulty with the Epilogue, which she found 'repugnant' because it meant addressing the audience not as Rosalind or Ganymede, but as herself; she believed in the total submergence of the actor in the character. Like all those then playing Rosalind, she omitted passages which would have been thought offensive by the audience. Any suggestion of what was considered coarseness was usually removed or altered, sometimes by textual editors as well as by actors and directors. As early as 1714, for instance, Rowe emended Rosalind's wishful thinking about Orlando as her 'child's father' (1.3.11) to a self-centred thought about her 'father's child'—a change not endorsed by Theobald but enthusiastically supported by Coleridge and many others; and an eighteenth- or nineteenth-century Rosalind usually decided to wear a gallant curtal-axe upon her 'side', as 'thigh' (1.3.116) was considered indelicate. She did not make a joke about Touchstone losing his 'old smell' (1.2.98) and Celia hardly ever charged her with wanting to learn Orlando's whereabouts so that she could put a man in her belly (3.2.197). She sometimes bantered with Orlando about a wife taking her wit to a neighbour's bed, however, because the sexual meaning of 'wit' (4.1.155) had been lost and so the word did not threaten the perceived femininity of the role. The rediscovery of meanings and the reinstatement of lines in more liberally-minded times has led to further exploitation of the gender ambiguity in the role, giving it a depth and intricacy denied by, for example, W. Robertson Davies who, in *Shakespeare's Boy Actors* (1939), advised that the modern actress should consider a Shakespearian heroine from the boy actor's point of view; 'it will emerge', he wrote, 'as a simple and direct conception . . . she will be spared the necessity to deal with complexities which are not inherent in the part.'[46] Particularly in the case of Rosalind, complexities in fact arise

[46] p. 199.

especially because the part was written for a boy to act, and doubleness is redoubled.

Names and Places

As You Like It is notorious for having characters with the same names, a 'fault' sometimes seen as evidence of hasty playwriting or revision.[47] Oliver de Boys and Sir Oliver Martext cause little trouble, but the melancholy Jaques and Jaques de Boys can cause confusion to an audience, and even occasionally to theatre reviewers.[48] Helen Gardner suggests that it 'seems possible that the melancholy Jaques began as this middle son and that his melancholy was in origin a scholar's melancholy. If so, the character changed as it developed, and by the time that Shakespeare had fully conceived his cynical spectator he must have realized that he could not be kin to Oliver and Orlando.'[49] Perhaps. Shakespeare did have lapses. But the mirroring aspects of the play support the idea that Jaques/Jaques de Boys is another significant double. The cynic goes through the play pessimistically moralizing on the unpleasant state of the world, likening people to beasts, professing to a preference for solitude, but in fact needing an audience. Jaques de Boys, mentioned only in the first few lines of the play, appears at the end (giving the actor of the part only fifteen and a half lines and two words to succeed or fail) with news that is the final denial of his namesake's pessimism. Similarly, if less incisively, Oliver and Sir Oliver are linked. Oliver's second line in the play is his question to Orlando, 'What mar you then?', when it is he who mars his brother's life, just as Martext, it is implied, mars religious teaching; but Oliver remakes the text of his life when he repents. Shakespeare's alteration to the source is relevant here. Lodge's Saladyne repents earlier in the story and searches for Rosader in the forest of Arden to seek his pardon as a first step on a pilgrimage to Jerusalem. Oliver is seeking Orlando to kill him, and repents when his intended victim saves his life. The religious context of Oliver's sudden conversion,

[47] Wilson, p. 112.

[48] Reviewing Michael Elliott's 1961 production for the London *Evening News*, Julian Holland wrote, 'Jacques [sic], with his freezing, exciting wit, could never have had a brother so wet as Ian Bannen makes Orlando' (5 July 1961).

[49] '*As You Like It*', in *More Talking of Shakespeare*, ed. John Garrett (1959), p. 19.

so ably discussed by Richard Knowles,[50] is in strong contrast to the farcical and irreligious context of Touchstone's dismissal of the comical hedge-priest.

The most problematic name in the play is not the name of a character, but of a place, Arden. Ever since Malone noted in 1790 that 'Ardenne is a forest of considerable extent in French Flanders lying near the Meuse, and between Charlemont and Rocroy' (iii. 123), it has been customary to equate the forest of Arden with the forest of the Ardennes in that rugged mountain region. Some editions, like that in the Cassell's School Shakespeare series [1921], even supply a map of the area, and the Oxford (1986) editors modernize 'Arden' to 'Ardenne'.[51] The theatre of horrific fighting in World War II, the Ardennes forest was from ancient times the setting for numerous legends, including tales of St Hubert, and of the five sons of Amyon. Malone, however, concludes his note thus: 'But our author was furnished with the scene of his play by Lodge's novel.' That 'But' and the sentence it introduces are significant, and they have been largely ignored by subsequent editors and commentators. Lodge's Arden is not on France's north-east border at all, but over 650 kilometres to the south-west, between Bordeaux and Lyons. A. Stuart Daley suggests the area which formed the ancient territory of Périgord, now incorporated in the Department of Dordogne; he notes that in Henry Roberts's *Haigh for Devonshire* (1600) the forest of Arden is between Bordeaux and Rouen, to the north-east of Bordeaux.[52]

In Roberts's 'pleasant discourse of six gallant merchants of Devonshire', the heroes[53] are ambushed by robbers in the forest of 'Ardine' (sig. C2^{r}). The name occurs in several other works of the period, in various spellings. In Chapman's *Revenge of Bussy d'Ambois* (1613) Charlotte refers to 'the desperat'st ruffians, | Outlaws in Arden' (3.2.151–2; the Q spelling is 'Acden', which

[50] 'Myth and Type in *As You Like It*', *ELH*, 33 (1966), 1–22. Some of Knowles's ideas are taken up by René Fortin in ' "Tongues in Trees": Symbolic Patterns in *As You Like It*', *Texas Studies in Literature and Language*, 14 (1973), 569–82.

[51] The case is argued in Stanley Wells, *Re-Editing Shakespeare for the Modern Reader* (Oxford, 1984), pp. 28–30.

[52] 'Observations on the Natural Settings and Flora of the Ardens of Lodge and Shakespeare', *English Language Notes*, 22, 3 (1985), 20–9.

[53] Piquantly, one of the heroes is called Oliver and another, called James, shares an inn bed with a Spaniard who turns out be a woman—'how so ever it fell out between them', comments the author, 'the lady was exceedingly well pleased' (sig. H3^{v}).

all editors have taken to be a misprint for 'Arden'); Greene's Orlando talks of 'Ardenia woods, | Where all the world for wonders do await' (*Orlando Furioso* 2.1.589–90), the context indicating that the 'wonders' would be unpleasant; Spenser's Astrophel comes to a forest more 'wide and waste', and more filled with wild beasts than 'famous Ardeyn' ('Astrophel', l. 96). A gentler aspect appears in Act 2 of Chapman's *Tragedy of Charles Duke of Byron* (1607), where Cupid ushers in a masque of 'nymphs, part of the scattered train | Of friendless virtue, living in the woods of shady Arden' (2.1.3–5), and in his translation of Ariosto's *Orlando Furioso* (1591) Harington describes a fountain in 'Ardenna', which caused the drinker to fall in love (I. 78). This fountain, also mentioned by Spenser as 'that same water of Ardenne, | The which Rinaldo drunck' (*Faerie Queene* IV. iii. 45), is one of two; the other turns love to aversion, instead of aversion to love.

The name 'Arden' is derived from Gaulish, *arduo-* (a hypothetical form) in *Arduenna silva*, the Latin name for the Ardennes, related to Old Irish *ard* (high) and Latin *arduus* (high, steep).[54] In his *Britannia*, which was first published in 1586 in Latin, and had six editions before being translated into English in 1610, William Camden writes of '*Arden*; which word the Gauls and Britons heretofore seem to have used for a *wood*, since two great forests, the one in *Gallia Belgica*, the other amongst us in Warwickshire, are both called by one and the same name of *Arden*.' After describing Warwickshire as being divided into 'the *Feldon* and the *Woodland*', he later says, 'As it is now called the *Woodland*, so by a more ancient name it was called *Arden*: which in my opinion are words importing the same thing.'[55] Support for this view is found in the entry for Arden in the fourth edition of the *Encyclopedia Britannica* (1810): 'the common name of forests among the Celtae, from the widely extensive one which ranged for 500 miles across the country of Gaul, or that which covered more than half the county of Warwick in Britain, and the sites of which still retain the appellation of *Arden*, to the much smaller one of the ancient Mancenion, that covered and surrounded the site of the present Manchester.'

[54] See the entry for *arduous* in *The Oxford Dictionary of English Etymology* (Oxford, 1967).

[55] *Camden's Britannia* (Newton Abbot, 1971), facsimile of the edition of 1695, pp. 231, 499, 503.

The fact that the Warwickshire Forest of Arden was so close to Stratford, coming in Shakespeare's day near to Shottery where Anne Hathaway lived, and that Shakespeare's mother's family name was Arden as well, has been irresistible to commentators. In the Temple edition of the play, for example, Israel Gollancz remarks that 'the locality of the play is . . . in the north-east of France but Shakespeare could hardly help thinking of his own Warwickshire Arden, and there could be little doubt that his contemporaries took it the same way,'[56] echoing Furness, who asserted in his 1890 Variorum note that 'to every listener at the play the "Forest of Arden" was no forest in far-away France, but was the enchanted ground of their own home', even though Knight had testily complained fifty years earlier about those who wanted to localize Arden, and was 'sure that Shakespeare *meant* to take his forest out of the region of the literal when he assigned to it a palm-tree and a lioness'.

There is no doubt that Shakespeare provides a French setting—Oliver says Orlando is 'the stubbornest young fellow of France' (1.1.133–4)—but it is not localized in the Ardennes mountains. Nor is it localized to Arden in Warwickshire, the Bordeaux district, or anywhere else. Though its name could be applied to any of them, it is none of them. This ambiguity contributes to the informing idea of doubleness in the play, exciting and freeing our imaginations. Le Beau is a courtier with a descriptive French name, Touchstone a fool with an English one, and Corin calls him 'Master Touchstone' (3.2.11–12). Jaques combines French and English in his, and the Duke calls him 'monsieur' (2.7.9). Audrey, William, and Sir Oliver Martext are undeniably English. Other characters are not so nationally defined; but to confine them to a forest in the north-east of France, or a wood near Stratford, is limiting and unnecessary. Arden is a fabulous forest where extraordinary things happen. There is no map for it.

Charles the wrestler's romantic view is that Arden is like the Golden World, the world in the time when no work had to be done, spring was eternal, and animals were not slaughtered, even for food. Duke Senior's view of nature and adversity as the great teachers for himself and his exiled courtiers agrees with this view at first but the necessity to kill the forest deer to survive, which 'irks' him, and the ruminations of Jaques on the sobbing

[56] 1894, p. xiii.

deer undercut the complacency of his opening speech (2.1.1–17). The harder realities of life in Arden, which some modern directors have tried, rather desperately, to use as a basis for gloomy interpretations of the play, are presented next in the unhappiness of the lovelorn Silvius, the 'churlish disposition' of Corin's master, the 'bleak air' of the forest, and the reminder in Amiens's song that 'Most friendship is feigning, most loving, mere folly' (2.7.182). These problems, however, are all sooner or later resolved. Silvius eventually marries his Phoebe, Corin gets a benign new employer, and Amiens's song is immediately followed by Duke Senior's welcoming Orlando, and telling him how much he loved the young man's father.

Arden is not a golden world, though to those outside it may seem to be. It does, however, become something of a schoolroom. As well as sermons in stones and books in the running brooks, there are human teachers, pre-eminently Rosalind, but also Touchstone, who attempts to teach Corin the virtues of the court compared with those of the country, but has more success in demonstrating to William why the country boy cannot marry Audrey. Jaques would also teach, and he does help Touchstone, but his wish to 'Cleanse the foul body of th'infected world' (2.7.60) meets with no success; his methods are too negative. Jaques has no sense of the marvellous.

He is therefore inevitably set apart from the other characters, for there is a progression through the play of the presentation of the marvellous in Arden, from the human to the supernatural. It is wonderful enough, but a coincidence, realistic, if barely believable, that the characters all come to Arden as they do. It is wonderful, but unrealistic that a 'green and gilded snake' should wreathe itself around a sleeping man's neck and that a hungry lioness should lie crouching nearby, waiting for the man to awaken before seizing him for food. But a snake and lioness are still real creatures. A god is not. With the appearance of Hymen the marvellous is at its most complete in the play.

Hymen is a pagan god, but the sound of 'Arden' is close to 'Eden', and the forest is to an extent a recovered Paradise. The play's opening scene of a fraternal quarrel in a garden and a faithful servant named Adam recalls Genesis 4, and the biblical allusions throughout the play support an insistent, if not obviously strong, connection between Arden and Eden. As Harry

Levin remarks in *The Myth of the Golden Age in the Renaissance* (1970), by the fourteenth century the world of the classical golden age was being moralized as Eden. In the Epistle to Arthur Golding's translation of Ovid's *Metamorphoses* Shakespeare would have read

> Moreover by the golden age what other thing is meant,
> Than Adam's time in Paradise, who being innocent
> Did lead a blest and happy life until that thorough sin
> He fell from God? From which time forth all sorrow did begin.
> (ll. 469–72)

In Book 1 Ovid describes the characteristics of the three subsequent ages of silver, bronze, and 'hurtful iron'. During the iron age, 'Men live by ravin and by stealth' (1, 162), war and quarrelling are rife, brother fights with brother. In *As You Like It*, the world outside Arden is in the Iron Age, which is Christianized as the fallen world. The characters are banished from it, flee from it, or, if evil, try to bring their fallen natures into the forest. They find, variously, contentment, love, and forgiveness. As often, it is given to one of Shakespeare's minor characters to hint at mighty issues, here the possibility of such a place, when Le Beau advises Orlando to leave Frederick's dangerous court: 'Hereafter, in a better world than this,' he says, 'I shall desire more love and knowledge of you' (1.2.269–70). Orlando finds both love and knowledge in Arden.

Pastoral

Love, always, and the attainment of self-knowledge, sometimes, were among the themes of pastoral, a well-enjoyed literary mode by the end of the sixteenth century. In poetry the idylls of Theocritus and the eclogues of Virgil and in prose the *Daphnis and Chloe* of Longus, together with romances like the *Aethiopica* of Heliodorus, were among the principal classical models for the fashion that had spread through Renaissance Europe. In England, Spenser's *Shepheardes Calender* (1579) and Book VI of *The Faerie Queene* (1596), and numerous longer poems and short lyrics, fed the growing interest in pastoral poetry while Sidney's *Arcadia*, begun in 1580 as an entertainment for his sister but not published until 1590, four years after his death, was the pre-eminent prose work of pastoral romance. Sidney probably owed something to the *Diana* of the Portuguese Jorge de Montemayor, which was translated from the original Spanish in 1598 by Bartholomew Young. By then, as well as Lodge's *Rosalynde*, several other pastoral novels had been published, including Robert Greene's *Menaphon* (1589), which was reprinted in 1598 with the catch-penny title of *Greene's Arcadia*, and *Pandosto* (1588), which Shakespeare later transformed into *The Winter's Tale*.

There was no classical tradition of pastoral drama, but, as David Young notes in his suggestive study of Shakespeare and pastoral, *The Heart's Forest*, 'pastoral' was in use as a generic term for plays or entertainments at least as early as 1579.[57] Several dramatists included pastoral elements in plays not predominantly concerned with shepherds. Margaret of Fressingfield in Greene's *Friar Bacon and Friar Bungay* (1594), for example, is an ancestor of Shakespeare's Perdita, though a rustic lass in reality, not a princess. John Lyly's *The Woman in the Moon* (*c.* 1595), which Agnes Latham (pp. lxi–lxii) suggests provided Shakespeare with ideas and style for parts of *As You Like It*, is set in a Utopia populated by shepherds who, lonely, ask Nature for a female; presented with Pandora, they all fall in love with her. Pandora, however, has been created by being imbued with temperamental aspects of each of the planets, which take it in turns to influence her. She is thus capricious and unpredictable, as Rosalind says she herself will be when married to Orlando (4.1.135–43). Under the moon's influence Pandora goes mad, and when she is restored to sanity Nature tries to place her in one planet, to ensure her temperamental stability; instead, Pandora chooses the moon because of its inconstancy. By these misogynistic means the shepherds are cured of their love.

Disguising as the opposite sex was a not unusual mechanism of pastoral. Sidney's Pyrocles, for instance, spends most of the *Arcadia* as Zelmane, an Amazon, in order to be near his beloved, the princess Philoclea. Complications follow when Philoclea's mother perceives the man beneath the feminine robes and falls in love with him, and Philoclea's father sees only the outer female and falls in love with 'her', just as the Phoebe of Lodge and Shakespeare becomes so mistakenly infatuated with Ganymede. In Lyly's play *Gallathea* (1586) two girls disguised as boys fall in

[57] New Haven and London, 1972, pp. 2–3.

love, each supposing the other to be what she appears to be; Venus obligingly changes one of them into a boy to allow a happy conclusion. Lyly's magical metamorphosis provides for enjoyable entertainment; Sidney's complexities serve his higher moral purpose of teaching the importance of distinguishing between truth and falsehood.

Sidney's heroes, Musidorus and Pyrocles, are strangers in Arcadia, arriving by way of shipwreck and battle. Their adventures happen in a place where they find 'here a shepherd's boy piping as though he should never be old; there a young shepherdess knitting and withal singing'.[58] This element of travel and sojourn was grafted on to classical pastoral from epic and romance, and it means that many Renaissance pastoral stories are not primarily about shepherds and shepherdesses but about people who arrive among them. Madeleine Doran illuminatingly shows how Shakespeare uses this convention along with another, 'the mode of criticism of court and city seen from the vantage point of sheepcote and forest glade',[59] the forest becoming a place where, for a time, people from beyond it can observe their usual world.

The court/ or city/country dichotomy is as old as Theocritus, but it took on special significance for the Renaissance in relation to the examination of political morality. The corruption of a real court that moved Ralegh to say in 'The Lie' 'it glows | And shines like rotten wood' and a dramatized court that led to a dying father's hope, 'let my son fly the courts of princes',[60] had wished-for alternatives in the woods which were 'More free from peril than the envious court' (2.1.4) and where a 'rank of osiers by the murmuring stream' could bring one to a 'sheepcote fenced about with olive trees' (4.3.80, 78). Shakespeare gives his doleful King Henry VI over thirty lines of comparison between the threat-filled existence of a king and the quiet life of a shepherd in tune with the great, regular swings of Nature's rhythms (*3 Henry VI* 2.5.21–54). *As You Like It*, set not in the harsh historical world of battles and treachery, but in the light, glad realm of romantic comedy, not on Towton Heath but in the forest of Arden, can

[58] Philip Sidney, *The Countess of Pembroke's Arcadia*, ed. Maurice Evans (Harmondsworth, 1977), pp. 69–70.

[59] '"Yet am I inland bred"', *SQ*, 15, 2 (1964), 113.

[60] John Webster, *The Duchess of Malfi*, 5.4.72.

afford to consider both these aspects, to accommodate both points of view, and to return its courtiers, those who wish to go, back to where they came from. All of them have gained something by their pastoral experience, even if, for Touchstone, it is only Audrey, 'an ill-favoured thing'.

Most of the characters are content to fleet the time carelessly; time is of small consequence, except to the most conscious lover in the forest, Rosalind. She is, of course, wrong in claiming that because Orlando says there is 'no clock in the forest' there is 'no true lover' there (3.2.291–3). Time has not the same importance for him as it now has for her. Because, so far as he is concerned, she is not physically present in the forest, he can only think of her, not be with her, and thought is not bound by time as physical action and being are. He is on time for his wedding, when there is promise of her being there in reality. As Hazlitt remarked, 'It is not what is done, but what is said, that claims our attention' in *As You Like It*;[61] the central acts of the play particularly have a static character, the action is all in the words and the brilliant play of wit they convey. Time stretches out, and even the punctuations of dawn and dusk and the necessities of shepherd life with which Lodge marks off his narrative's progress are dispensed with.

Apart from Rosalind, those for whom time matters most are Jaques and Touchstone. Touchstone, aptly called 'the time-keeper of the play' by Harold Jenkins in an excellent essay,[62] carries a dial to tell the time by, and Jaques is so amused by the fool's moralizing on the time that he laughs, so he says, for an hour, without stopping. Not long after, he is platitudinously dividing life into seven ages, mostly dismal. At the end, Jaques is again both specific and pessimistic when he says that Touchstone's and Audrey's 'loving voyage | Is but for two months victualled' (5.4.186–7). His and Touchstone's concern with time is related to their being the two characters who are least satisfied with being away from the court. On arriving in Arden, Touchstone declares, 'When I was at home I was in a better place', then adds philosophically, 'but travellers must be content' (2.4.15–16). Soon after, Jaques is ridiculing Amiens's song extolling the pleas-

[61] *Characters of Shakespeare's Plays* (1817; repr. 1962), p. 240.
[62] *'As You Like It', Shakespeare Survey 8* (1955), p. 49.

ures of forest life, in a parody which says that any man 'Leaving his wealth and ease' is no more than an ass (2.5.48); he either excludes himself from the jibe, or else changes his mind during the course of the play, for at the last he decides to stay in Duke Senior's 'abandoned cave' (5.4.191).

The timelessness which is a convention of pastoral is found in Arden. The disharmony of life outside Arden at the beginning of the play is reflected in the dislocations of time. How long, for instance, is it since Duke Senior was banished by his brother? When Oliver asks Charles for news of the 'new court', the wrestler replies that 'three or four loving lords have put themselves into voluntary exile with him' and that 'many young gentlemen flock to him every day' (1.1.96–7, 111–12), as if the event were quite recent. Yet Celia speaks as if there has been a considerable period between the banishment of Rosalind's father and the present, time enough for her to grow mature in her affection for her cousin (1.3.69–74). Fleeting the time carelessly allows time for contemplation, discussion, debate, songs, and love games. Michael Jamieson, developing an idea of C. L. Barber,[63] draws the distinction between the holiday spirit of Arden and the 'cares of Everyday' outside it; Rosalind's term 'working-day world' (1.3.12) makes the contrast even more strongly. Jay L. Halio goes further, comparing 'the timelessness of the forest world with the time-ridden preoccupations of court and city life'.[64] As the play draws towards its end, and the return to that world (although the characters are unaware of that), time takes up its slack, and gains definition. Orlando promises he will return to Rosalind 'By two o'clock' (4.1.164); Touchstone tells the disappointed Audrey that they will 'find a time' to be married (5.1.1); and in 5.2 the word 'tomorrow' becomes a kind of refrain, linked with the promise of marriage. The move back to regular, ordered time is given urgency by the pages' song, which advises lovers to 'take the present time'; the *carpe diem* tone is lighter than Marvell's, or even Herrick's, but the message is the same. And the idea of

[63] Michael Jamieson, *'As You Like It'* (1965), p. 49; and C. L. Barber, *Shakespeare's Festive Comedy* (1959), p. 239, referring to 'holiday and everyday perspectives'.

[64] Jay L. Halio, '"No Clock in the Forest": Time in *As You Like It*', in *Twentieth Century Interpretations of 'As You Like It'*, ed. Jay L. Halio (Englewood Cliffs, 1968), p. 94.

regularity is underscored by the page's insistence that he and his friend 'kept time', that they did not lose their time (5.3.42–3).

From the disordered time of the play's beginning through the apparent timelessness of the forest, which is really nature's time, which regulates 'the seasons' difference', the play comes to the ordered tones of music and regular rhythms of dance, with 'Earthly things made even' and at one together. John Russell Brown finds that what he calls 'the exceptional elaboration of the conclusion—its formal groupings, music, song, dancing, and attendant god—suggests that *As You Like It* is informed to an exceptional degree by Shakespeare's ideal of love's order'.[65] And indeed both here and elsewhere Shakespeare uses dance for its powerful symbolic qualities to signify order and harmony.

Dance is a near-essential part of Renaissance pastoral. In the May Eclogue of *The Shepheardes Calender* Palinode sees 'a shoal of shepherds' dancing 'each one with his maid' (ll. 20–4), and, most famously, in the pastoral Book VI of *The Faerie Queene* Calidore sees the Graces dancing on Mount Acidale, 'All ranged in a ring, and dancing in delight' (VI. x. 11).

The dance in *As You Like It* is the visual representation of Hymen's opening line, 'Peace, ho, I bar confusion' (5.4.120). The 'eight that must take hands' (l. 123) do so not only for the marriage ceremony, but also for their dance: as Sir Thomas Elyot wrote in *The Book Named The Governor* (1531), 'In every dance, of a most ancient custom, there danceth a man and a woman, holding each other by the hand or the arm, which betokeneth concord.'[66] The conflict and confusions of the play are over, the resolution reached, and the graceful regularity of the dance reflects this harmony achieved and the promise of married harmony to come. It also affirms the play's movement back to the city and the court, as the measures, 'full of state and ancientry', as Beatrice describes them in *Much Ado About Nothing* (2.1.69), are dances of the court; they had a special place in court entertainments because they were the first dances after the conclusion of a masque, when the courtier-masquers came down from the stage and took partners from the audience to begin the revels.

[65] *Shakespeare and His Comedies* (2nd edn., 1962), p. 142.

[66] Elyot, p. 94. These words have been given modern currency by T. S. Eliot's use of them in 'East Coker' (*Four Quartets* (1944)).

After the measures came quicker dances like galliards, corantos and lavoltas.[67]

That not only Silvius and Phoebe, but even Audrey (who must have heeded Touchstone's admonition to bear her body 'more seeming') join in this dance is indicative of Shakespeare's amused attitude to pastoral in *As You Like It*, for he both uses and mocks the artificiality of the pastoral mode. Silvius's description of love in 2.4, for instance, is comically extravagant, and rhetorically apt, but it serves to remind Rosalind of her own love. The scornful shepherdess and her unrequited lover are a commonplace of pastoral, from the third Idyll of Theocritus, 'The Despairing Lover', on; here, Rosalind's scolding, her lack of sympathy for Silvius, and the comic tone of the situation invite laughter both at the characters and at the convention they represent. In a provocative study of anti-pastoral sentiment in the English Renaissance, Peter Lindenbaum suggests that Phoebe is not especially beautiful, as she 'needs to be told by Rosalind that she should sell when she can' (3.5.61);[68] if that were so, Rosalind's sarcasm would be pointless, as would Phoebe's recalling that Ganymede had said her eyes and hair were black, which should have given offence (but did not because she was so smitten by Ganymede). Phoebe and Silvius are counterbalanced by Audrey, who is indeed 'foul', and William, who is as taciturn as Silvius is mellifluously fluent. Between the extremes of these two pairs, Corin is the shepherd closest to reality—his hands are hard and smelly from handling his sheep, and he is 'a true labourer' (3.2.69). Mary Lascelles's denial that *As You Like It* is a satire[69] is true in so far as 'satire' is too strong a term, but these rustics are among Shakespeare's tools for examining pastoral; many aspects of the convention are displayed for us to laugh at, sometimes guided to that laughter by characters in the play, Rosalind, Touchstone, Jaques particularly. The litany of love for Silvius, Phoebe, Orlando, and Rosalind in 5.2, for example, is initially attractive in its antiphonal verse, and it was set to music in Trevor Nunn's 1977 RSC production ('"No more of this," says Rosalind; and I agree with her', wrote J. C. Trewin in the

[67] For further discussion see my *Shakespeare and the Dance* (1981), pp. 54–6.

[68] *Changing Landscapes* (Athens, Georgia, 1986), p. 100.

[69] 'Shakespeare's Pastoral Comedy', in *More Talking of Shakespeare*, ed. John Garrett (1959), p. 81.

Birmingham Post, 12 September 1977), but its artificiality is shown up by the reality of Rosalind's sharp question to Orlando and her exasperated description of the incantations as 'like the howling of Irish wolves against the moon' (5.2.104–5). Finally, Shakespeare uses, without mockery, a device beyond the usual bounds of pastoral romance, the appearance of a god. Sometimes, as in Book VI of *The Faerie Queene*, divinity is seen from afar; more frequently, as in *Pandosto*, oracles speak; but in few pastoral romances, and in relatively few pastoral plays and poems, do gods appear.

In these ways, Shakespeare gets inside pastoral, uses it, and exposes it, making not only what David Young calls 'a sort of survey of the tradition' but as well an anatomy of pastoral, and, within that, an anatomy of love.[70]

The Play in Performance

The first recorded performance of *As You Like It* was at the Theatre Royal Drury Lane on 20 December 1740. The first concrete allusion to it in the theatre is its presence in a list now in the Public Records Office (LC 5/12, pp. 212–13), made in January 1669, of 108 plays, 21 of them by Shakespeare, formerly acted at the Blackfriars Theatre by the King's Men, and 'now allowed of' to Thomas Killigrew, Master of the Theatre Royal in Bridges Street; inclusion in such a list, however, is no guarantee of performance. It is a tantalizing thought, but one which must be seriously considered, that this play, immensely popular since 1740, may not have been performed at the time it was written. If that were the case, contributing reasons could be found among those suggested earlier for its not being printed until 1623. (See pp. 2–4 above.)

An historian, William Cory, wrote in August 1865 that on a visit to Wilton House he had been told of a letter 'from Lady Pembroke to her son, telling him to bring James I from Salisbury to see *As You Like It*; . . . he came'.[71] The Court was at Wilton

[70] Young, p. 40, where he helpfully refers to R. P. Draper, 'Shakespeare's Pastoral Comedy', *Etudes Anglaises*, 11 (1958), 1–17. Devon L. Hodges uses *As You Like It* as the example for 'Anatomy as Comedy' in *Renaissance Fictions of Anatomy* (Amherst, 1985), Ch. 4.

[71] Chambers (1930), ii. 329.

between 24 October and 12 December 1603, and the King was at Salisbury on 1 November, but as Cory does not record actually seeing the letter, and as it has never been found, it cannot be taken as evidence of performance.

In a letter of 1605 to Lords Devonshire and Cranborne, Sir John Harington wrote, 'the world is a stage and we that live in it are all stage players; some are good for many parts, some only for dumb shows, some deserve a *plaudite* some a *plorate*', and he then discussed how he had played several parts in his own life—child, scholar, soldier, courtier, husband, and fool among them. Although this has been taken as evidence for the play's performance, it too is unsatisfactory, as Harington prefaced his remarks by saying, 'I conclude (as one prettily argued last day in the Schools)'—a clear reference to school, university, or the sphere of academic discussion generally, not to the theatre. The image of life as a theatre and people as actors was a commonplace, found in contemporary school textbooks.[72]

Although no performances of the play were recorded in England until the eighteenth century, transcripts of six Shakespearian plays, including *As You Like It* (dated 9 March 1694/5), were prepared for theatrical performance, presumably by the students, at the English College at Douai in France; the transcripts were derived from the 1632 Folio, and are held in the Bibliothèque de Douai (MS 7.87), but, again, do not offer firm proof of performance.

Then in 1723 Charles Johnson plundered *As You Like It*, and several other Shakespearian plays, to create *Love in a Forest*, which keeps the main plot, omits Touchstone, Silvius, Phoebe, Audrey, William, and Sir Oliver Martext, names the banished duke Alberto, and marries Celia to Jaques. The wrestling-match becomes a sword combat, with challenges from *Richard II*, other speeches are purloined from *Much Ado About Nothing, Love's Labour's Lost* and *Twelfth Night*, and the mechanicals' 'Pyramus and Thisbe' from *A Midsummer Night's Dream* replaces Touchstone's diverting discourses on the degrees of the lie. The joint

[72] Harington's 27-page letter is in the Bodleian Library (MS Rawl. B162); he is here using 'last day' in the sense of 'yesterday; in time past' (*OED, last, a.* 3b; *yesterday*, B. *sb.* 2) and 'schools' in *OED* sense 7b. For the suggestion that the letter provides evidence of performance see Andrew Gurr, *Playgoing in Shakespeare's London* (Cambridge, 1987), pp. 97–8.

managers of the Drury Lane Theatre, where this gallimaufry was presented, all appeared in it. Colley Cibber was Jaques, Barton Booth Alberto, and Robert Wilks Orlando; Mrs Booth played Rosalind. In the Prologue, spoken by Wilks, the cobbler-playwright was said to have 'retrieved' the play, to have presumed 'to weed the beautiful parterre' of the original, and to have aspired to 'tune the sacred Bard's immortal Lyre; | The scheme from time and error to restore, | And give the stage from Shakespeare one play more'—claims which, as Knowles points out (p. 635), indicate the lack of a stage history for *As You Like It*. *Love in a Forest* itself had a very brief stage history, opening on 9 January 1723 and having only five more performances before disappearing from the stage for ever. But it signalled a growing interest in Shakespeare's comedies, which had not suited Restoration taste.

The revival of *As You Like It* in 1740 was due mainly to rivalry between John Rich, the owner of the Covent Garden theatre, and Charles Fleetwood and Charles Macklin, of Drury Lane, but from the beginning the history of the play's performance has been dominated by the actresses who have played Rosalind, and what follows deals largely with some of them. Breeches parts—actresses in men's roles or as women disguised as men—had become popular during the 1730s; in November 1740 Rich had had great success with Margaret Woffington in the cross-dressed role of Sylvia in Farquhar's *The Recruiting Officer* and then as Sir Harry Wildair in *The Constant Couple*. The members of the Shakespearian Ladies Club wanted more of their beloved Bard, and so Macklin, who probably had his eye on the part of Touchstone, which he played in the following season and for many after, decided on *As You Like It*, with Hannah Pritchard as Rosalind and the vivacious Kitty Clive as Celia. Thomas Arne composed music for the songs, including the Cuckoo Song from *Love's Labour's Lost*, given to Celia at first, but almost always after to Rosalind, provided the actress could sing; it remained in the play until the twentieth century. The great success of the comedy led to a twelve-night run, revivals of *Twelfth Night* and *The Merchant of Venice*, and a rise in Shakespeare's popularity which has continued ever since. From mid-December to the end of March 1741 there were only six acting nights without a Shakespearian production at one of the three London theatres. For six nights in October 1741, *As*

You Like It played simultaneously at both Drury Lane and Covent Garden: Mrs Woffington was Rosalind at the Lane and Mrs Pritchard at the Garden. And it was as Rosalind that the beautiful Peg made her last appearance. On 3 May 1757 she suffered a stroke while halfway through the Epilogue, a frightful occurrence described by John Doran: 'that once saucy tongue became paralysed . . . and at the sense that she was stricken, she flung up her hands, uttered a wild shriek in abject terror, and staggering towards the stage-door, fell into the arms stretched to receive her; and amidst indescribable confusion of cheering and commiserating cries, Margaret Woffington disappeared from the stage for ever.'[73]

Other eighteenth-century Rosalinds avoided such a dramatic exit from this role, which was so popular that even Sarah Siddons, the greatest Lady Macbeth of the age, attempted it. Although a successful Rosalind in the provinces a decade earlier, when she played the part in London in 1785 and 1786 Siddons failed both times. Embarrassed by appearing as a man, she devised a Ganymede costume neither clearly masculine nor feminine, inciting such scorn as the *Morning Post*'s: 'Her hussar boots, with a gardener's apron and petticoat behind, gave her a most equivocal appearance which rendered Orlando's stupidity astonishing in not making a premature discovery of his mistress.'[74] A further reason for Mrs Siddons's failure is indicated by Charles Young's remark that her Rosalind 'wanted neither playfulness nor feminine softness; but it was totally without archness, not because she did not properly conceive it—but how could such a countenance be arch?'[75] Where Sarah Siddons failed, Dorothy Jordan triumphed. This good-natured, buoyant actress, whose trim figure and perfect legs, so admired by Sir Joshua Reynolds, were well suited to male costume, played Rosalind first on 13 April 1787 and continued in the part until she left the London stage in 1814; she was probably one of the reasons that from 1776 to 1817 *As You Like It* was acted at Drury Lane more often than any other Shakespeare play. Her portrayal of Rosalind as an arch rogue, with something of the hoyden, typified the eighteenth-century concept of the part, though Mrs Spranger Barry (formerly

[73] *'Their Majesties' Servants'*, 3 vols. (1888), ii. 210.

[74] Cited by Linda Kelly, *The Kemble Era* (New York, 1980), p. 54.

[75] Cited by Mrs Clement Parsons, *The Incomparable Siddons* (1909), p. 124.

6. Mrs Barry, Drury Lane, *c.* 1773, with a boar-spear in her hand (1.3.117). No. VI in a series, 'How the Old Actors Dressed "Shakespeare"'. A caption describes this as 'a portrait of Mrs Barry as Rosalind, in a costume which defies archaeology, and might indeed, be the fellow to the one her husband played Timon in.' The fur trimming was common until late into the nineteenth century. (*Illustrated London News*, 15 April 1893)

Mrs Dancer and later Mrs Crawford), who played her every season at Drury Lane from 1766 to 1778, appears to have been less boisterous (Fig. 6).

The sight of actresses in men's clothes seems to have become increasingly attractive from the 1720s on. This may be one aspect of a more generally intensified interest in cross-dressing which was then developing, partly through cases of women who disguised themselves as men and joined the army or navy to be with lovers or husbands. According to Alice Browne, although women discovered to be masquerading as soldiers and sailors were discharged and not allowed to re-enlist, 'accounts of women who lived in male disguise were often quite sympathetic. In 1776 a jury convicted a blackmailer who had revealed a transvestite woman's true gender'.[76] Among published accounts of such women were *The Life and Adventures of Mrs. Christian Davies, the British Amazon* (1740) and *The Female Soldier; or the Surprising Life and Adventures of Hannah Small* (1750). Christian Davies, it is interesting to note, who was a veteran of Marlborough's wars, spent her old age as a Chelsea pensioner. Another reason for the popularity of breeches parts may have been the social attitude that cross-dressing implied sexual wantonness. Girls who were tomboys were probably not, it was thought, likely to uphold the highest standards of female propriety. In the scandalous *Memoirs of the Remarkable Life and Surprizing Adventures of Miss Jenny Cameron* (1746), the author, Archibald Arbuthnot, links the ebullient Miss Cameron's tomboyish romping with her seduction at an early age. Both male and female members of the theatre audience could therefore have been titillated by the appearance of a Rosalind, a Viola, or a Harry Wildair. And in this attitude is a clue to that quality of archness which eighteenth-century critics found so praiseworthy in actresses who played Rosalind.

The last major Rosalind in the prevailing eighteenth-century mode of arch hoyden was Mrs Nesbitt, who was the first to play the role in William Charles Macready's Drury Lane production of 1842, the most influential production of the play ever staged. Macready himself played a distinguished, contemplative Jaques. An engraving (Fig. 7) shows the wrestling scene, with a great castle, over eighty spectators, including Rosalind and Celia downstage right, and a fence around the wrestling ring. There were ninety-seven in the cast altogether, and seventy-eight of them appeared in the grand processional entry of Duke Frederick and his court. The actors playing Charles and Orlando were trained in Cornish wrestling and the fight was exceedingly realistic: excited members of the audience would shout at Rosalind and Celia to move out of the way because they were blocking the view.

Macready's close attention to historical accuracy in the lavish sets and costumes—the place chosen was France in the fifteenth century—contributed to the growing movement to realism in

[76] *The Eighteenth Century Feminist Mind* (Brighton, 1987), p. 128.

7. The wrestling scene (1.2) with Rosalind and Celia downstage right in W. C. Macready's production, Drury Lane, 1842. An illustration by T. H. Shepherd in *London Interiors* (1844).

staging which led in turn to Shakespearian plays' being heavily cut to accommodate lengthy scene changes, a kind of theatrical equivalent to the increasing encrustation of annotation which tended to obscure the texts they were meant to clarify.

Mrs Nesbitt's Rosalind, however, was generally felt to be inadequate (even Macready thought so), and the description in the *Spectator* indicates the changed, more romantic, perception of the role. Mrs Nesbitt was considered to be

> utterly devoid of sentiment, and deficient in depth and earnestness: it [was] a very pleasant performance of the 'saucy lacquey' that Rosalind affects to be, the arch manner and joyous spirit of the actress giving piquancy to the assumption; but there [was] no under-current of tender and impassioned feeling.[77]

[77] Cited by N. R. Schroeder, '*As You Like It* in the English Theatre 1740–1955' (unpublished Ph.D. dissertation, Yale University, 1962), p. 96.

The desired 'tender and impassioned feeling' soon became the hallmark of the successful Rosalind. When the young Helen Faucit took over the role on three occasions in the first season, including a Royal Command Performance, and then more regularly, under Macready's tutelage she developed a different, sentimental interpretation which dominated the English stage until the 1920s. It was the part she loved above all others and she made her last appearance on the stage when she played it at a charity performance in 1879 in Manchester when almost sixty-five (Fig. 9).

A review of Helen Faucit's Rosalind in the *Edinburgh Observer* for 20 February 1845 makes a useful comparison:

> As we have but too often seen the Rosalind of the stage, she was merely the pretty coquette, roguish and knowing in the small artifices of a cold nature; or, what is worse, a coarse and not over nice woman of fashion, who had laid down her maidenhood with her dress, as if she thought, in despite of the author, that it was actually necessary that she should wear doublet and hose in her disposition. How different is it with this lady's Rosalind! In the most joyous outbursts of the sparkling fancy amid the freedom of the forest, we never miss the duke's daughter, whom, in the first act, we have seen, in the gentleness and unconscious grace of her deportment, the leading ornament of the court of her usurping uncle. She is never less than the high-born and high-bred gentle-woman.[78]

Twenty-six years after she had first performed the role, Helen Faucit was being praised by *Once A Week* in these terms:

> She is an actress who unites to singular physical graces a rare intelligence, whose charming voice is exquisitely modulated and managed—who can be both merry and wise, as Rosalind should be—who can be playful and tender too, humorous yet pathetic, arch and yet kind—can rail and love all the while—can wear doublet and hose, and, not forgetting Rosalind in Ganymede, be womanly still. Among the things to be properly prized by a public making any pretension to cultured taste—that should be seen, while yet it *can* be seen—is the representation of Rosalind by Miss Helen Faucit.[79]

Writing to Robert Browning in September 1884, Faucit said, 'To me *As You Like It* seems to be essentially as much a love-poem

[78] Cited by George Fletcher, *Studies of Shakespeare* (1847), p. 239.
[79] 10 June 1865, p. 686.

8. Ada Rehan, a great American Rosalind, with weapons and palm fronds. Augustin Daly's production at his New York theatre, 1889.
9. Helen Faucit, the most influential nineteenth-century English Rosalind, represented saying 'Come, woo me, woo me, for now I am in a holiday humour, and like enough to consent' (4.1.62–3). A surreptitious drawing made by J. D. Watson during rehearsal for her last stage appearance, at the Theatre Royal, Manchester, 1 October 1879 (*The Graphic*, 18 October 1879).

as *Romeo and Juliet*, with this difference, that it deals with happy love'.[80] Her approach to the role, and her personal involvement in it, are indicated by her account of how overcome with emotion she always was at the discovery that the unknown poet of Arden is Orlando: 'Oh happiness beyond belief, oh rapture irrepressible! The tears at this part always welled up to my eyes,' she writes,

[80] Helena Faucit (Lady Martin), *On Some of Shakespeare's Female Characters* (1885), p. 321. Carol J. Carlisle gives a usefully detailed discussion of Faucit's interpretation in 'Helen Faucit's Rosalind', *Shakespeare Studies*, 12 (1979), pp. 65–94.

'and my whole body trembled.' There was further occasion for the lachrymose on the line 'I do take thee, Orlando, for my husband'. 'I could never speak these words', she confesses, 'without a trembling of the voice, and the involuntary rushing of happy tears to the eyes, which made it necessary for me to turn my head away from Orlando.' Ellen Terry remarked that Miss Faucit indeed 'flushed up' when making her vow, and spoke with 'deep and true emotion'.[81]

On the other side of the Atlantic, Mary Anderson was being praised for similar, if not such emotional, feminine qualities. In October 1885 William Winter wrote in the *New York Tribune* of the 'sweet woman-nature' that characterized her portrayal and went on to say,

> Her Rosalind is neither a sensual rake nor a flippant hoyden; nor, on the other hand, is it in the least degree suggestive of an insipid prude. It is a noble, brilliant, pure, lovely woman, glorious in the affluent vitality of her beautiful youth, and enchanting in the healthful, gleeful, sparkling freedom of her bright mind and her happy heart.[82]

When Mary Anderson had made her debut in the role earlier in the year at Stratford, the English critics had not been so complimentary. The *St James Gazette* found her Rosalind 'of the earth earthy, belong[ing] to prose and not to poetry', lacking refinement and 'natural girlish charm' (3 September 1885); the *Manchester Courier*, while finding she acted with 'grace and charm', declared that 'the true ring of womanly sympathy could not be detected. . . . We have yet to see', the writer continued, 'the ideal Rosalind who with high spirits, first-rate comedy, power and womanly sympathy combines the capacity to express all those with perfect poetic feeling and truth to nature idealised through a romantic camera' (31 August 1885).

The *Courier* critic may have found a Rosalind close to his wish in Ada Rehan (Fig. 8), the greatest American Rosalind of the time, who was coached by Augustin Daly. She gave her first performance in his New York theatre on 17 December 1889, opened in London at the Lyceum on 15 July 1890, and took the play to the Vaudeville in Paris in the following year. Daly cut,

[81] Faucit, p. 340; Ellen Terry, *The Story of My Life* (1908), p. 189.
[82] Cited, *Dramatic Notes*, 1886 [Jan.–Dec. 1885], pp. 57–8.

changed, and bowdlerized the text to emphasize his star, and her combination of refinement, vigour, eager energy, and impulsiveness captivated a susceptible George Bernard Shaw when he saw her at the Grand, Islington, in 1897, though he disliked Daly's rather brash production overall. On 26 August 1897 the play was given as the first open-air production at Stratford, but rain forced its removal into the Memorial Theatre; Rehan reaped praise as 'the ideal Rosalind', whose 'by-play . . . was admirably suggestive of the woman's tender heart beating under the doublet in her interviews with Orlando' (*Daily News*, 27 August 1897). The *Leamington Courier* claimed that 'never has a more charming Rosalind been seen upon the boards' and commented further on her 'womanliness' (28 August 1897).

The reviewers' attitude is at one with Alfred Cann's description of Rosalind in his edition of the play which appeared in 1902: 'Rosalind . . . is cheerful under adverse circumstances, bright, vivacious and witty; but with it all she is most tender-hearted, a true womanly woman, with great capacity for sympathy and feelings for others.'[83] In 1907 Lily Brayton was felt by some to lack womanliness, but, according to the *Standard*, 'the girl-youth in the forest [was] blithe and warm with life' (8 October 1907). Her Orlando, Henry Ainley, was praised in the same review as 'manly and romantic' and for having, like Brayton, 'caught the trick of naturalness'. They were appearing in Oscar Asche's lavish production at His Majesty's, in which Asche himself played a controversially old Jaques, with a bald head and tufted beard, who munched an apple during the Seven Ages speech. The production was praised for its scenic realism—justifiably, as in the forest scenes, two thousand pots of fern and large clumps of bamboo were used, the forest floor was covered with cartloads of autumn leaves, and moss grew on the fallen logs. For the first time, Rosalind as Ganymede was dressed as a shepherd, with smock and crook (Fig. 10); another innovation, and a welcome one according to Gordon Crosse, an avid playgoer, was 'the happy introduction of a fire & a caldron [which]' he wrote, 'saved us from the usual absurdity of the outlaws appearing to live entirely upon apples'.[84] The text was cut and rearranged into

[83] *As You Like It* (1902), p. 30.

[84] 'Shakespeare Performances which I have seen. Vol. IV. July 1905–May 1909', MS in Birmingham Ref. Library S649.

10. Lily Brayton, in Oscar Asche's production, His Majesty's, 1907. Her wearing a shepherd's smock and leggings and carrying a crook broke with tradition.

thirteen scenes in three acts, specially printed copies being given as souvenirs to the first-night audience. Asche's realism was surpassed at the Queen's, Manchester, the following year, where Richard Flanagan provided a forest of Arden 'peopled with knotty trees, carpeted with luxurious moss and grass, traversed by a brook of rippling water, [and] enlivened by a flock of deer, who seemed to be quite at home in the make-believe of their haunt' (*Sunday Times*, 15 March 1908); the Orlando, Harcourt Williams, was less than happy at sharing the stage with Duke Senior's 'poor dappled fools' when they began to chase him, though he tried to look 'as heroic as he could in the circumstances'.[85]

[85] W. J. Harcourt Williams, *Four Years at the Old Vic* (1935), p. 192.

11. Claude Lovat Fraser's set for 1.1, Stratford, 1919. The stylized foliage was in light and darker tones of blue-green, the costumes for Orlando and Adam in ochre and brown. The colours in the court scenes were clear and vivid: vermilion, emerald, lemon, cobalt, crimson; those in the forest more subdued, but still fresh (*The Studio*, 77, 316 (1919), p. 65).

The womanly heroine, if not so sentimental as Faucit portrayed her, was the prevailing style of English Rosalinds until Nigel Playfair's revolutionary *As You Like It* at Stratford in 1919, which outraged some local Stratfordians. Like Macready's, it was a strong influence on subsequent productions, though unfortunately lacking similar commercial success. Playfair, who restored virtually the whole text, directed for clarity and speed, and his designer, Claude Lovat Fraser, dressed the cast in bright, clearly coloured clothes of medieval cut; the scenery, too, was simple and stylized (Fig. 11). There was no place here for the stuffed deer that had appeared in the hunting-chorus scene (4.2) in every Stratford production since 1879 when it was first brought on stage as a carcass, newly slaughtered from among the Charlecote deer herd (which was descended from the very herd from which, according to local myth, Shakespeare had poached a buck). This was the place, however, for a fresh approach to characterization; John Gielgud has remarked that 'The whole production was strikingly simple and bold in its conception, but it was before its time—and at Stratford-on-Avon . . . the Press was outraged and the company almost mobbed in the streets'.[86]

By no means, however, was all the press 'outraged'. The *Spectator* remarked that Athene Seyler was 'Rosalind complete', and commented on her 'gaiety, good humour, and tenderness'. The *Manchester Guardian* said that she 'takes the part at a tremendous rate, but the delicacy and perfection of her technique wonderfully bring out the invincible gaiety and tenderness which lie in Rosalind' (23 April 1919). *The Times* found her 'tingling with life and humour and femininity from start to finish' (23 April 1919). The *Morning Post* thought Herbert Marshall's Jaques a 'most striking performance . . . curiously individual and altogether a most interesting study of a morbidly intelligent cynic' and Playfair himself a 'fresh and entertaining Touchstone' (23 April 1919).

For several critics the production was experimental, and not an especially successful experiment at that. But what few realized at the time was that it freed the play from Macready's heavy medieval realism, from Faucit's sentimentalism, and, to a large extent, from directorial scissors and paste. William Poel, whose experimentation was of a more academic kind, had not included the play among those he produced for the Elizabethan Stage Society in the early years of the century, but his theories were the basis for the creation of the Maddermarket Theatre in Norwich, which opened on 23 September 1921 with an uncut version of the play performed in Elizabethan costume on what the director, Nugent Monck, called 'the first practical model of a sixteenth-century stage since Shakespeare's day'.[87] In 1932 there came Harcourt Williams's production at the Old Vic in Elizabethan dress with Peggy Ashcroft (Fig. 12), and four years later the famous Old Vic production by Esmé Church, dressed à la Watteau, with 48-year-old Edith Evans wooing and winning an Orlando half her age, in Michael Redgrave (Fig. 13). The romance was off-stage as well as on; in his autobiography Redgrave says

[86] *Early Stages* (1948), p. 71.
[87] *Shakespeare Survey 12* (1959), p. 72.

12. The first major modern production in Elizabethan dress, directed by Harcourt Williams at the Old Vic (1932). Valerie Tudor as Celia, Peggy Ashcroft as Rosalind, Geoffrey Wincott as Touchstone and Marius Goring as Le Beau. (1.2.91)

13. Edith Evans as Rosalind in blue satin with Michael Redgrave as Orlando. Esmé Church's Watteau-inspired production at the Old Vic (1936) and the New Theatre (1937). (5.4.118)

that the best advice he can give any Orlando is to fall in love with his Rosalind. Redgrave was, in fact, an expectant father at the time. His wife, Rachel Kempson, gave birth to their first daughter in 1937 and it is a nice irony that in 1961 that daughter, Vanessa Redgrave, succeeded Edith Evans as the most acclaimed Rosalind of her generation.

For all her Watteau costume of blue silk, Edith Evans was a thoroughly modern Rosalind: Alan Dent wrote that she gave 'a romantic and a witty performance';[88] for A. V. Cookman in the *London Mercury* on the other hand, she was 'anti-romantic' (vol. 35, p. 499). All agreed, however, that Edith Evans was enchanting and, even though somewhat old for the part, she was, depending on which reviewer you read, radiant, bewitching or even 'young love incarnate'.[89]

Vanessa Redgrave's Rosalind had audiences and critics alike at her feet. J. W. Lambert in *The Sunday Times*: she 'smiles away all problems, striking a silver note unheard on our stages for years, a note which sings of radiance without effort, of an unrestrained charity' (9 July 1961). In the *Daily Express* Bernard Levin rapturized, 'This Rosalind is a creature of fire and light . . . her body a slender supple reed rippling in the breeze of her love' (5 July 1961). In the *Spectator* Bamber Gascoigne began his paean with 'Her performance was a triumph' (14 July 1961). Redgrave's interpretation was in certain ways an anticipation of what later became the 'swinging sixties'. Slightly gawky in Elizabethan dress in the opening scenes at court, in Arden she became a free-spirited gamin; her long hair tucked up under a cap, she had a simple smock, pedal pushers (close-fitting pants coming to just below the knee), and bare calves and feet (Fig. 14). The women in the audience could respond to the lithe, lanky boy, the men to the lithe, slim girl beneath the disguise. Tony Church, who played Duke Frederick, has remarked that Ian Bannen, as Orlando, complicated his part, and the relationship, by reacting to the boy Ganymede rather than to the woman beneath the disguise—very different from Michael Redgrave, who made it clear that he would really prefer to pine for Rosalind than woo her proxy. The director, Michael Elliott, who trusted Shakespeare and used a very lightly cut text, gave the early scenes a chilly

[88] *Preludes and Studies* (1942), p. 112.

[89] For A. V. Cookman's and a variety of other views see Schroeder, pp. 222–3.

14. Rosalind in pedal-pushers. Vanessa Redgrave with Ian Bannen as Orlando in Michael Elliott's RSC production (1961). (5.2.19–20)

setting, emphasized by the fur hat and coat of Max Adrian's Jaques, a characterization which J. W. Lambert could 'hardly praise too highly for its restraint, its cankered pathos, its exquisite timing' (*Sunday Times*, 9 July 1961). Most reviewers remarked on Richard Negri's unit set, dominated by a large tree centre stage on top of a grassy slope, a 'great tree of life perched on a grave-like knoll', Edmund Gardner called it (*Stratford-upon-Avon Herald*, 20 October 1961).

The move to directors' rather than actors' Shakespeare led to greater freedom and experimentation, including Clifford Williams's 1967 all-male production for the National Theatre at the Old Vic. It was not the first recorded, Ben Greet having staged an all-male version in Elizabethan costume on 23 April 1920 at the Central YMCA buildings, with Duncan Yarrow as Rosalind, Leslie French as Celia and the dancer Anton Dolin as Phoebe. Critical anxiety was allayed when it was found to contain nothing to cause offence.[90] On 21 November 1893 a cast of women, some in false beards, presented the play at Palmer's Theatre in New York, and thereafter at a number of New York theatres until 3 February 1894. The idea, if not the cast, travelled across the Atlantic and an all-woman production was staged at London's Prince of Wales Theatre on 27 February 1894. Like the men's production twenty-six years later, this was more curious than satisfactory.

The 1967 Old Vic programme carried extracts from Jan Kott's essay on the play in *Shakespeare Our Contemporary*, and a comment by the director that he used a male cast so that the 'atmosphere of spiritual purity which transcends sensuality in the search for poetic sexuality' could be attained allowing 'the interior truth' of the play to emerge. Whether this ambitious aim was achieved was a matter for individual opinion, but the interpretation was coherent and stimulating. Ralph Koltai designed contemporary costumes and an effective abstract setting, with dangling clear plastic strips for the forest. Ronald Pickup (Fig. 15) was a somewhat intellectual Rosalind, Charles Kay a shrewd Celia, in spectacles, and Jeremy Brett a manly Orlando. The sex of the actors became irrelevant, except in the case of Audrey, who had a thick blonde pigtail and a five o'clock shadow. Taken to America with a different cast and costumes in 1974, the production was criticized for being coarse and extreme, a drag act lacking the purpose and achievement of the original.

Declan Donnellan's joyous production for Cheek By Jowl, however, which opened on 11 July 1991 at the Redgrave Theatre, Farnham, and toured internationally before closing in Madrid in March 1992, was justifiably praised. Its all-male cast included two black actors, Adrian Lester, an outstanding Rosalind, sensitive, passionate, and funny, and Joe Dixon, a slow-speaking, homosexual Jaques. Tom Hollander gave a home-counties surface to his watchful, tender-hearted Celia, who had a wonderful capacity for eloquent silence, and Patrick Toomey was a strong, boyish, but firmly masculine Orlando. The bare stage was walled with white canvas, broad strips of green silk unfurling from the

[90] On 19 April 1742 a Mr Page played Rosalind at his own benefit performance at the Haymarket Theatre. This must have been something of a curiosity, as Page is listed only once in the index to Charles Hogan's *Shakespeare in the Theatre 1701–1800*, 2 vols. (Oxford, 1957), in this role.

flies to represent Arden. Nick Ormerod dressed Frederick and his courtiers in tail suits, and gave the exiles Edwardian country clothes; Ganymede and Aliena wore modern dress. Among many felicitous touches, when the audience returned after the interval, which followed Act 2, Orlando was discovered sitting downstage centre writing his verses, so that the whole of 3.1, the banishment of Oliver, gained particular resonance by being enacted behind him.

Buzz Goodbody's production in 1973 made her the first woman to direct a play on the main stage of the Royal Shakespeare Theatre at Stratford; she, too, used modern dress (Fig. 16), but elicited the comment from Robert Cushman in *The Observer* that 'In her tight-fitting jacket and jeans, Eileen Atkins could just as easily be a boy as a girl. She could, however, just as easily be a girl as a boy, and I have never felt less inclination to suspend my disbelief' (17 June 1973). Four years later Trevor Nunn turned the play into a kind of baroque opera (Michael Billington, *Guardian*, 10 September 1977) or pantomime (John Peter, *Sunday Times*, 11 September 1977), swamping good performances by Peter McEnery as Orlando and Kate Nelligan as a Rosalind who was a 'nervous thoroughbred' (Peter), 'flashing eager smiles and using her nervy wit to camouflage her true feeling' (Billington). J. C. Trewin wryly ended his review in the *Birmingham Post*: 'As a musical variation . . . it has probably a certain charm. After all, its title is *As You Like It*, and this is a director's world' (12 September 1977); the musical content was quickly reduced during the early weeks of its run. At the Olivier in 1979 John Dexter mounted an imposing concluding masque as a spring celebration following a wintry first half of the play; influenced by Sir James Frazer's *Golden Bough*, he created what Ian McEwan of the *New Statesman* called a 'season of pre-Christian English country lore, lusty, blood-daubed, drunken, erotic and, of course, fertile, a time of holiday misrule and mating' (10 August 1979). Elaborately Elizabethan in costume, intellectualized and initially slow-moving, it divided critics. John Elsom called it 'a definitive illustration of how not to direct *As You Like It*', weighed down with 'academic interpretations, often startling in their silliness' (*Listener*, 9 August 1979), and considered Sara Kestelman and Simon Callow wildly miscast as Rosalind and Orlando. J. C.

15. Ronald Pickup as Rosalind in Clifford Williams's all-male *As You Like It* for the National Theatre (Old Vic, 1967). (3.2.84)

16. Rosalind in jeans. Hewison's cartoon of Eileen Atkins with David Suchet as Orlando and Richard Pasco as Jaques. Buzz Goodbody's RSC production (1973).

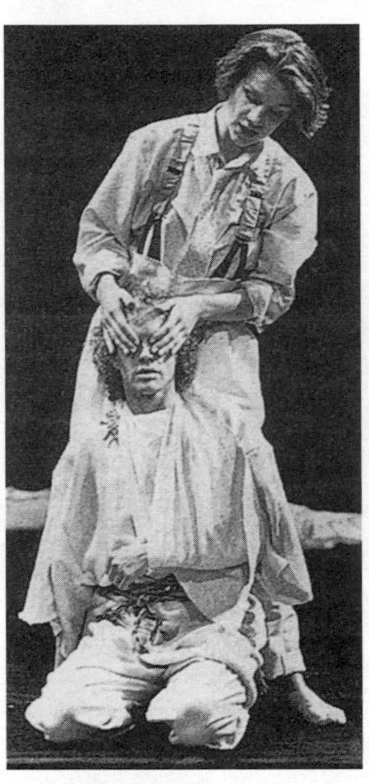

17. Juliet Stevenson with Hilton McRae as Orlando (5.2) in Adrian Noble's RSC production (1985).

Trewin thought Kestelman a Rosalind 'who knows all about the part, refuses to be arch, enjoys the forest masquerade and—most important—understands what to do with her vowels and consonants' (*Birmingham Post*, 3 August 1979); B. A. Young wrote, 'Simon Callow's Orlando really is a young man in love, and he speaks the verse to perfection' (*Financial Times*, 2 August 1979), and Michael Bryant drew nearly universal praise for his sardonic Jaques (who emulated Asche in eating an apple during the Seven Ages speech).

Adrian Noble's modern dress production for the RSC in 1985 brought acclaim to Juliet Stevenson (Fig. 17), though for some critics she was at first overshadowed by Fiona Shaw's Celia. The two actresses have written lucidly about their playing of the roles in *Players of Shakespeare 2*, edited by Russell Jackson and Robert Smallwood (Cambridge, 1988). Their third paragraph is an indication of the impact of feminist theory on Shakespearian interpretation in the theatre, and provides an intellectual platform for the philosophy of their presentation:

> To liberate Shakespeare's women from the confines of literary and theatrical tradition requires an analysis of the nature and effects of those social structures which define and contain them—the opening of this play sees Rosalind and Celia already contained within a structure that is oppressive and patriarchal, namely the court of Duke Frederick, Celia's father. The modern dress decision served to remind us that such structures are by no means 'ancient history', and that the freedom and self-definition that the two girls are seeking remain prevalent needs for many of their contemporaries today. (p. 57)

They make a particularly acute comment about the play's conclusion:

> in the play's closing moments it is Duke Senior who resumes charge, and traditional values seem in danger of being celebrated. This, at the end of a play which so fully and radically explores the complexities of sexuality, maleness, and femaleness, and sends gender boundaries flying, was endlessly difficult to play. (p. 70)

Some reviewers remarked on the development of Rosalind away from the repressive court, and touching the heart with 'Men have died from time to time, and worms have eaten them; but not for love' (Martin Hoyle, *Financial Times*, 25 April 1985); of her succumbing to 'an erotic spell which comes over in great waves of musky intoxication' (Irving Wardle, *Times*, 19 December 1985). There was initially a feeling that the play's comic gaiety had been sacrificed for the concept that 'Arden is a cruel mirror-image of the court where people come to self realisation' (Michael Billington, *Guardian*, 18 December 1985), but in retrospect, Nicholas Shrimpton thought it 'frank, funny and, above all, intellectually alive' (*Shakespeare Survey* 39 (1987), p. 203).

Searching for new interpretations, directors produced odd and idiosyncratic versions. Tim Albery's at the Old Vic in 1989 turned Frederick's court into a malevolent fortress, and later, according to *Punch*, sent Fiona Shaw 'lolloping and whooping her way through a scruffy Forest of Arden' (19 August 1990). Stratford director John Caird was reprimanded by *The Guardian*'s Nicholas de Jongh for 'playing with Shakespeare again . . . Shakespeare has been hurt in the rough and tumble'; another casualty was

Sophie Thompson's Rosalind (Fig. 18), who 'emerged as a simpering St. Trinian's schoolgirl . . . Eschewing any hint of androgynous appeal', he wrote, 'Miss Thompson runs a gamut from bawling declamation to doleful quaver . . . there is small hint of sexual pathos, flirtatious mockery or erotic tension in her larkish, gamey performance' (13 April 1990). So much for womanly tenderness.

In his biography of Peggy Ashcroft, Michael Billington remarks,

> Rosalind, whom Peggy played [at Stratford in 1957] in Byam Shaw's opening production of *As You Like It*, has never been one of her favourite Shakespeare parts . . . But what she brought to the role—and she was admirably partnered by Richard Johnson as a virile Orlando—was a passionate sincerity. When she cried, 'But what talk we of fathers when there is such a man as Orlando?' it was with the moonstruck rapture of one fathoms-deep in love.
>
> This seems to me the crucial test of any Rosalind. Do you actually believe she is smitten by Orlando? I have seen Rosalinds lately who look as if they would much rather have a good natter with Celia about the works of Betty Friedan or Kate Millett than waste their time in the arduous business of wooing. There is also the Restoration Rosalind who enjoys raillery for its own sake and the hoydenish thigh-slapper who looks as if she is awaiting the arrival of Dick Whittington's Cat. Peggy had the feverish vivacity of the woman in love.[91]

Billington has here neatly pictured three of the main types of Rosalind—the hoyden, the wit, and the modern intellectual. To these must be added the serious and sentimental Rosalind of the nineteenth century, given something of a nudge but not displaced from the English stage by the American actresses Mary Anderson and Ada Rehan.

Although the first American Rosalind was Mrs Kenna, who appeared at the John Street Theater, New York, on 14 July 1786, the popularity of *As You Like It* in America began fifty years later, when Ellen Tree acted the role at the Park Theatre on 12 December 1836, three years after first playing it at Drury Lane. From then until the end of the century, the play was staged in New York with more regularity than in London and Stratford together. Helena Modjeska played a refined, elegant Rosalind in

[91] *Peggy Ashcroft* (1988), p. 170.

18. Rosalind as schoolgirl. Sophie Thompson, with Gillian Bevan as Celia, in John Caird's RSC production (1989).

19. Katharine Hepburn as a leggy Rosalind in Michael Benthall's production for the Theatre Guild, Cort Theater, New York (1950).

her own heavily cut version, published in 1883, and Julia Marlowe acted the role in New York between 1890 and 1910, though without, it seems, much distinction.

American productions, like the English, long remained traditional and vehicles for a star actress. Henrietta Crosman had a run of 60 performances at the Republic from 27 February 1902, a record which stood until Katharine Hepburn's season of 145 performances at the Cort Theater for the Theatre Guild, beginning 26 January 1950 (Fig. 19). A famous film star, directed by Michael Benthall from the Old Vic in her first Shakespearian role, Hepburn brought to Rosalind physical charm but little enchantment, despite her stated intention of playing 'for romance—pure, idealized, fabulous romance' (*New York Times*, 22 January 1950). 'She is not', wrote Brooks Atkinson, 'a helpless, bewitched, moonstruck maiden swooning through a magic forest . . . [she] has too sharply defined a personality for such romantic make-believe [and] her acting lacks the softness and warmth that commend Rosalind so passionately to Orlando' (*New York Times*, 27 January 1950). The critics generally agreed; audiences ignored them. Word Baker directed the first modern-dress production of the play for the American Shakespeare Festival, Connecticut, in June 1961, with a crop-haired Kim Hunter as Rosalind and a barefoot David Harron as Orlando in overalls. John McClain in the *New York Journal-American* approved the innovation of modern dress, as bringing the speech and behaviour of the players closer to the audience. Joseph Morgenstern of the *Herald Tribune*, however, felt that Baker had given his actors a 'conflicting collection of maps printed in different centuries' (17 June 1961).[92]

Romance in the setting at least returned with Romanian-born Andrei Serban's 1980 production in the La Mama Annex, New York, which began on a narrow apron stage before a street scene and then changed to a warehouse-size space for an Arden with pond, bridge, and dozens of real trees through which the actors led the audience. Serban, who had directed open-air productions in France (see below), saw the play in traditionally pastoral terms, love coming 'not in a romantic or sentimental sense, but as an energy for discovery' which the characters took back to the city

[92] Cited by Alice Anne Margarida, 'Shakespeare's Rosalind. A Survey and Checklist of the Role in Performance, 1740–1980' (unpublished Ph.D. dissertation, University of New York, 1982), p. 131.

(*New York Times*, 18 January 1980). Mel Gussow of the *New York Times* enjoyed the 'carnival-like' staging because '*As You Like It* should be feather-light and fanciful', and seemed unaware of Serban's serious intentions for the play. The environmental setting may have had similarities with that of Peter Stein's 1977 Berlin production (see below), but conceptually as well as geographically the two were oceans apart.

Among notable productions of *As You Like It* elsewhere, the most famous was Jacques Copeau's, which ran for 150 performance at the Théâtre de l'Atelier in Paris from 6 October 1934 and was remounted in the open air at the Boboli Gardens in Florence in May 1938 with an Italian cast. Copeau, who himself played Jaques, wrote, 'All my efforts have been concentrated on that wonder of wonders—on Rosalind. A gigantic role beneath its fragile envelope'.[93] The Rosalind of this detailed production was Madeleine Lambert, Jean-Louis Barrault played Touchstone, and the music, which included twenty-seven items, was composed by Georges Auric. Philip Carr commented in the *New York Times* (11 November 1934) that Lambert gave a 'very intelligent, if insufficiently homely and natural' performance, but that Copeau's direction was too heavy handed, missing the play's poetic essence. The Italian film director Luchino Visconti's production at Rome's Teatro Eliseo which opened on 26 November 1948 was more notable for the decor and costumes by Salvador Dali than for a cogent interpretation of the play. Robert Speaight considered that the 'combination of a realist director and a surrealist designer who had turned his back on surrealism, was to get the worst of both conventions'.[94]

Academic criticism became increasingly influential in the theatre during the second half of the twentieth century. Peter Stein's elaborate philosophical production in 1977 for the Schaubühne am Halleschen Ufer company in Berlin, for example, claimed in its programme inspiration from Northrop Frye and Jan Kott. Staged in a film studio, it included Robin Hood, Robinson Crusoe, a wild man and some present-day hikers among its characters and ran for four and a half hours. At the end of Act 1 the audience, limited to 300 because most available space was needed for acting and staging, had to take a difficult fifteen-

[93] Cited by Robert Speaight, *Shakespeare on the Stage* (1973), p. 191.

[94] Speaight, p. 263.

20. Robin Phillips's Regency *As You Like It* for the 1977 Stratford (Ontario) festival, with Domini Blythe as Celia, Bernard Hopkins as Touchstone, Bob Baker as Le Beau and Maggie Smith as Rosalind (1.2).

minute walk before arriving in an open forest area with a stream, pond, trees, and singing shepherds. Werner Habicht remarked in *Shakespeare Quarterly* that 'the sense of having experienced "total Shakespeare" prevailed, though several critics complained that they had been unable to take in all the details' (*SQ*, 29 (1978), p. 299).

Untouched by such elaborate theorizing and experiment, but with a strong concern for elegance, in Canada Robin Phillips directed the play for the 1977 Stratford Ontario Festival with Regency costumes designed by Robin Fraser Paye, a winning Rosalind in Maggie Smith (Fig. 20) and an unusually young, dashing Jaques in Brian Bedford. Ralph Berry saw the production as being placed in the world of a Jeffrey Farnol romance, and Phillips as 'particularly successful in imparting a sense of organic life to the societies of the play' (*SQ*, 29 (1978), p. 225).

Until the Stratford Festival was established in 1953, Canada was at first mainly dependent for its Shakespeare productions on touring companies, and *As You Like It* did not figure largely in their repertoires probably because Jaques, much less Orlando, was not meaty enough for such nineteenth-century stars as Edmund Kean, his son Charles, W. C. Macready or, certainly, Henry Irving (see p. 82 below). The play was occasionally presented at the Lyceum Theatre, Toronto, during the management of John Nickinson (1852–8), and during the late 1870s was performed by Mrs Morrison's Stock Company at the Grand Opera House there. During the first half of the twentieth century Shakespeare performances were chiefly the province of amateur and semi-professional groups, including the Players' Club, founded at the University of Toronto in 1903, and the Shakespearean Society of Montreal, which began in 1945. The most important of these groups was that led by the English actor Earle Grey and his wife, Mary Godwin, from 1949 to 1958 in Toronto.[95]

During the nineteenth century the situation was similar in other English-speaking parts of the then British Empire such as Australia, where Shakespeare's plays were staged only sporadically until the Irish actor, Gustavus Brooke, arrived in Melbourne in February 1855, although *As You Like It* had been first performed in that country at Sydney's Royal Victoria Theatre ten years before. By his departure in 1861 Brooke had given 134 performances of Shakespeare among his other productions but his main line was tragedy, and there were only five presentations of *As You Like It*.[96] Before the end of the century, however, and in this Australia differed from Canada, several rival theatre managements were well established, and a number of theatre companies performed some Shakespeare. W. J. Holloway and Essie Jenyns, for example, included *As You Like It* in their repertoire at Sydney's Criterion Theatre in 1887, and the challenge of playing Rosalind led Nellie Stewart, the leading musical comedy actress of the day, to make her Shakespearian debut at Her Majesty's Theatre, Sydney, on 14 July 1909. (Part of the last scene was incorporated into one of Stewart's successes, *Peg Woffington*, presumably allowing a melodramatic departure from the stage (see above, p. 53).) *As You Like It* was in the repertoire of Allan Wilkie's Shakespeare company—the country's first professional

[95] See Herbert Whittaker, 'Shakespeare in Canada Before 1953', *Stratford Papers on Shakespeare*, ed. B. W. Jackson (Toronto, 1965), pp. 71–89.

[96] See Dennis Bartholomeusz, 'Shakespeare on the Melbourne Stage, 1843–61', *Shakespeare Survey* 35 (1982), 31–41.

Shakespeare company—which toured both Australia and New Zealand for ten years from 1920, and in that time produced no less than twenty-seven of the plays, but there were few other professional performances of Shakespeare generally during the next two decades. In Glen Byam Shaw's 1952 Stratford production, however, the play was one of three taken to Australia and New Zealand in 1953 by a Shakespeare Memorial Theatre company led by Anthony Quayle. Quayle's dignified, ageing Jaques was well-contrasted with the eager young Rosalind of Barbara Jefford, an athletic Orlando from Keith Michell and Leo McKern's quizzical Touchstone.

Growing interest in the 1960s led to an increasing number of productions, fresh attitudes and greater variety in presentation. Jim Sharman, the successful director of *Hair* and other rock musicals, mounted a brash, colourful version for the Old Tote, Sydney, in 1971, with Darlene Johnson as Rosalind, perspex properties, rock music, and Touchstone on roller skates. The Sydney *Daily Telegraph*'s Barbara Hall praised it as a 'celebration of youth and happiness' (25 January 1971). In the *Sydney Morning Herald* H. G. Kippax damned it for having 'a great yawning void of incomprehension behind the gimmickry'; 'Sharman', he wrote, 'has turned the vintage champagne of "As You Like It" into ginger pop' (25 January 1971). Kippax was more delighted by the Nimrod Theatre's 1983 production, directed by John Bell and Anna Volska, which gave the play an Australian 1930s setting, with Frederick a city mobster, Duke Senior a squatter (i.e. country landowner) and Orlando a jackeroo (Fig. 21). Anna Volska's Rosalind, 'a kind of young Gertrude Lawrence of the Cowardy twenties at the beginning', he wrote, 'gives a beautifully studied progress towards maturity' (*Sydney Morning Herald*, 25 July 1983). Roger Hodgman's 1982 production for the Melbourne Theatre Company at the Playhouse moved into the 1960s, Rosalind and Celia at first in school uniforms (anticipating John Caird's at Stratford in 1989), then jeans, with Orlando in the blue singlet and moleskins of an outdoor labourer.

As You Like It lends itself happily to outdoor performance, of course, through its forest setting, but the first recorded was not until 22 July 1884, in the grounds of Coombe House, Kingston-upon-Thames, with the most famous Jaques of the day, Hermann Vezin (he played it from 1875 to 1900), a Californian actress,

21. An outback *As You Like It*. Anna Volska as Rosalind, Deirdre Rubenstein as Celia and John Walton as a jackeroo Orlando. Nimrod Theatre production by John Bell and Anna Volska, Sydney (1983).

Eleanor Calhoun, as Rosalind and an otherwise largely amateur cast, including Lady [sic] Archibald Campbell as Orlando. Ben Greet presented the forest scenes of the play in the open air at Hinchingbrooke Park, Huntingdon, on 27 June 1888 and thereafter in both England and America at various times until 1912. The brilliant American actress Maude Adams gave one performance in 1910 before an audience of 8,000 (surely the largest for a live presentation of the play) in the Greek theatre of the University of California, Berkeley, but it was not considered a great success. On the other side of the world, the Allan Wilkie company, which had begun touring India in 1911, gave the first of its many 'Pastoral' performances of the play in the Lawrence Gardens at Lahore in 1912. In the Regent's Park Open Air Theatre in London it was performed on average every two years between 1933 and 1958. The New York Shakespeare Festival in Central Park saw productions in 1963 and 1973 by Joseph Papp and in France in 1976 Andrei Serban began his production in a village near La Rochelle then had everyone walking to a forest a mile away for the Arden scenes. Three years later he directed it again, in the forest of the Ardennes (but see above, pp. 39–41). In October 1981 John Tasker directed a large and lavish production for the Queensland Theatre Company in Albert Park, Brisbane, with Carol Burns as Rosalind, four horsemen, and various livestock including goats, a bloodhound, and a piglet.

Unlike some of the other comedies, the play has not inspired any of the great operatic composers, but the first two acts of Francesco Maria Veracini's *Rosalinda* are loosely based on the early part, and the libretto by Paolo Rolli paraphrases a few passages. Performed first on 31 January 1744 at the King's Theatre, Haymarket, the opera itself is now lost, but it is perhaps another sign of the play's rapid popularity after its revival. The plans of Claude Debussy during 1902–4 for an opera based on the play came to nothing; however, *Comme il vous plaira*, an opera by a later French composer, Pierre Hasquenoph, with a libretto by Francis Didelot, was first performed at the Théâtre Municipal de Strasbourg on 14 January 1982 by Opéra du Rhin, directed by Maté Rabinovsky. A programme note on the primary role of the percussion indicates the contemporary nature of the music.

As You Like It has also been the basis for several lighter musical works. An operetta, *Rosalind*, with music and German libretto by Florence Wickham, was performed at the Theater des Volkes, Dresden, in 1938, and in America a musical by John Balanos with book and lyrics from the play, by Dran and Trani Seitz, was produced in New York's Theatre de Lys on 27 October 1964, after a summer tryout at the White Barn Theatre, Westport, Connecticut. Another variation was a rock musical directed by Martin L. Platt at the Festival Playhouse, Anniston, for the Alabama Shakespeare Festival in 1973. Five other musicals based on the play exist in manuscript, the most intriguing being a 1981 country-western adaptation, 'Tanglin' Hearts', by Peter Spelman.

Of Shakespeare's comedies *A Midsummer Night's Dream* has most inspired choreographers, but 'Touchstone, Audrey and William' from Hans Werner Henze's *Royal Winter Music* (1976) was adapted and used for a ballet with choreography by Günter Pick in Munich in 1986, and in 1988 John Neumeier choreographed

Mozart und Theme aus 'Wie es euch gefällt' for the Hamburg Ballet to perform at the Salzburg Festival.

Three silent films were produced, the earliest a ten-minute, open-air version produced by the Kalem Company in 1908. Vitagraph's was made in 1912 with Rose Coghlan, aged 61, as Rosalind, a part she had first played in 1880; the London Film Company called its modern-dress version made in 1916 'Love in a Wood'. Then in 1935–6 Paul Czinner directed a production with his wife, Elisabeth Bergner, as a German-accented Rosalind, Laurence Olivier as Orlando, and flocks of sheep which Olivier later said 'ran away with the film'.[97] Television brought Shakespeare to audiences of previously unimagined size, and on 6 February 1937 a BBC programme based on 3.2, with Margretta Scott and Ion Swinley, presented the first scenes from Shakespeare ever to be televised. In 1946 Ian Atkins directed the first full BBC production, transmitted on 14 July, with Vivienne Bennett as Rosalind, John Byron as Orlando and David Read as Jaques. Margaret Leighton, Laurence Harvey and Michael Hordern, from Glen Byam Shaw's 1952 Stratford production, led the cast of the next, seen on 15 March 1953, and an adaptation of Michael Elliott's Stratford production with Vanessa Redgrave, Patrick Allen and Max Adrian was screened on 22 March 1963, directed by Ronald Eyre. Basil Coleman's production for the BBC Shakespeare series, first shown on 17 December 1978, had a vigorous, rather knowing, Rosalind in Helen Mirren, a maturing Orlando in Brian Stirner, and Richard Pasco as a sardonic, deep-thinking and alcoholic Jaques.

'Your very, very Rosalind'

It was inevitable that the preceding discussion of *As You Like It* in performance should have been largely a history of famous Rosalinds. It is the part which Hannah Pritchard and Margaret Woffington played simultaneously in rival theatres for six nights in 1741, and the part for which Helen Faucit created the most influential interpretation of the nineteenth century. It is the role which Ellen Terry's father said his daughter was born to act, and which she herself bitterly regretted never having had the

[97] Laurence Olivier, *On Acting* (1986), p. 177. This version is notable for being the first Shakespeare film for which William Walton composed a score.

opportunity to act because, as there was no part in the play sufficiently grand for Henry Irving, his company never performed it. Katharine Hepburn chose the part for her Shakespeare debut in New York in 1950, and in 1961 the 24-year-old Vanessa Redgrave's performance in Stratford and London won her the Evening Standard award for Best Actress. And as well as playing Rosalind in 1932 when she was nearly 25, then again in 1957 at nearly 50, Peggy Ashcroft spoke the epilogue to close the gala celebrating her eightieth birthday in December 1987.

The truth is that, more than any other of the comedies, *As You Like It* belongs to its main character. When Shaw declared 'who ever failed, or could fail, as Rosalind?'[98] he was wrong, of course—actresses have failed in the part—but his implication was right. Rosalind is the most various and delightful of Shakespeare's comic heroines. She also has the longest female part in all the plays—according to Spevack, her 721 lines exceed Cleopatra's 670, the next longest, and more than double Viola's 339 in *Twelfth Night*. As the Egyptian queen dominates *Antony and Cleopatra*, Rosalind is the controlling figure of *As You Like It*. Properly, Celia is the leader initially—she is the daughter of the current ruler, even if he is a usurper—but her opening words direct us to her downcast cousin, and then it is Rosalind who suggests falling in love as a sport to cheer them up. The girls' thinking and dialogue are evenly matched until they reach the Forest of Arden (and it is Celia's suggestion that they go there) but once into man's clothing Rosalind takes on responsibility, authority and the freedom to speak and behave both as a male and, when with either or both Touchstone and Celia, as a female. The dichotomy is clearly established at the beginning of 2.4. Weary in spirit on their arrival in Arden, she says 'I could find in my heart to disgrace my man's apparel and to cry like a woman. But I must comfort the weaker vessel' (ll. 4–6); then on hearing Silvius's love complaint she relapses back into loving womanhood, to be briskly returned to her male role by the practical necessities of needing an occupation and somewhere to live.

It is in Act 3 that Rosalind begins to sparkle. She gives better than she gets from Touchstone, and, teased by Celia about

[98] *Shaw on Shakespeare*, ed. Edwin Wilson (Harmondsworth, 1969), p. 50.

Orlando's presence in the forest, she draws out to a delicious, self-luxuriating length her cousin's riddling revelation. When her lover's name is pronounced her womanly reaction of 'Alas the day, what shall I do with my doublet and hose' is swept away in a spate of questions flung at her cousin, which in turn gives way to self-mocking sentimentalism. When Orlando appears, the love game, the 'sport' Rosalind had proposed in 1.2, can begin. Inventing 'an old religious uncle' who taught her a cure for love, and reinventing herself as 'Rosalind', as Ganymede she denigrates women for their capriciousness, mocks Orlando for not having the signs of love about him, and inveigles him into undertaking the cure. Her own femininity is comically exposed in 3.4 when she petulantly claims the right to weep because Orlando has not arrived, criticizes him herself, then quickly defends him against Celia's criticism. The strength of her feeling for Orlando engenders sympathy for Silvius and annoyance with the scornful Phoebe; secure in her own love, she wants others in love, like Silvius, to be happy too. As Ganymede she gives stringent advice to Phoebe; as 'Rosalind' she emulates Phoebe and gives Orlando a tongue-lashing when he comes late. But this is the prelude to the play's most brilliant scene, in which Rosalind manipulates her disguise so that she changes from a ribald male to a tender female in the space of a few lines (4.1.77–86), and speaks some of the most poignant words in the play—'Men have died from time to time, and worms have eaten them, but not for love.' Here, reality begins to break in, and it continues, put into action, when Rosalind seizes on Orlando's 'And wilt thou have me?' (l. 106) to make Celia perform the apparently mock marriage ceremony which is, in fact, a binding one (see note to 4.1.116).[99] The success of her ploy releases her into even greater exuberance. She mockingly rails against women, grows daringly bawdy, and then is momentarily stunned into dropping her mask when Orlando coolly announces that he has to leave her for a couple of hours. Recovering, she scoldingly extracts his promise to return, and when he is gone she is free to express her wild

[99] In the 1961 American Shakespeare Festival production (Connecticut, dir. Word Baker) Orlando realized 'Rosalind' was Rosalind when he took her hand at this point; he let the audience know he knew, but kept it from Rosalind until his reply to her line 'Why do you speak too, "Why blame you me to love you?"' (5.2.101–2). The play apparently survived this unusual interpretation.

exhilaration of love, cruelly oblivious of the effect her absorption in Orlando and herself is having on Celia. Indeed, so self-absorbed is she that she calls her cousin 'Aliena' when the situation demands 'Celia'. Love here makes her blind, just as in 4.3 the sudden love of Celia and Oliver blinds them to Rosalind's distress on seeing Orlando's bloody handkerchief.

Empowered by her disguise, she lectures others on love, while revelling in her own, exploiting the tension between her two roles. But she finds the business of acting increasingly irksome, and her impatient 'Pray you, no more of this' of 5.2 could apply as much to her own role-playing as to the others' love-litany. She hastens towards the restoration of her feminine self and the open revelation of her feelings that this will allow, for, even while she decries the romantic love of Orlando and the sentimentalism of Silvius, she is herself the most romantic, the most sentimental lover of the play. It is her capacity to contain and give expression to such diversity in love that makes her the greatest of Shakespeare's comic heroines.

The Text

As You Like It is the tenth of the thirty-six plays in the First Folio, where it was first printed. Coming between *The Merchant of Venice* and *The Taming of the Shrew*, it occupies signatures Q3–S2, pages 185–207 of the section of the Folio assigned to the comedies; in all copies p. 189 is misnumbered 187. Of the eight or nine compositors who worked on the Folio, as discussed by Gary Taylor and William Montgomery in *William Shakespeare: A Textual Companion*,[100] three, B, C, and D, set up type for *As You Like It*. To speed up the job, they appear to have set up simultaneously, casting off the copy, that is, estimating how much space would be needed for a given amount of manuscript. If the calculation proved incorrect, then verse could be set as prose, to squeeze it into the room available, or prose could be printed as verse to fill out the space, as appears to have happened in 2.6. Sheets were proofread as they came from the press, and corrections, none of major significance, were made to pages 193, 204 and 207. As the uncorrected as well as the corrected sheets were used (as was

[100] *Textual Companion*, pp. 148–9.

customary—paper was expensive) different copies of the Folio have variant readings on those three pages.

It is generally agreed that the compositors had a very neat, clean manuscript—their 'printer's copy'—to work from. There are no signs of the copy's being foul papers (the author's draft); there are few recognizably Shakespearian spellings, characters are named for the most part consistently, and, as Greg points out, it is particularly notable that Duke Senior and Duke Frederick are distinguished in speech headings and stage directions 'with a meticulous care that we do not naturally associate with Shakespeare'.[101] Such care is, however, usually associated with a prompter (the 'book-keeper'), who needs to be sure of such distinctions. Act and scene divisions are not especially needed in a prompt-book, and their clarity and completeness in the text of *As You Like It* suggest some kind of editing. M. M. Reese suggested in his edition (1969) that Orlando's appearance at the beginning of 3.2 to hang a poem on a tree and then make his exit ten lines later could be a separate scene, but the action is continuous, Corin and Touchstone entering on Orlando's exit. Speech headings are unusually consistent, and only two are omitted (1.1.152, 2.3.16). Since Theobald, the ascription of 1.2.77–9 to Rosalind has been generally held to be an error for Celia, although the Folio's reading has had some defenders.

The few stage directions are mainly sharp imperatives—*Wrastle* (1.2.196.1) and *Shout* (1.2.199.1), for example—which some editors, including Latham, take to indicate that the copy text was probably 'a transcript by a playhouse scribe' of which the purpose 'was normally to serve as a prompt book' (p. x). Both Chambers and Greg are more cautious. Speaking generally of prompt copy, Chambers remarks, 'I do not think one need regard the imperative as a special note of the book-keeper.' He finds that in *As You Like It* the stage-directions 'only occasionally suggest the hands of the author ([2.1.0; 2.4.0; 3.2.118.1]) and the book-keeper ([1.2.134.1, 196.1, 199.1; 2.4.0; 2.5.34.1; 4.2.9.1; 5.4.102.1])'.[102] Curiously, 2.4.0.1–3, *Enter Rosaline for Ganimed, Celia for Aliena, and Clowne*, alias *Touchstone*, appears in both his lists of examples; Greg, who is in general agreement, considers

[101] W. W. Greg, *The Shakespeare First Folio* (Oxford, 1955), p. 294.

[102] Chambers (1930), i. 118, 402; see i. 105–8, 117–22 for Chambers's discussion of the important functions of the book-keeper.

that this stage direction suggests the author, but he concludes that 'On the whole the evidence points to F having been printed from a prompt-book that retained a few features of the author's papers but had in other respects been carefully prepared. If the company was reluctant to risk their prompt-copy, a transcript may have been made for the printer.'[103] Knowles suggests that the printer's copy may have been 'some kind of transcript from foul papers, perhaps embodying some annotations by the prompter' (p. 334).

Much of the argument for prompt copy depends on the stage directions, which are sparse and brief; some could as easily be the author's as the prompter's or the scribe's. Directions like *Enter Duke Senior : Amyens, and two or three Lords like Forresters* (2.1.0.1–2), and *Enter Amyens, Iaques, & others* (2.5.0.1–2), for example, might be considered too imprecise for a prompter, who would want to know how many actors would need to be on stage, and are more likely to reflect the author's hurry in the flow of writing, though Chambers remarks that the book-holder 'is often lacking in precision, particularly with regard to supernumeraries'.[104]

What can be said is that the copy was prepared for the printing house probably from a transcript of the author's draft or fair copy, and that the transcript may have been made as the playhouse prompt-book. If that sounds indecisive, it can be stated with certainty that, whatever its source, the copy text was well prepared and resulted in a printed text with few problems.

[103] Greg, p. 294.
[104] Chambers (1930), i. 120.

EDITORIAL PROCEDURES

THE text of this edition is based on the Folio of 1623, modernized in general following the principles of Stanley Wells set out in *Modernizing Shakespeare's Spelling* (Oxford, 1979) and *Re-Editing Shakespeare for the Modern Reader* (Oxford, 1984), and in Gary Taylor's Introduction to *Henry V* (Oxford, 1982). Quotations from other contemporary and earlier works are modernized except for certain documentary evidence used in the Introduction, and in the collation, where the lemma in the modernized form is followed by the original spelling in the rest of the entry. I am grateful to the State Library of New South Wales for supplying a photographic copy of the text from the First Folio in its Shakespeare Tercentenary Memorial Library.

Substantive departures from the Folio are given in the collation below the text. Emendations are recorded in the usual way, the lemma giving the reading of this edition, the edition immediately following the lemma that in which it first occurred, and then the Folio reading:

shorter] ROWE 1714; taller F

For modernizations of a substantial (and perhaps controversial) kind, the Folio spelling is given in brackets:

goodbye] F (God buy you)

Such instances are discussed in the explanatory notes.

Speech headings are normalized, substantive changes being collated, a consistent change being collated on the first occasion. Headings are printed on the same line as the first line of a prose speech, a line above the first line when the speech is in verse unless the speech begins with an incomplete line. Substantive changes to stage directions are collated, but where the action is certain there is no indication in the text; where there is doubt, for instance, as to where the action or character might be, then partial square brackets are used (⌈ ⌉) in the text. All asides and indications of speaking to another character are editorial; they are placed in round brackets and are not collated. This is also the case with stage directions placed between speech headings and speeches, except for those which emend a Folio direction, like *reads* at 4.3.40, which are collated.

The Folio punctuation is the compositors' rather than Shakespeare's, but it is generally sensitive, if somewhat heavy by modern standards. Changes to it are necessarily numerous, and only those which affect meaning are collated, as at 4.3.104. The Latin act and scene headings of the Folio have been silently altered to numerals, and the line numbering for this and other Shakespeare plays is from *The Complete Works*, edited by Stanley Wells and Gary Taylor (Oxford, 1986). Unless otherwise stated, references to other plays are from readily available modern editions, where possible those in the Revels series. Quotations from the Bible are modernized from a 1602 edition of the Geneva Bible (1560) and, where relevant, from a 1572 edition of the Bishops' Bible (1568).

Since *As You Like It* is more dependent on a single source than any other of Shakespeare's comedies, I have quoted frequently from that source, Thomas Lodge's *Rosalynde*, modernizing the text and giving the folio numbers of the first volume of *The Complete Works of Thomas Lodge*, edited by Edmund Gosse (4 vols., New York, 1963; repr. of 1883 edn.).

Abbreviations and References

The following abbreviations are used in the Introduction, explanatory notes and collations. The place of publication is London unless otherwise specified.

EDITIONS OF SHAKESPEARE

F, F1	The First Folio, 1623 (F1 is used when needed to distinguish it from later Folios)
F2	The Second Folio, 1632
F3	The Third Folio, 1663
Cambridge	W. G. Clark and W. A. Wright, *Works*, The Cambridge Shakespeare, 9 vols. (Cambridge, 1863–6)
Capell	Edward Capell, *Comedies, Histories and Tragedies*, 10 vols. (1767–8)
Collier	J. P. Collier, *Comedies, Histories, Tragedies, and Poems*, 'The Second Edition', 6 vols. (1858)
Cowden Clarke	Charles and Mary Cowden Clarke, *Plays*, 3 vols. [1864–8]

Dyce	Alexander Dyce, *Works*, 6 vols. (1857)
Dyce 1864	Alexander Dyce, *Works*, 9 vols. (1864–7), vol. 3.
Furness	Horace Howard Furness, *As You Like It*, A New Variorum edition of Shakespeare (Philadelphia and London, 1890; repr. New York, 1963)
Gibson	Colin Gibson, *As You Like It*, The Kennet Shakespeare (1965)
Grant White	Richard Grant White, *Comedies, Histories, Tragedies & Poems*, 3 vols. (Boston, 1883)
Halliwell	J. O. Halliwell[-Phillipps], *Works*, 16 vols. (1853–65)
Hanmer	Thomas Hanmer, *Works*, 6 vols. (Oxford, 1743–4)
Harrison	G. B. Harrison, *As You Like It*, The Penguin Shakespeare (Harmondsworth, 1955)
Johnson	Samuel Johnson, *Plays*, 8 vols. (1765)
Knight	Charles Knight, *Works*, Pictorial Edition, 8 vols. (1838–43)
Knowles	Richard Knowles, *As You Like It*, A New Variorum Edition of Shakespeare (New York, 1977)
Latham	Agnes Latham, *As You Like It*, The Arden Shakespeare (1975)
M Col 1	J. P. Collier's notes in the Perkins Folio (1632), (–1853)
Malone	Edmond Malone, *Plays and Poems*, 10 vols. (1790)
Moberly	[Charles E. Moberly,] *As You Like It* (Rugby, 1868)
Neilson	W. A. Neilson, *Works*, Cambridge edition (Boston, 1906)
H. J. Oliver	H. J. Oliver, *As You Like It*, New Penguin Shakespeare (Harmondsworth, 1968)
Oxford	Stanley Wells and Gary Taylor, gen. eds. with John Jowett and William Montgomery, *Complete Works*, The Oxford Shakespeare (Oxford, 1986)
Pope	Alexander Pope, *Works*, 6 vols. (1723–5)
Rann	Joseph Rann, *Dramatic Works*, 6 vols. (Oxford, 1786–94)
Rowe	Nicholas Rowe, *Works*, 6 vols. (1709)
Rowe 1714	Nicholas Rowe, *Works*, 8 vols. (1714)
Singer 1856	Samuel Weller Singer, *Dramatic Works*, 10 vols. (1856)
Steevens	Samuel Johnson and George Steevens, *Plays*, 10 vols. (1773)
Steevens 1778	Samuel Johnson and George Steevens, *Plays*, 10 vols. (1778)
Theobald	Lewis Theobald, *Works*, 7 vols. (1733)

Theobald 1740 Lewis Theobald, *Works* (second edition), 8 vols. (1740)

Wilson Arthur Quiller-Couch and John Dover Wilson, *As You Like It*, The New Shakespeare (Cambridge, 1926)

OTHER WORKS

Abbott E. A. Abbott, *A Shakespearian Grammar*, third edition (1873)

Bullough Geoffrey Bullough, ed., *Narrative and Dramatic Sources of Shakespeare*, 8 vols. (1957–75)

Burton Robert Burton, *The Anatomy of Melancholy*, ed. Holbrook Jackson, 3 vols., Everyman (1932)

Capell N. Edward Capell, *Notes and Variant Readings in Shakespeare*, 3 vols. (1779 [1774]–83)

Cercignani Fausto Cercignani, *Shakespeare's Works and Elizabethan Pronunciation* (Oxford, 1981)

Chambers (1923) E. K. Chambers, *The Elizabethan Stage*, 4 vols. (Oxford, 1923)

Chambers (1930) E. K. Chambers, *William Shakespeare: A Study of Facts and Problems*, 2 vols. (Oxford, 1930)

Child Helen Child Sargent and George Lyman Kittredge, eds., *English and Scottish Popular Ballads*, edited from the Collection of Francis James Child (1904)

Colman E. A. M. Colman, *The Dramatic Use of Bawdy in Shakespeare* (1974)

Dent R. W. Dent, *Shakespeare's Proverbial Language: An Index* (Berkeley and Los Angeles, 1981)

Elyot Sir Thomas Elyot, *The Boke Named the Governour*, ed. Foster Watson, Everyman (1907)

Harington *Sir John Harington's A New Discourse of a Stale Subject, Called the Metamorphosis of Ajax*, ed. Elizabeth Story Donno (1962)

Johnson (1989) *Samuel Johnson on Shakespeare*, ed. H. R. Woudhuysen (Harmondsworth, 1989)

Kökeritz Helge Kökeritz, *Shakespeare's Pronunciation* (New Haven, 1953)

Lodge *Rosalynde. Euphues Golden Legacie*, in *The Complete Works of Thomas Lodge*, ed. Edmund Gosse, 4 vols. (New York, 1963; repr. of 1883 edn.)

MED *Middle English Dictionary*, eds. Hans Kurath and Sherman M. Kuhn (Ann Arbor, 1954–)

Nashe	*The Works of Thomas Nashe*, ed. R. B. McKerrow (1904–10) . . . With supplementary notes . . . by F. P. Wilson, 5 vols. (Oxford, 1958)
OED	*The Oxford English Dictionary*, second edition, prepared by J. A. Simpson and E. S. C. Weiner (Oxford, 1989)
Ovid	*Shakespeare's Ovid. Being Arthur Golding's Translation of the Metamorphoses*, ed. W. H. D. Rouse (1961)
RSC	Royal Shakespeare Company
Schoenbaum	Samuel Schoenbaum, *William Shakespeare : A Documentary Life* (Oxford, 1975)
Spevack	Marvin Spevack, *A Complete and Systematic Concordance to the Works of Shakespeare*, 9 vols. (Hildesheim, 1968–80)
Sprague	Arthur Colby Sprague, *Shakespeare and the Actors* (New York, 1944; repr. 1963)
SQ	*Shakespeare Quarterly*
Strutt, Joseph	*The Sports and Pastimes of the People of England*, ed. William Hone (1876)
Textual Companion	Stanley Wells and Gary Taylor with John Jowett and William Montgomery, *William Shakespeare : A Textual Companion* (Oxford, 1987)
Tilley	M. P. Tilley, *A Dictionary of the Proverbs in England in the Sixteenth and Seventeenth Centuries* (Ann Arbor, 1950)
Vickers	Brian Vickers, *The Artistry of Shakespeare's Prose* (1968)
Whiter	Walter Whiter, *A Specimen of a Commentary on Shakespeare* (1794), eds. Alan Over and Mary Bell (1966)
Wiles	David Wiles, *Shakespeare's Clown* (Cambridge, 1987)
Wilson	F. P. Wilson, *The Proverbial Wisdom of Shakespeare* (Cambridge, 1961)

As You Like It

THE PERSONS OF THE PLAY

DUKE SENIOR, deposed and living in banishment

ROSALIND, his daughter, later disguised as Ganymede

AMIENS }
JAQUES } Lords attending on him

TWO PAGES

DUKE FREDERICK, the usurper

CELIA, his daughter

LE BEAU, a courtier attending on him

CHARLES, Duke Frederick's wrestler

TOUCHSTONE, the court jester

OLIVER, eldest son of Sir Rowland de Boys

JAQUES }
ORLANDO } his younger brothers

ADAM, a former servant of Sir Rowland

DENNIS, Oliver's servant

CORIN, an old shepherd

SILVIUS, a young shepherd, in love with Phoebe

PHOEBE, a shepherdess

AUDREY, a goatherd

WILLIAM, a countryman, in love with Audrey

SIR OLIVER MARTEXT, a country clergyman

HYMEN, god of marriage

Lords, pages, and other attendants

Rowe was the first editor to provide a list of characters.

As You Like It

1.1 *Enter Orlando and Adam*

ORLANDO As I remember, Adam, it was upon this fashion bequeathed me by will but poor a thousand crowns, and, as thou sayst, charged my brother on his blessing to breed me well—and there begins my sadness. My brother Jaques he keeps at school, and report speaks goldenly of his profit. For my part, he keeps me rustically

1.1 The play begins with a quarrel, with a conflict between good and evil, with a conspiracy to murder, and with information about the principal worlds of the action: the corrupt court, and the healing green world of Arden. The parallel events from which the action develops are firmly described: the repression of Orlando by his brother Oliver and the usurpation of Duke Senior's dukedom by his brother, Frederick.

0.1 ***Orlando*** Shakespeare gives Lodge's Rosader a name from medieval and later romances: *Orlando* is the Italian form of Roland, the hero's name in the twelfth-century *Chanson de Roland*; and Sir John Harington's translation of Ariosto's *Orlando Furioso* (1516–32) was published in 1591. Italian names were popular in Elizabethan England: that of the composer *Orlando* Gibbons (1583–1625) is one example. To provide 'a Roland for an *Oliver*'—the name of Orlando's elder brother in *As You Like It*—was proverbial for indicating a match or more than a match.

Adam In both *The Tale of Gamelyn* and Lodge the name of the faithful servant is Adam Spencer (i.e. steward); the simplified 'Adam', the name of the first created human being, initiates with the play's opening words a current of religious, particularly Christian and biblical, allusiveness which continues until the last lines before the Epilogue. See Introduction, p. 42.

1–4 **As . . . well** Orlando and Adam enter in mid-conversation. Although the syntax is odd and has led to much editorial comment, the meaning is simply that Orlando has been left a miserable 1,000 crowns (£250) and his brother has been entrusted with bringing him up and giving him a good education.

2 **poor a thousand** only a thousand (Abbott §85)

3 **on his blessing** as a condition of gaining his blessing

4 **breed** bring up, educate

5 **Jaques** pronounced 'Jakes', 'Jakus' or 'Jakwis'. In Lodge the second brother is called Fernandyne; Shakespeare gives him an English form of the French 'Jacques', making him, with his brother Oliver (see 1.1.23.1n.), one of two characters in the play with the name of another, in this instance the melancholy courtier of Duke Senior's court in exile (see 2.1.27n.). Theatre-goers have at times taken the two Jaqueses to be the same character, and Harold Jenkins is among critics who suggest that they were originally meant to be one, the melancholy of the second arising from the study of schoolbooks rather than, as the cause later became, foreign travel and experience ('*As You Like It*', *Shakespeare Survey 8* (1955), 42). One such error on the part of a dramatist looks like carelessness; two, however, raises questions of purpose. See Introduction, p. 38.

keeps at school maintains at university. Compare Hamlet, who, like modern American university students, intends to go 'back to school' (*Hamlet* 1.2.113) after being away for a time.

6 **goldenly** excellently. This is the only example quoted by *OED* (*adv.* 1) before 1840.

profit proficiency (*OED*, *profit*, *sb.* 3) or the benefit it has been to him

6–7 **keeps me . . . home** restrains me here in

at home—or, to speak more properly, stays me here at home unkept; for call you that keeping for a gentleman of my birth, that differs not from the stalling of an ox? His horses are bred better, for besides that they are fair with their feeding, they are taught their manège, and to that end riders dearly hired. But I, his brother, gain nothing under him but growth, for the which his animals on his dunghills are as much bound to him as I. Besides this nothing that he so plentifully gives me, the something that nature gave me his countenance seems to take from me. He lets me feed with his hinds, bars me the place of a brother, and as much as in him lies, mines my gentility with my education. This is it, Adam, that grieves me; and the spirit of my father, which I think is within me, begins to mutiny against this servitude. I will no longer endure it, though yet I know no wise remedy how to avoid it.

Enter Oliver

ADAM Yonder comes my master, your brother.

ORLANDO Go apart, Adam, and thou shalt hear how he will shake me up.

Adam stands aside

1.1.11 manège] OXFORD *after* F: mannage

26.1 *Adam . . . aside*] Adam *retires* M COL 1; *not in* F

the country (with a possible pun on '*rus*tically' in contrast to '*gold*enly')

7 **properly** accurately

stays detains (*OED v.*[1] 20). Compare 1.3.65: 'Ay, Celia, we stayed her for your sake'—a verbal link between Orlando and Rosalind.

8 **unkept** uncared for (with a pun on *keeps* in ll. 5 and 6)

11 **manège** movements proper to a trained horse (*OED*, *manège*, *sb.* 2). Editors (except Oxford) read 'manage' but *OED* gives this as '*Obs.* exc. *arch.*'

12 **riders dearly hired** expensive horse-trainers employed

12–15 'All he does for me is let me grow as well as I may, like the lowliest animals on his rubbish heaps.'

16 **nature** The first of a recurrent series of references to nature, and another link with Rosalind (compare 1.2.39).

countenance (a) the way he regards me (b) his behaviour towards me

17 **hinds** servants, especially agricultural labourers

18–19 **as much . . . lies** with all the power he has (*OED*, *lie*, *v.*[1] B. 12c)

19 **mines my gentility** undermines my status as a gentleman

23.1 ***Oliver*** Lodge's unpleasant Saladyne is given the name of Roland's great friend in the *Chanson de Roland*, which is set in the time of Charlemagne. That Orlando's elder brother is named nowhere in the dialogue of *As You Like It*, only in stage directions and speech headings, is one of the puzzles concerning names in the play, along with there being another character, with the same name, the hedge-priest, Sir *Oliver* Martext (3.3); as the bad brother, Oliver, mars the good brother, Orlando, the bad priest, Sir Oliver, mars the good book, the Bible. See Introduction, p. 38.

25 **thou** the pronoun mostly used by a good-humoured master to a servant

26 **shake me up** Verbal rather than physical violence is suggested by Orlando's 'hear'.

OLIVER Now, sir, what make you here?

ORLANDO Nothing, I am not taught to make anything.

OLIVER What mar you then, sir?

ORLANDO Marry, sir, I am helping you to mar that which God made, a poor unworthy brother of yours, with idleness.

OLIVER Marry, sir, be better employed, and be nought awhile.

ORLANDO Shall I keep your hogs, and eat husks with them? What prodigal portion have I spent, that I should come to such penury?

OLIVER Know you where you are, sir?

ORLANDO O sir, very well; here in your orchard.

OLIVER Know you before whom, sir?

ORLANDO Ay, better than him I am before knows me. I know you are my eldest brother, and in the gentle condition of blood you should so know me. The courtesy of nations allows you my better, in that you are the first-born; but the same tradition takes not away my blood, were there twenty brothers betwixt us. I have as much of my father in me as you, albeit I confess your coming before me is nearer to his reverence.

27 **make** do. The 'make/mar' antithesis is proverbial (Tilley M48) and appears in ten other Shakespeare plays. Orlando puns on 'make' = 'create'.

30 **Marry** indeed (originally, the name of the Virgin Mary used as an oath)

30–1 **which God made** Compare 3.2.198: 'Is he of God's making?'

33–4 **be nought awhile** begone; I don't want to see you around here (Dent N51.1)

36 **prodigal** Orlando ironically compares himself with the prodigal younger son in the parable, who would gladly have eaten the food of the swine he was reduced to minding (Luke 15: 16). This is the parable of the Gospels most frequently mentioned in the plays. Richmond Noble lists eight examples and notes that the use of 'husks' indicates that Shakespeare was familiar with the Geneva Bible (although the Rheims also has 'husks'); the Bishops' reads 'cods' (*Shakespeare's Biblical Knowledge*, 1935, pp. 277–8).

39 **orchard** a garden, with herbs and fruit-trees

42–3 **gentle . . . blood** 'as we are in the same well-born family'. This is the play's first allusion to the blood relationship which is perverted by Oliver's unnatural behaviour.

43 **know** acknowledge

43–4 **courtesy of nations** traditions of civilized society, which set the law of primogeniture, as opposed to natural law, by which Orlando and Oliver are sons of the same father. Compare Edmund, *Tragedy of King Lear* 1.2.2–4: 'Wherefore should I | . . . permit | The curiosity of nations to deprive me'.

46–8 **I have . . . reverence** 'I am as much our father's son as you are, even if your being older might make you think you ought to have the respect due to him.' Orlando's pride in his lineage is a significant part of his character; compare 1.1.21–2, 1.2.216–18.

OLIVER (*threatening him*) What, boy!

ORLANDO (*seizing him by the throat*) Come, come, elder brother, you are too young in this.

OLIVER Wilt thou lay hands on me, villain?

ORLANDO I am no villein. I am the youngest son of Sir Rowland de Boys. He was my father, and he is thrice a villain that says such a father begot villeins. Wert thou not my brother, I would not take this hand from thy throat till this other had pulled out thy tongue for saying so. Thou hast railed on thyself.

ADAM (*coming forward*) Sweet masters, be patient. For your father's remembrance, be at accord.

OLIVER (*to Orlando*) Let me go, I say.

ORLANDO I will not till I please. You shall hear me. My father charged you in his will to give me good education. You have trained me like a peasant, obscuring and hiding from me all gentleman-like qualities. The spirit of my father grows strong in me, and I will no longer endure it. Therefore allow me such exercises as may become a gentleman, or give me the poor allottery my father left me by testament. With that I will go buy my fortunes.

OLIVER And what wilt thou do—beg when that is spent? Well, sir, get you in. I will not long be troubled with

49 *threatening him*] This edition; *menacing with his hand* JOHNSON; *not in* F 50 *seizing . . . throat*] *collaring him* JOHNSON; *not in* F 53, 55 villein . . . villeins] OXFORD *after* F: villaine . . . villaines 59 *coming forward*] COLLIER

49 **What, boy!** Orlando reacts to this insult and a threatening movement from Oliver by seizing his brother by the throat. Many editors and directors have made Oliver 'the first to pass from words to deeds' (Sprague, p. 31) but the earliest known precedent for Orlando's being the first to make full physical contact dates from 1723: *Love in a Forest* has '*Laying his Hand on his Collar*' (l. 51), and '*shaking him*' after 'thrice a villain' (ll. 54–5). Dr Johnson, interestingly, gives '*Collaring him*' (l. 51).

51 **young** 'immature', rather than 'in the early stage of growth'. Compare 1.3.69: 'I was too young . . . to value her'.

52 **thou** Oliver's insulting change from the familiar 'you' is due to anger (Abbott §231.3).

52–5 **villain . . . villeins** Orlando puns on 'villain' = a wicked man, and 'villein' = a menial serf.

65 **qualities** accomplishments

67 **exercises** regular occupation, employment

68 **allottery** what has been allotted to him

69–70 **buy my fortunes** As he has been deprived of education, Orlando will try to buy some kind of position, presumably at court.

71–2 **thou . . . you** Oliver now changes from the contemptuous 'thou' to the even more insulting 'you', used by angry masters to their servants, thus degrading his brother to the level of the servant, Adam; 'you' used this way is distinct from the familiar 'you' (Abbott §232).

you. You shall have some part of your will. I pray you, leave me.

ORLANDO I will no further offend you than becomes me for my good.

OLIVER (*to Adam*) Get you with him, you old dog.

ADAM Is 'old dog' my reward? Most true, I have lost my teeth in your service. God be with my old master, he would not have spoke such a word.

Exeunt Orlando and Adam

OLIVER Is it even so? Begin you to grow upon me? I will physic your rankness, and yet give no thousand crowns neither. Holla, Dennis!

Enter Dennis

DENNIS Calls your worship?

OLIVER Was not Charles, the Duke's wrestler, here to speak with me?

DENNIS So please you, he is here at the door, and importunes access to you.

OLIVER Call him in. *Exit Dennis*

'Twill be a good way. And tomorrow the wrestling is.

Enter Charles

CHARLES Good morrow to your worship.

89 *Exit Dennis*] JOHNSON; *not in* F

73 **will** Oliver puns contemptuously on (a) their father's bequest (b) Orlando's wish.

78–9 **dog . . . service** A reference to Aesop's fable of the greyhound who could not hold a wild beast he had caught: 'The master rateth at the dog with stripes [i.e. lashes] and words. The dog answereth . . . Thou hast loved me catching game, thou hast hated me being slow and toothless' (William Bullokar, *Aesops Fablz* (1585), ed. J. R. Turner (Leeds Texts and Monographs, NS 1, 1969), D1^{r}).

79 The biblical allusiveness of this opening episode is rounded off with Adam's calling upon God as he leaves.

81 **grow upon** (a) take liberties (b) increase, like a troublesome plant

82 **physic** treat medically

rankness rebelliousness (*OED*, *rank*, *a.* 1). Used here in the medical sense of blood that is corrupt and/or in oversupply. 'Rankness' does not appear to have been current as a medical term 'for a condition requiring blood letting', *pace* G. B. Harrison, although it was in 1450 (*MED*, *rank*, *adj.* 4a); by 1600 the words used included 'fulness', 'plenitude', 'plethora' and 'repletion'. But compare *Caesar* 3.1.153: 'Who else must be let blood, who else is rank'. Oliver's image also relates to over-luxuriant plant growth, with which the image of blood-letting is associated in *Richard II* 3.4.58–61: gardeners 'wound' the bark of a fruit tree 'Lest, being over-proud in sap and blood, | With too much riches it confound itself'.

83 **Dennis** The surname, perhaps, rather than the Christian name though the form is still current for both. Oxford modernizes to 'Denis', which is equally English and French. Oliver is not the kind of master to be too familiar with servants, though deferential to a court employee such as Charles the wrestler (l. 92).

87 **door** Kitchen gardens and orchards were often walled, with doors giving access on the one hand to the park beyond and on the other to the house, a courtyard or other gardens.

OLIVER Good Monsieur Charles—what's the new news at the new court?

CHARLES There's no news at the court, sir, but the old news: that is, the old Duke is banished by his younger brother, the new Duke, and three or four loving lords have put themselves into voluntary exile with him, whose lands and revenues enrich the new Duke; therefore he gives them good leave to wander.

OLIVER Can you tell if Rosalind, the Duke's daughter, be banished with her father?

CHARLES O no; for the Duke's daughter her cousin so loves her, being ever from their cradles bred together, that she should have followed her exile, or have died to stay behind her. She is at the court, and no less beloved of her uncle than his own daughter; and never two ladies loved as they do.

OLIVER Where will the old Duke live?

CHARLES They say he is already in the forest of Arden, and a many merry men with him; and there they live like the old Robin Hood of England. They say many young

104 she] F3; hee F1

92–3 **new . . . court?** Oliver's attempt at jocularity leads to our learning of Duke Senior's banishment and of Rosalind and Celia. Charles's reply, references to love, to the golden world, and to Robin Hood, with the implication of the green world, suggest Paradise regained and prepare us for future developments.

100 **Rosalind** As well as having floral connotations the name is said to be connected with Spanish *linda*=sweet, beautiful, exquisite. E. Withycombe suggests a less romantic origin: 'Old German *Rosalindis*, compound of *(h)ros* 'horse' and *lindi* 'serpent' (*The Oxford Dictionary of English Christian Names* (Oxford, 1977)).

109 **already** The question of how long Duke Senior has been banished should not concern us. 'There's no clock in the forest' (3.2.291–2).

Arden The name comes from *Rosalynde*, where it refers to a forest between Bordeaux and Lyons; by its suggestion of the English forest of Arden, which in the sixteenth century extended from Stratford northward and westward through Warwickshire, it contributes to the theme of doubles in the play. For further discussion see Introduction, pp. 39–41.

110 **a many** This use of 'a' with numeral adjectives to indicate indefiniteness, common in the fourteenth to sixteenth centuries, survives in *a good many*, and in other expressions such as *a few* (Abbott §87).

111 **Robin Hood** The outlaw folk-hero's name establishes the idea of the greenwood, a place whose legendary carefree peacefulness contrasts with the aggressive atmosphere of the de Boys estate and the usurper's court. Through Lodge's Rosader, Orlando derives from Gamelyn, hero of a fourteenth-century narrative poem, who turns up in a later ballad, *Robin Hood Newly Revived*, as Gamwell, Robin's cousin. The popularity of two Robin Hood plays at the Rose Theatre in 1598 led Fleay (*A Chronicle . . . Life . . . of Shakespeare* (1886), p. 208) and others to see *As You Like It* as the Chamberlain's Men's pastoral answer to the rival Admiral's company.

of England In realistic terms the play's geographical setting is not England.

gentlemen flock to him every day, and fleet the time carelessly, as they did in the golden world.

OLIVER What, you wrestle tomorrow before the new Duke?

CHARLES Marry do I, sir, and I came to acquaint you with a matter. I am given, sir, secretly to understand that your younger brother, Orlando, hath a disposition to come in disguised against me to try a fall. Tomorrow, sir, I wrestle for my credit, and he that escapes me without some broken limb, shall acquit him well. Your brother is but young and tender, and for your love I would be loath to foil him, as I must for my own honour if he come in. Therefore out of my love to you I came hither to acquaint you withal, that either you might stay him from his intendment, or brook such disgrace well as he shall run into, in that it is a thing of his own search, and altogether against my will.

OLIVER Charles, I thank thee for thy love to me, which thou shalt find I will most kindly requite. I had myself notice of my brother's purpose herein, and have by underhand means laboured to dissuade him from it; but he is resolute. I'll tell thee, Charles, it is the stubbornest young fellow of France, full of ambition, an envious emulator of every man's good parts, a secret and villainous contriver against me his natural brother. Therefore

112 **fleet the time** pass the time away (*OED*, *fleet*, *v.*[1] 10d): a rare, transitive usage; earliest instance of *fleet* in this sense cited by *OED*

113 **carelessly** free from care or anxiety
golden world In the golden age of classical myth, 'Which we have named the golden world' (Ovid, *Metamorphoses*, 15, 104), no one needed to work for a living, no beasts were killed, 'The springtime lasted all the year' (1, 122), the streams ran milk, then wine, and honey flowed from the trees. Writers of pastoral followed Virgil (Eclogue 4) in linking the simplicity of shepherd life with this idyllic time referred to by Charles. The exiled Duke Senior and his courtiers, especially Jaques, know it is different in Arden (compare 2.1.5–11 and 45–63).

114 **What** an expression of impatience (Abbott §73a). The evil Oliver is irritated by Charles's pregnant description of the life of the good Duke.

119 **disguised** In Lodge the contest follows a chivalric tournament; in Elizabethan times wrestling was a lower-class sport, and, as well, professional wrestlers, like minstrels, tumblers and players, travelled the country as entertainers. Orlando wants to conceal his noble rank.

120 **credit** reputation

121 **shall** must, will have to (Abbott §315)

123 **foil** overthrow, defeat. Compare 2.2.14.

126 **stay . . . intendment** stop him carrying out his intention

129 **thee** As Oliver begins his corruption of Charles, he changes to the socially distancing 'thee' and 'thou'.

130 **kindly** fittingly

132 **underhand** secret, surreptitious

use thy discretion. I had as lief thou didst break his neck as his finger. And thou wert best look to't; for if thou dost him any slight disgrace, or if he do not mightily grace himself on thee, he will practise against thee by poison, entrap thee by some treacherous device, and never leave thee till he hath ta'en thy life by some indirect means or other. For I assure thee—and almost with tears I speak it—there is not one so young and so villainous this day living. I speak but brotherly of him, but should I anatomize him to thee as he is, I must blush and weep, and thou must look pale and wonder.

CHARLES I am heartily glad I came hither to you. If he come tomorrow I'll give him his payment. If ever he go alone again, I'll never wrestle for prize more. And so God keep your worship.

OLIVER Farewell, good Charles. *Exit Charles*

Now will I stir this gamester. I hope I shall see an end of him, for my soul—yet I know not why—hates nothing more than he. Yet he's gentle; never schooled, and yet learned; full of noble device; of all sorts enchantingly beloved; and, indeed, so much in the heart of the world,

153 OLIVER] F2; *not in* F1 153 *Exit Charles*] CAPELL; *Exit.* (*after l.* 152) F

137 **had as lief** should like as much

139–40 **do not . . . grace himself** does not bring himself great credit

140 **practise** plot, conspire against

141 **device** stratagem, trick

146 **anatomize** analyse in detail (*OED v.* 3); sinisterly appropriate here, as the literal meaning is '*esp.* To dissect a human body' (*OED v.* 1).

149–50 **go alone** walk without help

150 **prize** By 1600 the once-popular sport of wrestling had declined in England and was seen mainly at country fairs and celebrations and in London on St Bartholomew's day. In earlier times a ram was a usual prize; Chaucer's Miller 'At wrastlynge . . . wolde have alwey the ram' (*Canterbury Tales*, General Prologue, l. 548). In *The Courtier* (1528, tr. Thomas Hoby, 1561), Castiglione nevertheless commends wrestling as a gentlemanly pastime because it was useful in hand-to-hand fighting (1959, p. 40), and in *The Book Named the Governor* (1531), Elyot says that wrestling is 'profitable in wars, in case that a captain shall be constrained to cope with his adversary hand to hand, having his weapon broken or lost' (p. 74).

150–1 **God . . . worship** Charles's parting phrase is an ironic echo of Adam's at l. 79.

153 **gamester** athlete, perhaps with the special sense of 'wrestler', current in nineteenth-century Berkshire dialect (*OED* †1b).

154 **my soul** Jealousy is a motive for villainy in several of Shakespeare's characters, notably Iago, Edmund and Leontes.

156 **device** A word with a variety of meanings relevant here, all but the first *obs.* (and even that is *arch.* and *rare*): ingenuity (*OED* 1); purpose, intention (*OED* 2); will, inclination (*OED* 3); opinion, notion (*OED* 4); familiar conversation (*OED* 5). The general meaning contributes to our admiration for Orlando and dislike of the malevolent Oliver.

enchantingly as if by enchantment (*pace OED*, which cites this as the first example for 'In an enchanting manner')

and especially of my own people, who best know him, that I am altogether misprized. But it shall not be so long. This wrestler shall clear all. Nothing remains but that I kindle the boy thither, which now I'll go about.

Exit

1.2 *Enter Rosalind and Celia*

CELIA I pray thee Rosalind, sweet my coz, be merry.

ROSALIND Dear Celia, I show more mirth than I am mistress of, and would you yet were merrier: unless you could teach me to forget a banished father you must not learn me how to remember any extraordinary pleasure.

CELIA Herein I see thou lovest me not with the full weight that I love thee. If my uncle, thy banished father, had banished thy uncle, the Duke my father, so thou hadst been still with me I could have taught my love to take thy father for mine. So wouldst thou, if the truth of thy love to me were so righteously tempered as mine is to thee.

ROSALIND Well, I will forget the condition of my estate to rejoice in yours.

CELIA You know my father hath no child but I, nor none is like to have. And truly, when he dies thou shalt be

159 **misprized** despised, not appreciated. The earliest instance of this usage cited by *OED* is dated 1648, although *misprize* *v.*[1] a., To despise, is recorded in 1481.

161 **kindle . . . thither** incite the boy (used contemptuously) to go there

1.2 The first part of this scene, up to the wrestling match, introduces Rosalind, Celia and Touchstone; it owes nothing to Lodge. Rosalind's discontent links her with Orlando, and the formalized fight between Orlando and Charles echoes the quarrel between the brothers in Oliver's orchard. By the end of the scene the potential for tragedy has been dissipated.

0.1 *Celia* Probably derived from 'Cecilia' but having implications of 'heavenly', as in Jonson's *Volpone*.

1 **coz** abbreviated form of *cousin*, used here as an endearment

3 **were** Although most editors follow Rowe in adding *I* as the subject of *were*, the emendation changes F's meaning: 'I appear happier than I really am, and wish that you could be even more cheerful than I seem to be'.

5 **learn** teach (*OED*, *learn*, *v.* 4b), still in vulgar use

8–9 **so . . . still** provided that you were constantly with me (Abbott §133)

11 **righteously tempered** The metaphor may be (a) musical: correctly tuned (b) metallurgical: brought to a proper degree of hardness or resiliency or (c) more general: brought to the right consistency for use.

13 **estate** 'Condition with respect to worldly prosperity, fortune etc. . . . *arch.*' *OED sb.* 2.

15 **but I** Ungrammatical use common at the end of the sixteenth century (*OED pron.* 2); Abbott (§209) notes that the sound of *d* and *t* before *me* was avoided.

nor none Emphatic double negative (Abbott §406).

his heir; for what he hath taken away from thy father perforce, I will render thee again in affection. By mine honour I will, and when I break that oath, let me turn monster. Therefore, my sweet Rose, my dear Rose, be merry.

ROSALIND From henceforth I will, coz, and devise sports. Let me see, what think you of falling in love?

CELIA Marry, I prithee do, to make sport withal; but love no man in good earnest, nor no further in sport neither than with safety of a pure blush thou mayst in honour come off again.

ROSALIND What shall be our sport, then?

CELIA Let us sit and mock the good housewife Fortune from her wheel, that her gifts may henceforth be bestowed equally.

ROSALIND I would we could do so, for her benefits are mightily misplaced; and the bountiful blind woman doth most mistake in her gifts to women.

CELIA 'Tis true; for those that she makes fair she scarce makes honest, and those that she makes honest she makes very ill-favouredly.

ROSALIND Nay, now thou goest from Fortune's office to Nature's. Fortune reigns in gifts of the world, not in the lineaments of Nature.

18 **perforce . . . affection** Celia is opposing her father's violence towards Rosalind's father with her own love for Rosalind.

22 **devise sports** Thinking up amusement to divert melancholy is also attempted in a garden by Richard II's sad queen (*Richard II* 3.4). In her reply to Rosalind, Celia develops the bawdy sense of sport as 'amorous dalliance' (*OED sb.*[1] I. 1b. (*Obs.*)); Rosalind's proposal turns out to be ironically apt, and this part of the conversation is a preparation for her meeting and falling in love with Orlando. Discussing a set theme, a favourite Renaissance social pastime, is played with zest in *As You Like It* (see, e.g., 3.2.11–81, 3.2.290–320, 5.4.64–98).

26–7 **pure blush . . . come off** escape with nothing more than an unguilty blush

29 **housewife Fortune** Fortune was frequently depicted as a blindfolded woman turning a huge wheel on which men and women were moved from high to low points in their lives. The idea appears to have had its beginnings in Roman times. Celia satirically debases this to a domestic spinning wheel and Fortune herself to a housewife, with the connotation of 'hussy' (a common downgrading of the word), whom they can drive away by mockery. Rosalind's fortunes are at a low ebb now but they rise by the end of the play. The same derogatory image is used in *Henry V* 5.1.76 and *Antony* 4.16.46.

36 **honest** chaste. The idea that the ugly are chaste and the beautiful otherwise is proverbial (Tilley B163), as Audrey knows (compare 3.3.30); it is a basis for Hamlet's verbal attack on Ophelia in *Hamlet* 3.1.105–53.

39–40 **Fortune . . . Nature** Fortune deals in

Enter Touchstone the clown

CELIA No. When Nature hath made a fair creature, may she not by Fortune fall into the fire? Though Nature hath given us wit to flout at Fortune, hath not Fortune sent in this fool to cut off the argument?

ROSALIND Indeed, there is Fortune too hard for Nature, when Fortune makes Nature's natural the cutter-off of Nature's wit.

CELIA Peradventure this is not Fortune's work, neither, but Nature's, who perceiveth our natural wits too dull to reason of such goddesses, and hath sent this natural for our whetstone; for always the dullness of the fool is the whetstone of the wits. How now, wit: whither wander you?

TOUCHSTONE Mistress, you must come away to your father.

1.2.40.1 *Touchstone the clown*] Touchstone, *a clown* THEOBALD 1740; *Clowne* F (*and so throughout*) 50 and] MALONE; *not in* F

material and temporal things, like money and power, not in a person's physical beauty, which is Nature's province. The balanced, alliterative style of the ensuing conversation is unusual in Shakespeare, but characteristic of Lyly, Greene and others who relished euphuism.

40.1 ***Touchstone*** The clown's name, first mentioned in F at 2.4.0.1, possibly includes the name of the clown, Tutch, in the actor Robert Armin's play, *Two Maids of More-clack* (*c.* 1597), and that of a contemporary tavern-fool, John Stone, which may be alluded to in *Twelfth Night* 1.5.80–1 when Malvolio says he has seen Feste 'put down . . . with an ordinary fool that has no more brain than a stone'. The whole name is believed by some (e.g. Charles S. Felver, 'Robert Armin, Shakespeare's Source for Touchstone' (*SQ*, 7 (1956), 135–7) to refer to Armin's training as a goldsmith, in which a touchstone (a piece of dark quartz or jasper) was used to test the quality of gold and silver alloys by the colour of the streak made when the metal was rubbed on it. Figuratively, a touchstone serves to test genuineness or value—as Touchstone does, for example, with Jaques (2.7.12–42), Corin (3.2.13–81), and William (5.1.10–58). See Introduction, pp. 25–8.

42 **fall into the fire** (a) and so be disfigured (b) be tempted into unchastity

43 **wit** cleverness, intelligence. The word occurs 24 times in the play, with a wide range of functions and meanings. This amount of usage ranks *As You Like It* third after *L.L.L.* (32) and *Much Ado* (29), two other comedies with notably witty heroines.

46 **natural** an idiot. Rosalind says this for the sake of a witty pun; Touchstone is far from idiocy, though he may be dressed in the long-skirted coat often worn by simpletons and congenital idiots. See Introduction, p. 26.

50 **reason of** talk about

and Omitted in F, supplied by Malone; F2 alters 'perceiveth' in the previous line to 'perceiving', which makes acceptable sense.

51 **whetstone . . . dullness** The idea, if not the precise expression, was proverbial. Compare Tilley W299 and Dent W298.1, where six different items are listed as being the whetstone, including an arithmetic textbook, Robert Recorde's *The Whetstone of Wit* (1557).

52–3 **wit: whither . . . you?** Proverbial (Tilley W570). Said to an over-talkative person (compare 4.1.153), but here Celia turns it into 'Where are you off to?' Compare *Dream* 2.1.1: 'How now, spirit, whither wander you?'

CELIA Were you made the messenger?

TOUCHSTONE No, by mine honour, but I was bid to come for you.

ROSALIND Where learned you that oath, fool?

TOUCHSTONE Of a certain knight that swore 'by his honour' they were good pancakes, and swore 'by his honour' the mustard was naught. Now I'll stand to it the pancakes were naught and the mustard was good, and yet was not the knight forsworn.

CELIA How prove you that in the great heap of your knowledge?

ROSALIND Ay, marry, now unmuzzle your wisdom.

TOUCHSTONE Stand you both forth now: stroke your chins, and swear by your beards that I am a knave.

CELIA By our beards—if we had them—thou art.

TOUCHSTONE By my knavery—if I had it—then I were; but if you swear by that that is not, you are not forsworn. No more was this knight, swearing by his honour, for he never had any; or if he had, he had sworn it away before ever he saw those pancakes or that mustard.

CELIA Prithee, who is't that thou meanest?

TOUCHSTONE One that old Frederick, your father, loves.

⌈CELIA⌉ My father's love is enough to honour him

77 CELIA] THEOBALD; *Ros.* F

55 **messenger** Fools were notably unreliable, as Proverbs 26:6 says: 'He that sendeth a message by the hand of a fool, is as he that cutteth off the feet [glossed by the Geneva Bible "That is, receiveth damage thereby"] and drinketh iniquity'.

59–61 **honour . . . mustard** A now-obscure joke, which may possibly be related to Jonson's *Every Man In His Humour* (1598): Schoenbaum notes that some have seen in that play a jibe at Shakespeare's motto, *Non sanz droict* (Not without right), when the character Sogliardo, a rustic clown, pays £30 for his arms and is 'mocked with the "word" [i.e. motto] *Not without mustard*'. While finding the parallel suggestive, Schoenbaum shows it is unlikely, and remarks that if Shakespeare 'did choose "Non sanz droict" as his motto neither he nor his descendants seem ever to have used it' (p. 171).

68 **beards** This quip subtly introduces the complex joking with gender on which so much of the play's humour depends. Rosalind and Celia, being women, have no beards; the boys who played them on the Elizabethan stage were, presumably, too young to have beards either. Touchstone's sly drawing of attention to the male actors beneath the female costumes is taken further by Celia's reply.

76 **old Frederick** Touchstone's being both familiar and disrespectful earns him a rebuke.

77 CELIA F gives the line to Rosalind but most editors follow Theobald in assigning it to her cousin. Touchstone belongs to Frederick's court and adores Celia (1.3.128–32); he has no reason to jibe at Duke Senior, but he clearly appears to suggest that Duke Frederick's court is not honourable.

77–8 **him enough.** Most editors follow in principle Hanmer's punctuation 'him:

enough; speak no more of him: you'll be whipped for taxation one of these days.

TOUCHSTONE The more pity that fools may not speak wisely what wise men do foolishly.

CELIA By my troth, thou sayst true; for since the little wit that fools have was silenced, the little foolery that wise men have makes a great show. Here comes Monsieur Le Beau.

Enter Le Beau

ROSALIND With his mouth full of news.

CELIA Which he will put on us as pigeons feed their young.

ROSALIND Then shall we be news-crammed.

CELIA All the better: we shall be the more marketable. *Bonjour*, Monsieur Le Beau, what's the news?

LE BEAU Fair princess, you have lost much good sport.

CELIA Sport? Of what colour?

LE BEAU What colour, madam? How shall I answer you?

ROSALIND As wit and fortune will.

TOUCHSTONE Or as the destinies decrees.

CELIA Well said. That was laid on with a trowel.

85 Le Beau] STEEVENS; the *Beu* F 91 LE BEAU] STEEVENS *throughout*; *Le Beu* F

enough!' (i.e. 'you've said enough!'). F's punctuation, however, is satisfactory, and gives the reading, 'My father's love is enough to give him sufficient honour, even if he lacks his own personal honour.'

79 **taxation** (a) censure, satire (b) (possibly) a pun on Latin *tax* 'the sound of a whip-stroke'

80–1 Touchstone is the first of Shakespeare's wise fools—witty clowns allowed to comment on the behaviour of the households to which they are attached. Feste in *Twelfth Night* and King Lear's fool are developments of the type.

83 **silenced** Some, following Fleay, have seen in this a reference to the burning of satirical writings of Nashe and others at Stationers' Hall in June 1599; others, like Moberly, detect a reference to persecution of players by the Lord Mayor and aldermen of London. However, as Celia says it is *fools* who have been silenced, neither explanation is very satisfactory.

85 **Le Beau** 'The Beautiful' (French). Allied with the character's affected speech, the name gives an actor the opportunity to play the fop.

90 ***Bonjour*** 'Good day, hallo' (French). Celia is making fun of Le Beau, drawing attention to his Frenchness.

93 **colour** character, kind (*OED sb.* 16a): the earliest instance of *colour* in this sense cited by *OED*. Le Beau's confusion at Celia's question may be because she is using 'colour' in a new way, but the ensuing dialogue indicates that he is rather slow-witted. His advice to Orlando (ll. 246–52) shows he is also thoughtful for others.

94 **wit and fortune** Compare 'Little wit serves unto whom Fortune pipes' (Tilley W560).

95 **decrees** Although some suggest typographical error here, third person plurals ending in *-s* are 'extremely common' in F (Abbott §333).

96 **laid . . . trowel** fulsome, excessive. Now proverbial (Tilley T539) in its ironic and figurative use, which appears to have originated with Celia's quip, the phrase presumably comes from bricklaying.

TOUCHSTONE Nay, if I keep not my rank—

ROSALIND Thou loosest thy old smell.

LE BEAU You amaze me, ladies. I would have told you of good wrestling, which you have lost the sight of.

ROSALIND Yet tell us the manner of the wrestling.

LE BEAU I will tell you the beginning, and if it please your ladyships you may see the end, for the best is yet to do, and here, where you are, they are coming to perform it.

CELIA Well, the beginning that is dead and buried.

LE BEAU There comes an old man and his three sons—

CELIA I could match this beginning with an old tale.

LE BEAU Three proper young men, of excellent growth and presence.

ROSALIND With bills on their necks: 'Be it known unto all men by these presents'—

LE BEAU The eldest of the three wrestled with Charles, the Duke's wrestler, which Charles in a moment threw him, and broke three of his ribs, that there is little hope of life in him. So he served the second, and so the third. Yonder they lie, the poor old man their father making such pitiful dole over them that all the beholders take his part with weeping.

ROSALIND Alas!

TOUCHSTONE But what is the sport, monsieur, that the ladies have lost?

LE BEAU Why, this that I speak of.

TOUCHSTONE Thus men may grow wiser every day. It is the

97 **rank** professional standing

98 **loosest** Editors have emended to *losest* but Rosalind, taking 'rank' in the sense of 'Having an offensively strong smell' (*OED a.* 12), is saying that if Touchstone cannot keep his bad smells to himself then he must be releasing a fart. Considered indelicate today perhaps, but ladies, including Queen Elizabeth herself, once made jokes in public about farting (see Oliver Mawson-Dick's edition of Aubrey's *Brief Lives* (Harmondsworth, 1962), p. 357), and fools were associated with bad smells (compare 2.1.26n.).

99 **amaze** bewilder, perplex

107 **tale** *Rosalynde* and *The Tale of Gamelyn* are but two stories which have just such a beginning with an old man and three sons; but as well, Celia is still making fun of Le Beau, punning on *tale*/'tail' (as opposed to 'beginning').

110 **bills** Possibly a pun on 'bill' = (a) a long-handled weapon or pruning implement and (b) a legal document. In Lodge 'Ganymede . . . cast up her eye, and saw where Rosader came . . . with his forest bill on his necke' (42[r]). In the sense 'Labels round their necks', Rosalind puns on 'presence', since many legal documents began *noverint universi per praesentes*—'know all men by these presents'; she is mocking Le Beau's pomposity.

117 **dole** lamentation

first time that ever I heard breaking of ribs was sport for ladies.

CELIA Or I, I promise thee.

ROSALIND But is there any else longs to see this broken music in his sides? Is there yet another dotes upon rib-breaking? Shall we see this wrestling, cousin?

LE BEAU You must if you stay here, for here is the place appointed for the wrestling, and they are ready to perform it.

CELIA Yonder sure they are coming. Let us now stay and see it.

Flourish. Enter Duke Frederick, Lords, Orlando, Charles, and attendants

DUKE FREDERICK Come on. Since the youth will not be entreated, his own peril on his forwardness.

ROSALIND Is yonder the man?

LE BEAU Even he, madam.

CELIA Alas, he is too young. Yet he looks successfully.

DUKE FREDERICK How now, daughter and cousin; are you crept hither to see the wrestling?

ROSALIND Ay, my liege, so please you give us leave.

DUKE FREDERICK You will take little delight in it, I can tell you, there is such odds in the man. In pity of the challenger's youth I would fain dissuade him, but he will not be entreated. Speak to him, ladies; see if you can move him.

CELIA Call him hither, good Monsieur Le Beau.

134.1 *Duke Frederick*] ROWE; *Duke* F 135 DUKE FREDERICK] *Duke F.* MALONE; *Duke* F

124–5 **breaking . . . sport . . . ladies** The remarks of Touchstone and Celia point up the barbarity of Frederick's court, even though tournaments resulting in 'breaking of ribs' and worse injuries were watched by ladies both in medieval times and at the Accession Day tilts of Elizabeth's reign. (Boxing and wrestling are still 'sport for ladies'.)

127–8 **broken music** Music played by a combination of different kinds of instruments; Rosalind is making a pun comparing the fractured bones of the young man with the broken ribs of a smashed instrument, such as a lute. She may be punning as well, or instead, on 'side' as 'one of the two divisions of a choir' (*OED*, *side*, 21a).

134.1 ***Flourish*** a fanfare of trumpets or horns, usually signalling the entrance of a king, queen or other persons in authority

136 **peril . . . forwardness** 'the danger he puts himself in is due to his presumptuous self-confidence' (*OED* 4): earliest instance of *forwardness* in this sense cited by *OED*.

139 **looks successfully** seems likely to succeed

141 **crept** approached timorously. Frederick's use of the word indicates his (mistaken) perception of the weakness of the women.

144 **odds . . . man** such superiority in Charles

DUKE FREDERICK Do so. I'll not be by.

He stands aside

LE BEAU (*to Orlando*) Monsieur the challenger, the Princess calls for you.

ORLANDO I attend them with all respect and duty.

ROSALIND Young man, have you challenged Charles the wrestler?

ORLANDO No, fair Princess. He is the general challenger; I come but in as others do, to try with him the strength of my youth.

CELIA Young gentleman, your spirits are too bold for your years. You have seen cruel proof of this man's strength. If you saw yourself with your eyes, or knew yourself with your judgement, the fear of your adventure would counsel you to a more equal enterprise. We pray you for your own sake to embrace your own safety and give over this attempt.

ROSALIND Do, young sir. Your reputation shall not therefore be misprized. We will make it our suit to the Duke that the wrestling might not go forward.

ORLANDO I beseech you, punish me not with your hard thoughts, wherein I confess me much guilty to deny so fair and excellent ladies anything. But let your fair eyes and gentle wishes go with me to my trial, wherein if I be foiled, there is but one shamed that was never gracious, if killed, but one dead that is willing to be so. I

149.1 *He . . . aside*] Duke *goes apart.* THEOBALD; *not in* F

150–2 **Princess . . . them** Orlando has his eye, and mind, on both women and in any case does not know which is the princess. 'Princess' could be an uninflected plural (Abbott §471), which makes 'calls' either a third person plural in *-s* (Abbott §333) or a printing error.

155 **general challenger** Since Duke Frederick and Le Beau have both just named him as the challenger, this disclaimer by Orlando can be taken as indicating both his modesty and his bashful confusion at meeting Rosalind and Celia; he is strictly right, however, in that Charles is taking on anyone who dares.

156 **try** test

160–1 **your eyes . . . judgement** if you could see yourself compared to the brawny Charles, or judge your own inexperience against his experience

161 **fear** formidableness (*OED sb.* 5c)

166 **misprized** scorned. There is nice irony in Rosalind's choice of the same word that Oliver had used in angry self-pity at 1.1.159.

168–77 Orlando's balanced, courteous speech of loneliness and despair indicates his inborn gentility as well as the emotionalism which led to his attack on Oliver and will lead to his versifying in Arden. It may also be a half-deliberate appeal to the women's feelings.

169 **wherein** though

172 **foiled** Although 'foil' is a technical term in wrestling for 'a throw not resulting in a flat fall' (*OED sb.*[2] †1), Orlando simply means 'If I am defeated'.

shall do my friends no wrong, for I have none to lament me; the world no injury, for in it I have nothing. Only in the world I fill up a place which may be better supplied when I have made it empty.

ROSALIND The little strength that I have, I would it were with you.

CELIA And mine, to eke out hers.

ROSALIND Fare you well. Pray heaven I be deceived in you.

CELIA Your heart's desires be with you.

CHARLES Come, where is this young gallant that is so desirous to lie with his mother earth?

ORLANDO Ready, sir; but his will hath in it a more modest working.

DUKE FREDERICK You shall try but one fall.

CHARLES No, I warrant your grace you shall not entreat him to a second that have so mightily persuaded him from a first.

ORLANDO You mean to mock me after; you should not have mocked me before. But come your ways.

ROSALIND (*to Orlando*) Now Hercules be thy speed, young man!

CELIA I would I were invisible, to catch the strong fellow by the leg.

Charles and Orlando wrestle

196.1 *Charles . . . wrestle*] *wrastle.* F

184–6 **lie . . . mother earth . . . working** Charles makes a sexual joke; Orlando rebuts the bawdy by punning on *will* (a) sexual desire (b) non-sexual desire, and on *working* (a) sexual activity (b) performance, achievement; he reinforces the non-sexual meanings of these words with *modest*. 'Mother earth' is proverbial (Dent E28.1).

187 **fall** A *fall* consisted in either the adversary's back or one shoulder and the opposite heel touching the ground.

191–2 **You mean . . . before** Compare the proverbial 'Do not triumph before a victory' (Tilley V50) and 'He who mocks shall be mocked' (M1031), and 1 Kings 20: 11: 'Let not him that girdeth his harness [armour] boast himself as he that putteth it off', glossed in the Geneva Bible, 'Boast not before the victory be gotten'.

193 **Hercules be thy speed** may Hercules be your helper. Rosalind invokes the name of the demigod who wrestled with and defeated Antaeus, whose mother was Gaia, the Earth, and whose strength was renewed whenever he touched the ground. Compare Charles's gibe at l. 184. In Lodge it is the court wrestler who 'looked like *Hercules*' [7[v]].

196.1 The wrestling match can be a dramatic high point of the scene: Macready (Drury Lane, 1842) had the combatants trained in Cornish wrestling, put a fence around them and thronged the stage with upwards of 80 spectators (see p. 55). It can be coarsely vulgarized. And it can fail: in 1890 Furness noted dismally that 'Our stage Orlandos and Charleses are generally such feeble adepts . . . that the match . . . is far from thrilling, and we are amazed not so much at

ROSALIND O excellent young man!

CELIA If I had a thunderbolt in mine eye, I can tell who should down.

Orlando throws Charles. Shout

DUKE FREDERICK
No more, no more.

ORLANDO Yes, I beseech your grace.
I am not yet well breathed.

DUKE FREDERICK How dost thou, Charles?

LE BEAU He cannot speak, my lord.

DUKE FREDERICK Bear him away.

Attendants carry Charles off

What is thy name, young man?

ORLANDO Orlando, my liege, the youngest son of Sir Rowland de Boys.

DUKE FREDERICK
I would thou hadst been son to some man else.
The world esteemed thy father honourable,
But I did find him still mine enemy.
Thou shouldst have better pleased me with this deed
Hadst thou descended from another house.
But fare thee well, thou art a gallant youth.
I would thou hadst told me of another father.

Exeunt Duke Frederick, Le Beau, ⌈Touchstone,⌉ Lords, and attendants

CELIA (*to Rosalind*)
Were I my father, coz, would I do this?

199.1 *Orlando . . . Shout*] *Charles is thrown* ROWE; *Shout.* F 204.1 *Attendants . . . off*] CHA. *is borne off.* CAPELL; *not in* F 214.1–2 *Exeunt . . . attendants*] *Exit . . . with his train* THEOBALD; *Exit Duke.* F

Orlando's powers as at Charles's accommodating mortality.' Orlando need not be brawny; Elyot remarks 'it hath been seen that the weaker person, by the sleight of wrestling, hath overthrown the stronger, almost [before] he could fasten on the other any violent stroke' (p. 74).

201 **breathed** exercised, warmed up

203, 204.1 Acting editions as early as 1774 give Le Beau's line to Touchstone, who sometimes accompanied Charles's body off-stage.

208 The change to blank verse moves the play to another plane, from the foolery and physical activity of the earlier part of the scene to the more serious matters of court politics, and love. Frederick, though the usurper, is not yet shown as a very wicked villain—he had tried to dissuade Orlando from the wrestling match and now, even when so displeased, still calls him 'a gallant youth'.

210 **still** always

215 Although many directors have moved Celia's line to follow l. 223, they have thereby robbed Rosalind of the opportunity to be so struck by Orlando that she is oblivious of Celia and what she says.

ORLANDO
I am more proud to be Sir Rowland's son,
His youngest son, and would not change that calling
To be adopted heir to Frederick.

ROSALIND
My father loved Sir Rowland as his soul,
And all the world was of my father's mind.
Had I before known this young man his son
I should have given him tears unto entreaties
Ere he should thus have ventured.

CELIA Gentle cousin,
Let us go thank him, and encourage him.
My father's rough and envious disposition
Sticks me at heart.—Sir, you have well deserved.
If you do keep your promises in love
But justly, as you have exceeded all promise,
Your mistress shall be happy.

ROSALIND (*giving him a chain from her neck*) Gentleman,
Wear this for me—one out of suits with fortune,
That could give more but that her hand lacks means.
Shall we go, coz?

CELIA Ay. Fare you well, fair gentleman.

Rosalind and Celia begin to go

ORLANDO (*aside*)
Can I not say 'I thank you'? My better parts
Are all thrown down, and that which here stands up
Is but a quintain, a mere lifeless block.

229 *giving . . . neck*] THEOBALD; *not in* F 232.1 *Rosalind . . . go*] This edition; *not in* F

217 **calling** station in life. Some editors give 'name', for which this line is the latest example of usage in *OED* (*vbl. sb.* 4), but the contrast is between the social positions of being the youngest son of Sir Rowland de Boys and being heir to Frederick.

222 **unto** in addition to

225 **envious** full of ill-will; malicious, spiteful

227 **But justly** only exactly

230 **out of suits** out of favour, perhaps with the meaning of having failed in one's requests, though a sartorial sense may also be intended; Rosalind is putting herself in the same position as Orlando. Mary Anderson (1885) placed the chain in Orlando's hand, but most Rosalinds hang it about Orlando's neck; Helen Faucit (1839) surreptitiously kissed it first. Many Orlandos kneel to receive the chain with bowed heads. Lodge's Rosalynde merely sends hers to Rosader by a page.

233 **parts** abilities

235 **quintain** In its simplest form, a wooden post used for tilting practice by knights, who rode at it with their lances. By 1600 running at the quintain was a mainly rural sport, held especially at weddings. Queen Elizabeth watched it as part of a country bridal at Kenilworth in 1575 and Joseph Strutt, who discusses various types of quintains, quotes (p. 190) Dr Plott's *History of Oxfordshire* (1677): 'It is

ROSALIND (*to Celia*)
He calls us back. My pride fell with my fortunes,
I'll ask him what he would.—Did you call, sir?
Sir, you have wrestled well, and overthrown
More than your enemies.
CELIA Will you go, coz?
ROSALIND Have with you. (*To Orlando*) Fare you well.
Exeunt Rosalind and Celia

ORLANDO
What passion hangs these weights upon my tongue?
I cannot speak to her, yet she urged conference.
Enter Le Beau
O poor Orlando! Thou art overthrown.
Or Charles or something weaker masters thee.

LE BEAU
Good sir, I do in friendship counsel you
To leave this place. Albeit you have deserved
High commendation, true applause, and love,
Yet such is now the Duke's condition
That he misconsters all that you have done.
The Duke is humorous. What he is indeed
More suits you to conceive than I to speak of.

ORLANDO
I thank you, sir; and pray you tell me this,
Which of the two was daughter of the Duke
That here was at the wrestling?

241.1 *Exeunt . . . Celia*] *Exit* F

now only in request at marriages.' Orlando's simile indicates that his thoughts fly just as quickly to their target as Rosalind's do.
mere absolute, downright

236 **He calls us back** Of course he doesn't, but Rosalind may hear his anguished mutter of self-reproach. Most actresses milk the moment for comedy, dawdling almost into the wings before stopping suddenly and restraining Celia from going, then turning and hurrying back to Orlando; it is most effective when Orlando has his back to Rosalind, as this allows her to compose herself and be properly dignified when she begins to speak to him.

241 **Have with you** I'm coming
243 **conference** conversation, talk
249 **condition** disposition, temper
250 **misconsters** misconstrues. The accent is on the second syllable.
251 **humorous** moody, peevish, ill-humoured, out of humour: the first instance of *humorous* in this sense cited by *OED* (*a.* 3b). As Chapman's *An Humorous Day's Mirth* was played in 1597, and Jonson's *Every Man In His Humour* and *Every Man Out Of His Humour* were performed by the Lord Chamberlain's Men in 1598 and 1599 respectively, Le Beau may well be using a modish word, but Lodge's Torismond banishes Rosalynde in a 'humour, with a stern countenance full of wrath' (12[r]).

LE BEAU

Neither his daughter, if we judge by manners—
But yet indeed the shorter is his daughter.
The other is daughter to the banished Duke,
And here detained by her usurping uncle
To keep his daughter company, whose loves
Are dearer than the natural bond of sisters.
But I can tell you that of late this Duke
Hath ta'en displeasure 'gainst his gentle niece,
Grounded upon no other argument
But that the people praise her for her virtues
And pity her for her good father's sake.
And, on my life, his malice 'gainst the lady
Will suddenly break forth. Sir, fare you well.
Hereafter, in a better world than this,
I shall desire more love and knowledge of you.

ORLANDO

I rest much bounden to you. Fare you well.

Exit Le Beau

Thus must I from the smoke into the smother,
From tyrant Duke unto a tyrant brother.—
But heavenly Rosalind! *Exit*

257 shorter] ROWE 1714; taller F 271.1 *Exit Le Beau*] CAPELL; *not in* F 274 Rosalind] ROWE; *Rosaline* F (*this spelling also at* 1.3.0.1, 1.3.1, 89, 95, 2.4.0.1)

257 **shorter** Although F's *taller* has had its defenders, Rosalind herself says she is 'more than common tall' (1.3.114) and Celia is described as 'low' (4.3.88). As 'smaller' was not a sixteenth-century usage relating to height, Rowe's 1714 emendation, the correction of a Shakespearian slip rather than an error in transmission of the text, is the most acceptable. Lodge's Rosalynde says, 'I . . . am of a tall stature' (14r).

258 An eleven-syllable line, with the last accented. Read *other's*.

264 **argument** reason

268 **suddenly** shortly, very soon

269 **better world** Shakespeare's minor characters are often given significant lines. Charles drew attention to the 'golden world' when speaking of the exiled Duke (1.1.113); now Le Beau implicitly compares the cruel world of the usurper's court with a happier, morally better place elsewhere, in the future.

270 **knowledge** personal acquaintance, friendship, intimacy

272 **from the smoke into the smother** Proverbial (Tilley S570). Lines 272–3 are the first of seven of the play's rhymed couplets which denote the end of a scene (1.3.136–7; 2.3.76–7; 2.4.100–1; 2.7.203–4; 3.4.53–4; 5.4.192–3).

274 **heavenly Rosalind** More than half Shakespeare's heroines of comedy are described as having divine qualities. Compare, e.g., Ferdinand on seeing Miranda (*Tempest* 1.2.424–5). 'Most sure the goddess | On whom these airs attend'. For Orlando, Rosalind's existence compensates for his troubles. F's spelling, *Rosaline*, recalls the witty lady of *L.L.L.* and Romeo's obdurate mistress (*Romeo* 1.2.85). This spelling, which occurs five more times, occurs only in pages set by Compositor D, who had set the same name four times previously in *L.L.L.*, not long before working on *As You Like It*.

1.3 *Enter Celia and Rosalind*

CELIA Why cousin, why Rosalind—Cupid have mercy, not a word?

ROSALIND Not one to throw at a dog.

CELIA No, thy words are too precious to be cast away upon curs. Throw some of them at me. Come, lame me with reasons.

ROSALIND Then there were two cousins laid up, when the one should be lamed with reasons and the other mad without any.

CELIA But is all this for your father?

ROSALIND No, some of it is for my child's father. O how full of briers is this working-day world!

CELIA They are but burs, cousin, thrown upon thee in holiday foolery. If we walk not in the trodden paths our very petticoats will catch them.

ROSALIND I could shake them off my coat. These burs are in my heart.

CELIA Hem them away.

ROSALIND I would try, if I could cry 'hem' and have him.

CELIA Come, come, wrestle with thy affections.

ROSALIND O, they take the part of a better wrestler than myself.

1.3 Orlando's ecstasy is followed by Rosalind's quieter, more wry acknowledgement of love's arrival. Frederick's banishment of his niece motivates the movement of the action to Arden and the disguise which she and Celia wear for most of the play. The scene is usually played continuously on from 1.2.

3 **Not . . . dog** Proverbial (Tilley W762).

8 **mad** having lost her reason(s) she would be mad

11 **my child's father** Various editors from Rowe (1709) to Verity (1900) emend to 'my father's child', sharing Coleridge's view that F puts 'a very indelicate anticipation in the mouth of Rosalind' (*Coleridge's Shakespearian Criticism*, ed. T. M. Raysor, 2 vols. (1960), i. 94). Endemic in nineteenth-century stage performances, the emendation surprisingly turned up in Buzz Goodbody's RSC production in 1973. The meaning of F is perfectly clear, however, and intentional, and echoed by Celia at 3.2.197.

12 **briers** '(To leave one) (To be) in the briers' was proverbial (Tilley B673).

13 **burs** rough or sticky seed-vessels or flower-heads of plants, especially burdock, which little boys threw at one another for fun. Compare *Troilus* 3.2.108–9: 'They are burrs . . . they'll stick where they are thrown' and the proverb 'To stick like burs' (Tilley B724). Typically, Rosalind puns on the meaning of *bur* as an irritation in the throat that one coughs (*hems*) away; following on from 'petticoats' and 'coat', Celia puns on *hem* as in sewing and in coughing. Rosalind takes it further as a pun on *him* and is, perhaps, also saying she wishes she could call Orlando with a pre-arranged signal. (In less happy circumstances, Othello tells Emilia 'Cough or cry "hem" if anybody come' (*Othello* 4.2.31).)

18 **Hem them away** cough them away (*OED*, *hem*, *v.*² 3): earliest instance of *hem* in this sense cited by *OED*

19 **cry . . . him** Perhaps proverbial; Dent

CELIA O, a good wish upon you! You will try in time, in despite of a fall. But turning these jests out of service, let us talk in good earnest. Is it possible on such a sudden you should fall into so strong a liking with old Sir Rowland's youngest son?

ROSALIND The Duke my father loved his father dearly.

CELIA Doth it therefore ensue that you should love his son dearly? By this kind of chase I should hate him, for my father hated his father dearly; yet I hate not Orlando.

ROSALIND No, faith, hate him not, for my sake.

CELIA Why should I not? Doth he not deserve well?

Enter Duke Frederick, with Lords

ROSALIND Let me love him for that, and do you love him because I do. Look, here comes the Duke.

CELIA With his eyes full of anger.

DUKE FREDERICK (*to Rosalind*)
Mistress, dispatch you with your safest haste,
And get you from our court.

ROSALIND Me, uncle?

DUKE FREDERICK You, cousin.
Within these ten days if that thou beest found
So near our public court as twenty miles,
Thou diest for it.

ROSALIND I do beseech your grace
Let me the knowledge of my fault bear with me.

1.3.33.1 *Frederick*] *not in* F

includes it prefixed by two question marks (H413.1).

23–4 **try . . . fall** you will at some time try controlling your affections, but it will be with a disregard for failing (because that's what you in fact want). C. J. Sisson's suggested emendation *cry* for F's *try* with a consequent joking reference to childbirth is ingenious but unnecessary (*New Readings in Shakespeare*, 2 vols. (Cambridge, 1956), i. 147). Celia's words are an echo of her father's 'You shall try but one fall' (1.2.187), enriched by a common sexual allusion.

30 **chase** pursuit, hunting. Perhaps a pun following on 'dear(ly)', and an intimation of the impending move to Arden.

31 **dearly** deeply, keenly (in contrast to the immediately preceding meaning, 'affectionately')

33 **Why should I not?** What reason is there for me to hate him?

37 **your safest haste** such haste as to be as safe as possible for you
The change in the play's dramatic tempo and action is signalled by the reintroduction of verse. The formality of Frederick's banishment of Rosalind echoes his rejection of Orlando (1.2.208–14): both 'you' and 'thou' are used to indicate his rising anger. Compare Oliver's raging at Orlando (1.1.71–2).

40 **cousin** relative. Formerly 'very frequently applied to a nephew or niece' (*OED sb.* †1).

If with myself I hold intelligence,
Or have acquaintance with mine own desires,
If that I do not dream, or be not frantic—
As I do trust I am not—then, dear uncle,
Never so much as in a thought unborn
Did I offend your highness.

DUKE FREDERICK Thus do all traitors.
If their purgation did consist in words
They are as innocent as grace itself.
Let it suffice thee that I trust thee not.

ROSALIND
Yet your mistrust cannot make me a traitor.
Tell me whereon the likelihoods depends?

DUKE FREDERICK
Thou art thy father's daughter—there's enough.

ROSALIND
So was I when your highness took his dukedom;
So was I when your highness banished him.
Treason is not inherited, my lord,
Or if we did derive it from our friends,
What's that to me? My father was no traitor.
Then, good my liege, mistake me not so much
To think my poverty is treacherous.

CELIA Dear sovereign, hear me speak.

DUKE FREDERICK
Ay, Celia, we stayed her for your sake,
Else had she with her father ranged along.

CELIA
I did not then entreat to have her stay.
It was your pleasure, and your own remorse.

45 **intelligence** communication

51 **purgation** action of clearing oneself of guilt, by affirmation on oath in an ecclesiastical court, or by ordeal. By the sixteenth century these methods were obsolete, but Touchstone refers to them at 5.4.43.

52 **innocent as grace** Proverbial according to Tilley (T560) who, however, cites no other examples with 'grace'; Dent excludes it.

55 **depends** Compare 'decrees' at 1.2.95. Some editors follow F2 and emend to 'likelihood depends', others follow Malone's 'likelihoods depend'.

60 **friends** relatives

66 **ranged along** wandered about with him (in his exile)

68 **remorse** 'Compassion' is a probable meaning, but Celia may also be charging her father with having tried to assuage his feelings of guilt over the usurpation by caring for Rosalind.

I was too young that time to value her,
But now I know her. If she be a traitor,
Why, so am I. We still have slept together,
Rose at an instant, learned, played, eat together,
And wheresoe'er we went, like Juno's swans
Still we went coupled and inseparable.

DUKE FREDERICK

She is too subtle for thee, and her smoothness,
Her very silence, and her patience
Speak to the people, and they pity her.
Thou art a fool. She robs thee of thy name,
And thou wilt show more bright and seem more
virtuous
When she is gone. Then open not thy lips.
Firm and irrevocable is my doom
Which I have passed upon her. She is banished.

CELIA

Pronounce that sentence then on me, my liege.
I cannot live out of her company.

DUKE FREDERICK

You are a fool.—You, niece, provide yourself.
If you outstay the time, upon mine honour
And in the greatness of my word, you die.
Exit Duke Frederick, with Lords

CELIA

O my poor Rosalind, whither wilt thou go?
Wilt thou change fathers? I will give thee mine.
I charge thee, be not thou more grieved than I am.

88.1 *Frederick, with Lords*], *&c* F

69 **young** Although some have used Celia's comment to suggest inconsistency in the play's time-scheme, *young* here has the sense of 'immature'. Compare 1.1.51.

72 **eat** eaten

73 **Juno's swans** Swans were usually associated with Venus, goddess of love, peacocks with Juno, goddess of marriage, but gods and goddesses sometimes partook of one another's qualities, and could even be regarded as the same deity. Edgar Wind discusses this syncretism in *Pagan Mysteries in the Renaissance* (1958; rev. edn. Oxford, 1980), pp. 196–200. Juno was also associated with geese, which in ancient illustrations could be mistaken for swans. Kyd mentions 'Juno's goodly swans' in *Soliman and Perseda* 4.1.70 (*c.* 1592). Celia's description of the cousins' intimacy resembles Helena's account of the closeness of herself and Hermia (*Dream* 3.2.200–14).

75 **subtle** crafty, treacherously cunning

78 **name** reputation

86 **You are a fool** The repetition of this charge, with 'thou' of l. 78 replaced by the angry 'you', again emphasizes Frederick's fury.

ROSALIND
I have more cause.

CELIA Thou hast not, cousin.
Prithee, be cheerful. Know'st thou not the Duke
Hath banished me, his daughter?

ROSALIND That he hath not.

CELIA
No, hath not? Rosalind lacks then the love
Which teacheth thee that thou and I am one.
Shall we be sundered? Shall we part, sweet girl?
No. Let my father seek another heir.
Therefore devise with me how we may fly,
Whither to go, and what to bear with us,
And do not seek to take your change upon you,
To bear your griefs yourself, and leave me out.
For by this heaven, now at our sorrows pale,
Say what thou canst, I'll go along with thee.

ROSALIND Why, whither shall we go?

CELIA
To seek my uncle in the forest of Arden.

ROSALIND
Alas, what danger will it be to us,
Maids as we are, to travel forth so far!
Beauty provoketh thieves sooner than gold.

CELIA
I'll put myself in poor and mean attire,
And with a kind of umber smirch my face.
The like do you, so shall we pass along

95 This line has troubled editors. Concerned by F's shift from third to second person, Theobald emended 'thee' in the next line to 'me'. Oxford, assuming 'lacks' is 'lackest' abbreviated and that 'thou' was omitted, emends to 'lack'st thou'. F's reading, however, sounds natural and affectionate.

96 **thou . . . one** Compare 'A friend is one's second self' (Tilley F696).

101 **take . . . upon you** take your reversal of fortune upon yourself

102 **griefs** One of several Shakespearian variations on a proverbial saying (Tilley G447). Compare *Hamlet* 3.2.325–6: 'You do freely bar the door of your own liberty if you deny your griefs to your friend.' Dent excludes this example from *As You Like It*.

103 **pale** 'turned pale by our sorrows' rather than 'now we are at the extreme limit of our sorrows'

111 **umber** brown earth from *Umbria* in Italy used to make pigment. The girls' aristocratically pale complexions would too easily distinguish them among country folk.

And never stir assailants.
ROSALIND Were it not better,
Because that I am more than common tall,
That I did suit me all points like a man,
A gallant curtal-axe upon my thigh,
A boar-spear in my hand, and in my heart,
Lie there what hidden woman's fear there will.
We'll have a swashing and a martial outside,
As many other mannish cowards have,
That do outface it with their semblances.

CELIA
What shall I call thee when thou art a man?

ROSALIND
I'll have no worse a name than Jove's own page,
And therefore look you call me Ganymede.
But what will you be called?

CELIA
Something that hath a reference to my state.
No longer Celia, but Aliena.

ROSALIND
But cousin, what if we assayed to steal
The clownish fool out of your father's court.

118 will.] OXFORD; will, F

115 **suit . . . points** dress myself in every particular

116 **curtal-axe** a short broad cutting sword, a cutlass
upon my thigh Emended to 'by my side' in *Love in a Forest* and, owing to what was considered the indelicacy of the phrase, in many acting editions into the twentieth century.

117 **boar-spear** As this long-bladed spear was held firm by the hunter, if on foot, so that the onrushing boar impaled itself, Rosalind may be implying especial courage in the bearer. The spear was a usual stage property for Rosalinds down to the 1930s.

119 **swashing** blustering, swaggering

121 **outface it with their semblances** boldly present themselves to the world with false appearances; bluff it out. H. J. Oliver finds puns on the tailoring sense of 'face' meaning 'trim', and 'outside' in l. 119 as contrasted with lining.

124 **Ganymede** The start of the game of sexual ambiguity. Ganymede was a beautiful youth whom Jupiter (Jove), in the form of an eagle, carried off to become his cup-bearer, an event sometimes allegorized as pure thought and quick-mindedness rising above the earthly senses. The word was also a sixteenth-century term for a catamite, a youth who was the object of a male homosexual's passion. See Introduction, pp. 20–3.

126 **state** her change from princess to commoner (*OED sb.* †15)

127 **Aliena** The name, resonant with its sense of 'stranger', comes from Lodge.

129 **clownish fool** David Wiles (p. 66) suggests that this description 'helps identify the now absent character for the audience'.

Would he not be a comfort to our travel?

CELIA

He'll go along o'er the wide world with me.
Leave me alone to woo him. Let's away,
And get our jewels and our wealth together,
Devise the fittest time and safest way
To hide us from pursuit that will be made
After my flight. Now go in we content,
To liberty, and not to banishment. *Exeunt*

2.1 *Enter Duke Senior, Amiens, and two or three Lords dressed as foresters*

DUKE SENIOR

Now, my co-mates and brothers in exile,
Hath not old custom made this life more sweet
Than that of painted pomp? Are not these woods

2.1.0.2 *dressed as*] OXFORD; *like* F

130 **travel** F's 'travaile' includes the sense 'hardship, labour' as well as 'moving from one place to another'. Knowles remarks, 'In this play when the word refers to movement from place to place the spelling is always *trauel(l)* [1.3.108, 3.2.298, 4.1.17], as also in *Traueller* [2.4.15–6, 4.1.20, 4.1.30]. But when this sense is colored by that of 'exertion' etc., as here, the spelling is always *trauaile* (cf. [2.4.73, 4.1.27]).'

132 **Leave me alone** leave it to me

136 **go in we . . . banishment** F2's 'go we in' has been followed by most editors, but F's meaning 'Let us go into the palace—not to banishment, but, owing to our plan, to contentment instead', is acceptable, and more theatrical, as it has a greater sense of movement: the girls are about to leave the stage, to *go in* through the stage doors. This is an example of F2's tendency to 'make the language conform to the needs of written style rather than to the demands of oral delivery' (C. Alphonso Smith, in *Englische Studien*, 30 (1902), 4), and, it can be added, of stage practice. Compare 4.3.8 and 5.4.192.

2.1 The opening lines of the scene appear to confirm Celia's idea of content in banishment. Certainly Duke Senior's quiet philosophizing and the description of forest life contrast strongly with the fury and violence of Frederick's court. In Arden action is verbal rather than physical.

Macready (1842) transposed the scene to follow 2.3 and staged it in front of the Duke's cave (compare 5.4.191), with hunters playing a tune on their horns, falconers with birds on their wrists, hounds led across the stage leashed together, attendants preparing spears and crossbows—all before the Duke and his lords appeared. Adrian Noble (RSC, 1985) swathed the stage in wintry white sheeting and set the characters—the minimum number necessary—shivering.

0.1 *Duke Senior* The exiled duke's descriptive name in F stage directions and speech prefixes. Latham suggests (p. lxv) that it was provided by a scribe, no name having been supplied by the author.

Amiens The name of a French town eighty miles (129 km) north of Paris. Through its closeness to 'amiable', it here suggests friendliness.

0.2 **foresters** forest-dwellers, rather than officials in charge of a forest

2 **old custom** long-established practice. The line is perhaps a form of the proverb 'Custom [i.e. long experience] makes all things easy' (Tilley C933; Dent is doubtful), but the Duke may be rather referring to the attitudes and behaviour of an older, golden age.

More free from peril than the envious court?
Here feel we not the penalty of Adam,
The seasons' difference, as the icy fang
And churlish chiding of the winter's wind,
Which when it bites and blows upon my body
Even till I shrink with cold, I smile, and say
'This is no flattery. These are counsellors
That feelingly persuade me what I am.'
Sweet are the uses of adversity
Which, like the toad, ugly and venomous,
Wears yet a precious jewel in his head;
And this our life, exempt from public haunt,
Finds tongues in trees, books in the running brooks,
Sermons in stones, and good in everything.

AMIENS

I would not change it. Happy is your grace
That can translate the stubbornness of fortune
Into so quiet and so sweet a style.

5–11 One of Adam's penalties after the Fall was to have to endure seasonal change, which in classical myth was introduced by Jupiter in the Silver Age; there had been perpetual spring in the Golden Age, the classical equivalent of Paradise. Duke Senior, however, welcomes winter's honest chill because, unlike the flattery of insincere courtiers, it leads him to self-awareness. H. J. Oliver suggests that the Duke is asking a rhetorical question, 'and goes on to imply that it is nevertheless a good thing so to feel, for the reasons he gives'. The syntax is awkward in this passage, which has occasioned much comment since Theobald emended *not* to *but* in 1733. As the philosophical Duke finds 'good in everything', however, F's reading is perfectly acceptable.

5 **penalty of Adam** Glen Byam Shaw was the first director to seize upon this phrase to give the first few Arden scenes a wintry, early spring setting (Young Vic tour, Norwich, 1948).

6 **as** as, for instance

8 **Which** as to which (Abbott §272)

12–17 The ideas in Duke Senior's philosophizing, which are based in Stoic thought, are widely found in medieval and Renaissance literature. He is gracefully stating platitudes, discoursing on a theme, and may well be applauded by the lords who are present; the absent Jaques would have disapproved (compare 2.5.30–3).

12 **Sweet... adversity** Proverbial: 'Adversity makes men wise' (Tilley A42).

13 **toad** Toads have poisons of varying strengths in their skins. Michael Tyler cites records 'of human fatalities . . . following the eating of toads' and of local reaction on the skin merely from handling some European species ('Frog and Cane Toad Secretions' in J. Covacevich *et al.*, eds., *Toxic Plants and Animals* (Brisbane, 1987), p. 336). Once it was believed that in its head the toad had a stone, pearl or other gem which held great virtues, one being that it was an antidote to poison.

15 **exempt from public haunt** not visited by people in general

18 **I would . . . it** Many follow Upton (1746) in giving this sentence to Duke Senior but Capell N [1774] (i. 58) was surely right in restoring F's reading so that Amiens, speaking for the exiled lords, responds to the challenges implied in the Duke's opening questions.

19–20 **translate . . . style** (a) transform the difficult life forced upon them into a better one (b) render this difficult life into pleasant discourse about it, i.e. make everything, in the words of the play's title, 'as you like it'.

DUKE SENIOR
Come, shall we go and kill us venison?
And yet it irks me the poor dappled fools,
Being native burghers of this desert city,
Should in their own confines with forkèd heads
Have their round haunches gored.
FIRST LORD
Indeed, my lord,
The melancholy Jaques grieves at that,
And in that kind swears you do more usurp
Than doth your brother that hath banished you.
Today my lord of Amiens and myself
Did steal behind him as he lay along

21 **venison** Once used, as here, to describe both wild animals killed in the chase, especially deer, and the flesh of such animals, but now used only in the second sense. Harington remarks that 'venison . . . they say is a very melancholy meat' (pp. 205–6); except for Jàques, it does not seem to have affected the exiles in this way.

22 **irks** troubles
fools here a term of pity—simple creatures

23 **burghers** citizens. The Duke is giving the deer status above the ordinary plebeian forest-dwellers.
desert uninhabited, unpeopled. The Duke romantically exaggerates, carrying on the idea of l. 15. The word could once be applied 'to any wild, uninhabited region, including forest-land' (*OED sb.*[2] 1b). For other uses, compare 2.4.71 (*a.*), 2.6.16 (*sb.*), 2.7.110 (*sb.*), 3.2.120 (*sb.*), 4.3.142 (*a.*).

24 **confines** district, territory. Accented on the second syllable.
forkèd heads arrows with two points facing forwards. As a 'forked (i.e. horned) head' was also the sign of a cuckold, the Duke may be making a quiet joke, comparing the deer struck by double-pointed arrows with foolish citizens whose wives ('round haunches') are unfaithful ('gored' by their lovers) in their own homes. Compare *Winter's Tale* 1.2.187: 'o'er head and ears a forked one'.

27 **melancholy** Jaques is labelled as a 'humour' character having too much black bile, which makes him sullen and negative. (Compare Duke Frederick, 1.2.251.) The First Lord describes an emblematic picture of melancholy with such typical elements as the philosopher lying full length beneath a tree by a stream, and the deer. The description is heightened to exaggeration by the deer's weeping, having been wounded, and Jaques's own tears (l. 65). In *Love in a Forest* (1723) the First Lord lost this speech to Jaques himself, who kept it in most productions of *As You Like It* until Macready's (1842); despite the rewriting necessary to make the transposition credible, the practice lingered on during the nineteenth century, even Macready guiltily taking back the lines occasionally when playing Jaques. For further discussion see Introduction, pp. 28 ff.
Jaques Here two syllables; a monosyllable at ll. 41, 43, 54. The name is a pun on 'jakes', a current word for a lavatory, which is appropriate because in those afflicted with it melancholy produced 'continual, sharp, and stinking belchings, as if their meat in their stomachs were putrefied' (Burton, i. 383 (Pt I. Sec. 3. Mem. 1. Subs. 1)). Compare *1 Henry IV* 1.2.77–8, where Hal speaks of 'the melancholy of Moor-ditch', referring to the stinking ditch, virtually an open sewer, which drained the marshy area of Moorfields, north of the city.

28 **kind** manner, way

30 **lay along** lay at full length. This was a typical pose of the melancholic, and also a pastoral convention, as in the fourth eclogue of Richard Brathwait's *The Shepherd's Pipe* (1614): 'Under an aged oak was Willy laid | . . . O'ercome with dolours deep.' See Introduction, p. 28 and Fig. 3.

Under an oak, whose antic root peeps out
Upon the brook that brawls along this wood,
To the which place a poor sequestered stag
That from the hunter's aim had ta'en a hurt
Did come to languish. And indeed, my lord,
The wretched animal heaved forth such groans
That their discharge did stretch his leathern coat
Almost to bursting, and the big round tears
Coursed one another down his innocent nose
In piteous chase. And thus the hairy fool,
Much markèd of the melancholy Jaques,
Stood on th'extremest verge of the swift brook,
Augmenting it with tears.

DUKE SENIOR But what said Jaques?
Did he not moralize this spectacle?

FIRST LORD
O yes, into a thousand similes.
First, for his weeping into the needless stream;
'Poor deer,' quoth he, 'thou mak'st a testament
As worldlings do, giving thy sum of more
To that which had too much.' Then being there alone,

49 much] F2; must F1

31 **antic** Either 'grotesquely shaped' or 'venerable', or both.

32 **brawls** noisily makes its way 'over stones, etc.' (*OED v.*[1] 3): earliest instance of *brawl* in this sense cited by *OED*

33 **sequestered** separated (*OED pp. a.* †1): earliest instance of *sequestered* in this sense cited in *OED*. Fatally wounded deer proverbially withdrew themselves to die (Tilley D189); compare *Titus* 3.1.89–90: 'Seeking to hide herself, as doth the deer | That hath received some unrecuring wound.'

stag Strictly, a five-year-old male red deer, which could legally be hunted between 24 June and 14 September.

38 **tears** Other examples of weeping deer are found in *Hamlet* 3.2.259: 'Why, let the stricken deer go weep', and Michael Drayton's *Polyolbion*, Song 13, where a deer hunt is described in which 'the noble stately deer . . . He who the mourner is to his own dying corse, | Upon the ruthless earth his precious tears lets fall.' Michael Bath has shown that the weeping stag was a complex iconographical image involving death, healing and religion as well as melancholy ('Weeping Stags and Melancholy Lovers . . .', *Emblematica*, 1 (1986), 13–52).

42 **th'extremest verge** the farthest edge

44 **moralize** draw a moral from

46 **needless** Adding water to the sea by crying into it was a commonplace for an unnecessary act. Shakespeare applies the idea to a stream here and in *Complaint* 36–40.

47 **testament** P. J. Frankis proposes that there was a literary convention for describing a dying deer like a dying person and shows that the theme of the testament of a deer is found in earlier English poetry (*Neuphilologische Mitteilungen*, 59 (1958), 65–8).

48–9 **As worldlings do** like people devoted to the interests and pleasures of the world who make wealthy people their heirs in the hope that they will reciprocate and die first. This is a mainspring of plot in Jonson's *Volpone*.

Left and abandoned of his velvet friend,
''Tis right,' quoth he, 'thus misery doth part
The flux of company.' Anon a careless herd
Full of the pasture jumps along by him
And never stays to greet him. 'Ay,' quoth Jaques,
'Sweep on, you fat and greasy citizens,
'Tis just the fashion. Wherefore do you look
Upon that poor and broken bankrupt there?'
Thus most invectively he pierceth through
The body of country, city, court,
Yea, and of this our life, swearing that we
Are mere usurpers, tyrants, and what's worse,
To fright the animals and to kill them up
In their assigned and native dwelling place.

DUKE SENIOR
And did you leave him in this contemplation?

SECOND LORD
We did, my lord, weeping and commenting
Upon the sobbing deer.

DUKE SENIOR Show me the place.
I love to cope him in these sullen fits,
For then he's full of matter.

FIRST LORD I'll bring you to him straight.
Exeunt

50 **velvet friend** The comparison is between the velvety-skinned mate of the deer and a person's wealthy and extravagantly-dressed companion. Many editors follow Rowe in emending to 'friends'.

51–2 **misery . . . company** poverty separates a person from his neighbours. Proverbial (Tilley P529).

52 **flux** 'A continuous stream (of people)' (*OED sb.* 5b): earliest instance of *flux* in this sense cited by *OED*

55 **greasy** Applied to deer 'fat and fit for killing' (compare *OED, Grease, sb.* †1b); applied to citizens, rich, perhaps with an implication of ill-gotten gains (compare *OED v.* 4b and c), and as a contemptuous or abusive epithet (*OED a.* 1b).

56 **Wherefore . . . look** why do you even bother to look (much less stay and speak to)

59 **country, city, court** a common division of society. F2's 'the' before *country* regularizes the metre, but does not clarify meaning; the whole line is a tetrameter, 'body of' being elided. F1's reading emphasizes the generic quality of *country, city, court*.

61 **mere** absolute
tyrants usurpers (*OED sb.* 1) as well as cruel rulers (*OED sb.* 3). Just as Duke Frederick has deposed his brother (and banished Rosalind), Duke Senior himself and his exiled court are oppressive usurpers of the forest realm.
what's worse 'and what is even worse than these'

62 **kill them up** kill them off

67 **cope** meet with; encounter in debate

68 **matter** ideas; things to say
straight immediately

2.2 *Enter Duke Frederick, with Lords*

DUKE FREDERICK

Can it be possible that no man saw them?
It cannot be. Some villains of my court
Are of consent and sufferance in this.

FIRST LORD

I cannot hear of any that did see her.
The ladies her attendants of her chamber
Saw her abed, and in the morning early
They found the bed untreasured of their mistress.

SECOND LORD

My lord, the roynish clown at whom so oft
Your grace was wont to laugh is also missing.
Hisperia, the Princess' gentlewoman,
Confesses that she secretly o'erheard
Your daughter and her cousin much commend
The parts and graces of the wrestler
That did but lately foil the sinewy Charles,
And she believes wherever they are gone
That youth is surely in their company.

DUKE FREDERICK

Send to his brother; fetch that gallant hither.
If he be absent, bring his brother to me,

2.2.0.1 *Frederick*] POPE; *not in* F

2.2 A description of melancholy humour in 2.1 is followed by an example of a person affected by the choleric humour. Duke Frederick is so out of control of himself that in ll. 17–19 he becomes almost incoherent. (Compare 1.2.251 and 2.3.8.) This scene was once often omitted from productions, even though it is a preparation for Oliver's banishment and eventual arrival in Arden.

2 **villains** menial servants, but with the implication 'evil-doers'. Compare 1.1.52–5.

3 **consent and sufferance** agreement and toleration (and they are therefore treacherously involved)

7 **untreasured** Apparently coined by Shakespeare. *OED* cites this usage and no other until 1819. The word places a value on Celia; Rosalind is not included. Although Frederick refers to both girls, the First Lord's reply is about Celia only—it is the Second Lord who supplies information about Rosalind, and about Touchstone and Orlando as well.

8 **roynish** scurvy, coarse (French *rogneux*: mangy, scurvy). This refers more appropriately to Touchstone's jokes than to his person.

clown The lord is being socially dismissive, placing the fool among the villeins.

13 **wrestler** Probably pronounced with three syllables here.

14 **foil** defeat. *OED* (*v.*[1] 4) cites this passage as an instance of a wrestling term, where *foil* (*sb.*[2] †1), however, means 'The fact of being almost thrown; a throw not resulting in a flat fall'. As Charles is borne away speechless (1.2.204), Orlando has given him a complete fall. F. H. Mares suggests privately that the Second Lord is perhaps being politely euphemistic, knowing that Frederick dislikes Orlando.

17 **gallant** Orlando; the confusing babble of pronouns in these lines indicates Frederick's choler.

I'll make him find him. Do this suddenly,
And let not search and inquisition quail
To bring again these foolish runaways. *Exeunt*

2.3 *Enter Orlando and Adam, meeting*

ORLANDO Who's there?

ADAM
What, my young master, O my gentle master,
O my sweet master, O you memory
Of old Sir Rowland, why, what make you here!
Why are you virtuous? Why do people love you?
And wherefore are you gentle, strong, and valiant?
Why would you be so fond to overcome
The bonny prizer of the humorous Duke?
Your praise is come too swiftly home before you.
Know you not, master, to some kind of men
Their graces serve them but as enemies?
No more do yours. Your virtues, gentle master,
Are sanctified and holy traitors to you.
O, what a world is this, when what is comely
Envenoms him that bears it!

ORLANDO Why, what's the matter?

ADAM O, unhappy youth,
Come not within these doors. Within this roof
The enemy of all your graces lives,

2.3.0.1 *meeting*] CAPELL; *not in* F 10 some] F2; seeme F1 16 ORLANDO] F2; *not in* F1

19 **suddenly** at once

20 **quail** fail

21 **runaways** So overwhelming is Frederick's rage that he forgets he has banished Rosalind.

2.3 Rowe added 'Oliver's house' as a location and was generally followed by editors and producers. In 1770, for example, Francis Gentleman wrote that 'Orlando appears knocking at the door, and is answered by Adam'. Citing Gentleman, Sprague remarks, 'Orlandos not implausibly continued to knock on doors for over a century' (p. 34). The scene, which replaces a series of violent episodes in Lodge, further establishes the gentleness and virtue of Orlando, provides a moral example in Adam, and gets them on the road to Arden. It was particularly esteemed in the eighteenth and nineteenth centuries for its sentiment and because of the tradition that Shakespeare himself played Adam.

3 **memory** memorial

7 **fond to** foolish, imprudent as to

8 **bonny prizer** big, fine prize-fighter
humorous See 1.2.251n.

12 **No more do yours** your graces serve you no better (Abbott §414).

15 **Envenoms** poisons. Orlando's virtues have caused such people as Oliver and Duke Frederick to treat him as if he were poisonous, and so try to destroy him. There may be a reference to the poisoned garments of Greek myth (e.g. Medea's gift to Creusa, Deïaneira's to Hercules).

18 **Within this roof** inside this house

Your brother—no, no brother—yet the son—
Yet not the son, I will not call him son—
Of him I was about to call his father,
Hath heard your praises, and this night he means
To burn the lodging where you use to lie,
And you within it. If he fail of that,
He will have other means to cut you off.
I overheard him and his practices.
This is no place, this house is but a butchery.
Abhor it, fear it, do not enter it.

ORLANDO

Why, whither, Adam, wouldst thou have me go?

ADAM

No matter whither, so you come not here.

ORLANDO

What, wouldst thou have me go and beg my food,
Or with a base and boisterous sword enforce
A thievish living on the common road?
This I must do, or know not what to do.
Yet this I will not do, do how I can.
I rather will subject me to the malice
Of a diverted blood and bloody brother.

ADAM

But do not so. I have five hundred crowns,
The thrifty hire I saved under your father,
Which I did store to be my foster-nurse
When service should in my old limbs lie lame,

30 ORLANDO] F2; *Ad* <*am*>. F1

24 **use** are accustomed

27 **practices** plots, conspiracies

28 **place** appropriate place, therefore safe home, for Orlando (*OED sb.*[1] 12a)
butchery slaughter-house. The word succinctly summarizes the situation described by Lodge.

33 **base and boisterous** socially low and violent

38 **diverted blood** a blood relationship changed from its natural course. Compare 'unnatural': 4.3.123, 125.

39 **five hundred crowns** Probably coins of mixed denominations, but with a face value equal to 500 crowns (£125). If a household steward, as Lodge's Adam Spencer appears to have been, Adam would have been given board and lodging, and been able to save. In England in 1600 he could have earned up to £4 per year, so at that rate his 'thrifty hire' represents over thirty years' savings; Dr D. M. Metcalf of the Ashmolean Museum suggests privately that his 500 crowns would have weighed 1.25 to 1.5 kg—'more than a bag of sugar, but you wouldn't need both hands'. Stage Adams have produced their offerings in containers ranging from ridiculously tiny drawstring bags to comically large buckets, almost too heavy to lift.

40 **thrifty hire** wages thriftily saved

And unregarded age in corners thrown.
Take that, and he that doth the ravens feed,
Yea providently caters for the sparrow,
Be comfort to my age. Here is the gold.
All this I give you. Let me be your servant.
Though I look old, yet I am strong and lusty,
For in my youth I never did apply
Hot and rebellious liquors in my blood,
Nor did not with unbashful forehead woo
The means of weakness and debility.
Therefore my age is as a lusty winter,
Frosty but kindly. Let me go with you,
I'll do the service of a younger man
In all your business and necessities.

ORLANDO

O good old man, how well in thee appears
The constant service of the antique world,
When service sweat for duty, not for meed!
Thou art not for the fashion of these times,
Where none will sweat but for promotion,
And having that do choke their service up
Even with the having. It is not so with thee.

43 **thrown** i.e. should be thrown (Abbott §403)

44–5 **ravens . . . sparrow** God's feeding the ravens is found in Psalm 147: 9, Luke 12: 24 and Job 38: 41; God's concern for the sparrows, which Hamlet recalls (*Hamlet* 5.2.165–6), is mentioned in Matthew 10: 29 and Luke 12: 6.

48 **strong and lusty** The words echo, but invert the meaning of, Psalm 73: 4, 'For there are no bands in their death, but they are lusty and strong' (Geneva Bible); the psalmist is complaining that the wicked always seem better off. The tenor of Adam's speech is that he kept his strength because he has *not* given way to temptation; *lusty* = vigorous.

50 **Hot and rebellious** inflaming the passions and attacking mind and body, thus upsetting the right order of reason over will and will over passion, causing insurrection in the little world of man

51 **Nor . . . not** An emphatic double negative (Abbott §406).
forehead audacity (*OED sb.* †2b). The use of *woo* makes plain that Adam attributes his healthy old age not only to teetotalism but to sexual chastity as well.

53 **lusty** bracing

54 **Frosty** A reference to Adam's white hair. In its allusion to cold but not cruel winter, the passage anticipates Amiens's second song (2.7.175–94).
kindly genial

58 **antique** former, ancient

59 **service** Collier and others, considering the repetition from ll. 55 and 58 an error, emended or proposed to emend to another word, but the repetition adds to the high moral tone of the scene as a whole. Orlando praises Adam for retaining the values of an earlier time when people worked for others from a sense of responsibility, not for reward (*meed*).

62–3 **choke . . . having** As Orlando continues with an image of unfruitfulness, this phrase may be derived from the parable of the sower, Matthew 13: 22, 'He also that received seed into the thorns, is he that heareth the word: and the care of this world, and the deceitfulness of riches,

But, poor old man, thou prun'st a rotten tree,
That cannot so much as a blossom yield
In lieu of all thy pains and husbandry.
But come thy ways. We'll go along together,
And ere we have thy youthful wages spent,
We'll light upon some settled low content.

ADAM
Master, go on, and I will follow thee
To the last gasp with truth and loyalty.
From seventeen years till now almost fourscore
Here livèd I, but now live here no more.
At seventeen years, many their fortunes seek,
But at fourscore, it is too late a week.
Yet fortune cannot recompense me better
Than to die well, and not my master's debtor. *Exeunt*

2.4 *Enter Rosalind in man's clothes as Ganymede; Celia as Aliena, a shepherdess; and Touchstone the clown*

ROSALIND O Jupiter, how weary are my spirits!

TOUCHSTONE I care not for my spirits, if my legs were not weary.

ROSALIND I could find in my heart to disgrace my man's

72 seventeen] ROWE; seauentie F
2.4.0.1–2 *Enter . . . clown*] *Enter Rosaline for Ganimed, Celia for Aliena, and Clowne,* alias *Touchstone.* F 1 weary] THEOBALD (wearie); merry F

choke up the word, and he is made unfruitful' (Bishops' Bible).

66 **In lieu of** in return for

67 **come thy ways** come on

68–77 Orlando's speech ends with the same word, 'content', used by Celia in her final couplet before leaving the court (1.3.137); Adam's rhyming verse gives an incantatory, hieratic conclusion to this part of the play which, apart from the eighteen lines of 3.1, from now on takes place in the forest.

69 **low content** humble contentment

75 **too late a week** far too late (*OED, week, sb.* 6b): earliest instance of *week* in this sense cited by *OED*

77 **die . . . debtor** An allusion to the proverb 'I will not die in your debt (your debtor)' (Tilley D165).

2.4 The examination of love develops in this scene with Silvius's exaggerated romantic description, spoken in a contrived verse-form with a repeated refrain, Rosalind's introspective comments, and Touchstone's bawdy reminiscence. F's '*Clowne,* alias *Touchstone*' indicates that the fool, like Rosalind and Celia, has assumed a new identity, and probably a new costume too, changing from the long-skirted gown of the 'natural' idiot (compare 1.2.46n.) to the parti-coloured motley so frequently mentioned by Jaques in 2.7.

1 **Jupiter** Ganymede swears by 'his' master; as well, however, the planet Jupiter ruled the sanguine temperament, which was the happiest, the most given to love and directly opposed to the melancholy temperament, ruled by Saturn. Compare 'Jove, Jove' at l. 56.

apparel and to cry like a woman. But I must comfort the weaker vessel, as doublet and hose ought to show itself courageous to petticoat; therefore, courage, good Aliena!

CELIA I pray you, bear with me. I cannot go no further.

TOUCHSTONE For my part, I had rather bear with you than bear you. Yet I should bear no cross if I did bear you, for I think you have no money in your purse.

ROSALIND Well, this is the forest of Arden.

TOUCHSTONE Ay, now am I in Arden; the more fool I. When I was at home I was in a better place; but travellers must be content.

Enter Corin and Silvius

ROSALIND Ay, be so, good Touchstone. Look you, who comes here—a young man and an old in solemn talk.

CORIN (*to Silvius*)
That is the way to make her scorn you still.

SILVIUS
O Corin, that thou knew'st how I do love her!

CORIN
I partly guess; for I have loved ere now.

SILVIUS
No, Corin, being old thou canst not guess,
Though in thy youth thou wast as true a lover

6 **weaker vessel** Proverbial (Tilley W655) from 1 Peter 3: 7, 'Likewise, ye husbands, dwell with them as men of knowledge giving honour unto the woman, as unto the weaker vessel' (Geneva Bible).
doublet and hose jacket and breeches (the typical Elizabethan man's clothing)

7 **petticoat** The typically feminine garment, often a skirt (as distinct from a bodice) worn underneath a dress or outside it as a show petticoat.

9 **cannot go no further** An emphatic double negative. Compare 1.2.15.

11 **cross** A well-worn pun alluding to (a) bearing troubles (b) Matthew 10: 38 or Luke 14: 27 (c) money, as some Elizabethan coins had crosses on one side. Touchstone may know that Rosalind, and not Celia, has charge of their money.

14 **Arden** Kökeritz sees a pun on 'harden', a coarse material used for rustic clothes; but this is improbable, since Jaques makes much of Touchstone's motley (2.7.12–34) (unless he is wearing a rustic coat or cloak which he later discards).
more fool Proverbial (Dent F505.1). Compare *Shrew* 5.2.134: 'The more fool you for laying on my duty.'

16.1 ***Corin*** The name is perhaps from Lodge's Coridon, common in pastoral poetry. Bullough (ii. 155) believes it is from Corin, a shepherd in the play *Syr Clyomon and Clamydes*, which was printed in 1599.
Silvius From Latin *silva*, 'wood', appropriate for one so madly in love, as 'wood' was a current word for 'mad'.

17–18 Capell and others after him set these two lines as verse although only the last nine words, which serve to introduce the formal verse of Corin and Silvius, form a regular pentameter.

19–40 The play's sly mockery of the love traditions of literary pastoral is introduced by Corin and Silvius, whose

As ever sighed upon a midnight pillow.
But if thy love were ever like to mine—
As sure I think did never man love so—
How many actions most ridiculous
Hast thou been drawn to by thy fantasy?

CORIN

Into a thousand that I have forgotten.

SILVIUS

O, thou didst then never love so heartily.
If thou rememberest not the slightest folly
That ever love did make thee run into,
Thou hast not loved.
Or if thou hast not sat as I do now,
Wearing thy hearer in thy mistress' praise,
Thou hast not loved.
Or if thou hast not broke from company
Abruptly, as my passion now makes me,
Thou hast not loved.
O, Phoebe, Phoebe, Phoebe! *Exit*

ROSALIND

Alas, poor shepherd, searching of thy wound,
I have by hard adventure found mine own.

TOUCHSTONE And I mine. I remember when I was in love I broke my sword upon a stone and bid him take that for

41 thy wound] ROWE; their wound F2; they would F1

'solemn talk' amounts to an eclogue corresponding to the 34-stanza 'pleasant Eclogue between Montanus and Coridon' in Lodge.

28 **fantasy** desire

30–40 The formal patterning of Silvius's verse, with its unrhymed couplets followed by a repeated half-line, and his emotional exit, emphasize the artificiality of the pastoral mode which is being mocked.

35 **Wearing** Collier and others have followed F2 in emending to 'wearying', and in sixteenth-century Midlands spelling final *-y* was sometimes dropped before *-ing*, but 'wearing' is acceptable in the sense of 'exhausting' (*OED* *v.*[1] 10, and compare *ppl. a. wearing* = exhausting).

38 **passion** strong amorous feeling

40 **Phoebe** 'the shining one' (Greek), an epithet of the moon goddess Artemis (Diana), who was beautiful, virginal, and a huntress.

41 **searching** probing, as in surgery

42 **hard adventure** cruel chance

43–52 Touchstone's speech presents an aspect of love very different from the idealized romanticism of Silvius and, at this moment, Rosalind. The first part may be now-obscure bawdy involving punishment of Touchstone's penis for having an embarrassing orgasm in Jane Smile's presence, or ejaculating at the thought (or dream) of her during the night. Although the earliest instance of 'to come' = 'to experience sexual orgasm' in *OED* is dated 1650 (*OED* *v.* 17), Colman (p. 13) cites Dekker, 'a wench that will come with a wet finger', *1 Honest Whore* (1604), 1.2.4, and this seems to be the meaning of Mercutio's 'come to the

coming a-night to Jane Smile, and I remember the kissing of her batlet, and the cow's dugs that her pretty chopped hands had milked; and I remember the wooing of a peascod instead of her, from whom I took two cods, and giving her them again, said with weeping tears, 'Wear these for my sake.' We that are true lovers run into strange capers. But as all is mortal in nature, so is all nature in love mortal in folly.

ROSALIND Thou speak'st wiser than thou art ware of.

TOUCHSTONE Nay, I shall ne'er be ware of mine own wit till I break my shins against it.

ROSALIND

Jove, Jove, this shepherd's passion
Is much upon my fashion.

TOUCHSTONE And mine, but it grows something stale with me.

46 batlet] F2; batler F1

whole depth of my tale' (*Romeo* 2.3.91). There may also be an allusion to the tavern fool John Stone, cast here in the role of rival for the affections of the alluring Jane, as jealousy was a typical trait of fools. In Armin's *Two Maids of More-clack*, Sir Robert Toures, disguised as a tinker (who 'stops holes well') sings a bawdy song about a pregnant girl which has the chorus 'O stone, stone ne ra, stone na ne ra, stone' [$C4^{v}$], another possible reference to Stone.

46 **batlet** F's 'batler' was a wooden paddle for beating clothes when washing them, according to Johnson, but *OED* cites no other example, and F2's *batlet* is recorded by John Wise in a list of Warwickshire words (*Shakspere: his Birthplace and its Neighbourhood* (1861)); but as Jane Smile was a dairymaid, perhaps batlets were also used for making butter pats, and a pair of little bats is still used for shaping required amounts of handmade butter. Harold Brooks suggests that Shakespeare passed from laundry to milking by way of Golding's *Ovid*, 'udders full of batling (= nourishing) milk', 15, 526 (Latham). Milking has bawdy implications, however, as in *Two Gentlemen* 3.2.274–5 and Jonson, *Alchemist* 3.3.22, which suit the tenor of Touchstone's reminiscence. See Appendix A.

47 **chopped** chapped; cracked. Compare *Macbeth* 1.3.42: 'her choppy finger'.

48 **peascod** Lovers plucked peascods and gave them to their mistresses, and also used them to prophesy true or false love. But as the syllables of 'peascod' transposed give 'codpiece', 'cods' = 'testicles', 'wear' was slang for sexual intercourse, and 'capers' derives from the Latin for 'goat', symbol of lechery (compare 3.3.1–6), it is clear that Touchstone is being bawdy.

51 **mortal** (a) abundant (b) bound to die. Touchstone is saying that just as nature is plenteous (but everything natural must die) so it is natural that everyone in love is abundant in folly.

53 **Thou speak'st . . . ware of** Proverbial (Tilley M1158).

54 **ware** More puns: (a) aware (b) wary, scared.

55 **break my shins against it** am surprised by it; Touchstone is being ironical, alluding to a proverb, 'Fools set stools for wise men (folks) to stumble at (to break their shins)' (Tilley F543). Compare Dent S342.1, 'To break (burst) one's shins (fig.)' and *L.L.L.* 3.1.68: 'here's a costard broken in a shin'.

58 **stale** out of date; but Touchstone also continues his bawdy with a pun on *stale* = 'whore'.

CELIA
I pray you, one of you question yon man
If he for gold will give us any food.
I faint almost to death.
TOUCHSTONE (*to Corin*) Holla, you clown!
ROSALIND Peace, fool, he's not thy kinsman.
CORIN Who calls?
TOUCHSTONE Your betters, sir.
CORIN Else are they very wretched.
ROSALIND (*to Touchstone*)
Peace, I say. (*To Corin*) Good even to you, friend.
CORIN
And to you, gentle sir, and to you all.
ROSALIND
I prithee, shepherd, if that love or gold
Can in this desert place buy entertainment,
Bring us where we may rest ourselves, and feed.
Here's a young maid with travel much oppressed,
And faints for succour.
CORIN Fair sir, I pity her,
And wish, for her sake more than for mine own,
My fortunes were more able to relieve her;
But I am shepherd to another man,
And do not shear the fleeces that I graze.
My master is of churlish disposition,
And little recks to find the way to heaven
By doing deeds of hospitality.
Besides, his cot, his flocks, and bounds of feed

68 you] F2; your F1 73 travel] F1 (trauaile)

63 **clown** Touchstone as courtier addresses Corin as a socially inferior country fellow; Rosalind's rebuke puts him in his place, implying that he, not Corin, is the clown. Compare Second Lord's 'roynish clown' (2.2.8).

67 **wretched** In 1600 a common shepherd over twenty-one years of age could earn in a year up to £1 13*s*. and a set of clothes. Compare 2.3.39n.

70 **love or gold** Proverbial (Dent L479.1 and compare the still-current 'for love or money').

71 **entertainment** food and shelter

80 **little recks** takes no care. Corin's churlish master is like Nabal, who owned 3,000 sheep and 1,000 goats but refused hospitality to David (1 Samuel 25).

82 **cot** small cottage (see l. 91 below). Many editors keep F's 'cote', but '*Cote* in this sense having become obs., or merely dial., about 1625, *cot* has been revived as a poetical and literary term' (*OED, Cot, sb.* [1] 1). Compare W. S. Gilbert: 'Take a pretty little cot, quite a miniature affair' ('Take a Pair of Sparkling Eyes', *The Gondoliers* (1889)).

bounds of feed tracts of pasture

Are now on sale, and at our sheepcote now
By reason of his absence there is nothing
That you will feed on. But what is, come see,
And in my voice most welcome shall you be.

ROSALIND

What is he that shall buy his flock and pasture?

CORIN

That young swain that you saw here but erewhile,
That little cares for buying anything.

ROSALIND

I pray thee, if it stand with honesty,
Buy thou the cottage, pasture, and the flock,
And thou shalt have to pay for it of us.

CELIA

And we will mend thy wages. I like this place,
And willingly could waste my time in it.

CORIN

Assuredly the thing is to be sold.
Go with me. If you like upon report
The soil, the profit, and this kind of life,
I will your very faithful feeder be,
And buy it with your gold right suddenly. *Exeunt*

2.5 *Enter Amiens, Jaques, and other Lords dressed as foresters*

⌈AMIENS⌉ (*sings*)

Under the greenwood tree

93–4 And . . . place, | And . . . it.] CAPELL; And . . . wages: | I . . . could | Waste . . . it. F
2.5.0.1–2 *Enter . . . foresters*] *Enter . . . others.* F 1 ⌈AMIENS⌉ (*sings*)] *Ami.* CAPELL; Song. F

83 **sheepcote** Strictly, a shelter for sheep, but here the cottage of ll. 82, 91 and 4.3.78.

84–5 **nothing . . . feed on** i.e. nothing suitable for your delicate city tastes

86 **in my voice** so far as my vote is concerned

90 **if . . . honesty** if it would be fair dealing (so far as Silvius is concerned)

92 **have . . . of** receive (the wherewithal) . . . from

93 **mend** improve

94 **waste** spend

98 **feeder** (a) servant (*OED* 2b): earliest instance of *feeder* in this sense cited by *OED*; (b) shepherd; one who attends to the feeding of a flock (*OED* 4)

2.5 The pleasant forest life of the exiles is emphasized in this scene, which introduces music to the play. Opposed against the view of the agreeable Amiens is the cynicism of Jaques who is, however, not taken seriously by his fellows. The scene was much mangled in many early productions, the dialogue reduced, Amiens's song omitted or cut to the first verse, and Jaques's parody eliminated.

1 **Under . . . tree** This phrase reinforces the play's links with Robin Hood, as it occurs in several ballads in Child (e.g. 'A Gest of Robyn Hode', 195, 262, 312, 335, 377; 'Robin Hood and the Monk', 2; 'Robin Hood and Allen A Dale', 2, 7); it is also found in some Elizabethan songs. A prop-

Who loves to lie with me,
And turn his merry note
Unto the sweet bird's throat,
Come hither, come hither, come hither.
Here shall he see
No enemy
But winter and rough weather.

JAQUES More, more, I prithee, more.

AMIENS It will make you melancholy, Monsieur Jaques.

JAQUES I thank it. More, I prithee, more. I can suck melancholy out of a song as a weasel sucks eggs. More, I prithee, more.

AMIENS My voice is ragged, I know I cannot please you.

JAQUES I do not desire you to please me, I do desire you to sing. Come, more; another stanzo. Call you 'em stanzos?

AMIENS What you will, Monsieur Jaques.

JAQUES Nay, I care not for their names, they owe me nothing. Will you sing?

AMIENS More at your request than to please myself.

JAQUES Well, then, if ever I thank any man, I'll thank you. But that they call compliment is like th'encounter of

6–7 *Here . . . see* | *No enemy*] POPE; *Here . . . enemy* F 11–13] *as prose*, POPE; I . . . more, | I . . . song, | As . . . more. F

erty tree may be indicated by l. 28, although a stage post may have served for one.

3 **turn** adapt (so that he sings like a bird); some editors follow Rowe's unnecessary emendation to 'tune'.
note melody

4 **throat** voice

10 **Monsieur** The title indicates that Jaques is a nobleman of higher standing than his companion lords. Compare the use of 'Sir' in 4.2.

12 **weasel** Jaques typically thinks of a pestiferous small predator. Weasels suck eggs quickly, making a small hole at one end; they are also quarrelsome, sharp-toothed and irritable. Compare *Cymbeline* 3.4.160: 'As quarrelous as the weasel'. Edward A. Armstrong shows that 'weasel' is part of an image cluster, with 'dog-ape', 'melancholy', 'suck eggs' and 'song', which occurs in some form in five plays and *Lucrece* (*Shakespeare's Imagination* (1946), pp. 28, 34).

14 **ragged** harsh, rough (*OED a.*[1] 3b): earliest instance of *ragged* in this sense cited by *OED*. Amiens is displaying courtly manners in being self-deprecating.

16 **stanzo** Jaques, the traveller, is showing off and deriding Amiens at the same time; in 1600 the modern Italian form *stanza* was in use alongside *stanze* and *stanzo*. His response to Amiens's easy-going reply indicates his awareness of the different forms.

17 **What you will** Proverbial (Dent W280.5). Compare e.g. *Dream* 1.2.85, and the subtitle of *Twelfth Night*.

18 **names** A pun on a legal term: *Nomina*, the names of borrowers who have signed a loan document. Jaques would be interested if they were the names of people who owed him money.

two dog-apes, and when a man thanks me heartily methinks I have given him a penny and he renders me the beggarly thanks. Come, sing; and you that will not, hold your tongues.

AMIENS Well, I'll end the song.—Sirs, cover the while.

Lords lay out food and drink

The Duke will drink under this tree. (*To Jaques*) He hath been all this day to look you.

JAQUES And I have been all this day to avoid him. He is too disputable for my company. I think of as many matters as he, but I give heaven thanks, and make no boast of them. Come, warble, come.

AMIENS AND OTHER LORDS (*sing*)

Who doth ambition shun,
And loves to live i'th' sun,
Seeking the food he eats
And pleased with what he gets,
Come hither, come hither, come hither.
Here shall he see
No enemy
But winter and rough weather.

JAQUES I'll give you a verse to this note that I made yesterday in despite of my invention.

27.1 *Lords . . . drink*] This edition; *not in* F 30–3] *as prose*, POPE; And . . . him: | He . . . companie: | I . . . giue | Heauen. . . . them. | Come . . . come. F 34 AMIENS AND OTHER LORDS (*sing*)] This edition; *Song. Altogether heere.* F 2.5.39–41 see . . . weather] *see. &c.* F 42–3] *as prose*, POPE; I'll . . . note, | That . . . Inuention. F

23 **dog-apes** baboons. For Jaques, politeness is merely empty mutual congratulation. Compare l. 12n. above.

25 **beggarly thanks** effusive gratitude, like that given by a beggar who has received a very small gift

27 **cover the while** meanwhile, lay the table. A cloth may have been spread on the stage floor for a picnic (as is often done in modern productions) rather than a table brought on.

29 **look you** look for you

31 **disputable** ready to argue, disputacious. Jaques dislikes being made a butt by the Duke, who loves to 'cope' him in his 'sullen fits' (2.1.67), and can find 'good in everything' (2.1.17).

32 **give heaven . . . boast of them** Proverbial (Dent B487.1). Compare *Much Ado* 3.3.18–19.

35 **live i'th' sun** live a carefree, natural life (away from the city's competitiveness). *OED sb.* 4b quotes this line as its first example of the phrase which also, however, has the converse implication of living rough, as the proverb says, 'Out of God's blessing into the warm sun' (Tilley G272, though neither Tilley nor Dent notes this instance); compare Kent's remark to Lear, 'Thou out of heaven's benediction com'st | To the warm sun' (*Tragedy of King Lear* 2.2.152–3) and Hamlet's double-edged comment 'I am too much i'th' sun' (*Hamlet* 1.2.67). The 'winter and rough weather' in the last line of Amiens's song indicate this harsher side to alfresco living.

43 **in despite . . . invention** even though I have little imagination

AMIENS And I'll sing it.

JAQUES Thus it goes:

If it do come to pass
That any man turn ass,
Leaving his wealth and ease
A stubborn will to please,
Ducdame, ducdame, ducdame.
Here shall he see
Gross fools as he,
An if he will come to me.

AMIENS What's that 'ducdame'?

JAQUES 'Tis a Greek invocation to call fools into a circle. I'll go sleep if I can. If I cannot, I'll rail against all the firstborn of Egypt.

AMIENS And I'll go seek the Duke; his banquet is prepared.

Exeunt

2.6 *Enter Orlando and Adam*

ADAM Dear master, I can go no further. O, I die for food.

45 JAQUES] F2; *Amy⟨ens⟩*. F1

50 **Ducdame** A nonsensical trisyllable, best accented to agree metrically with 'come hither'. Commentators have suggested origins and meanings in at least six languages besides English, but they have fallen into the trap set by Jaques; the joke loses its point if the word has meaning. Jaques probably speaks or reads the verse rather than sings it, as the First Lord later tells Duke Senior that the malcontent was 'merry, hearing of a song' (2.7.4), not 'singing' it. The lines were frequently omitted in nineteenth-century productions; when included, they were the cue, as often nowadays, for the lords to crowd around Jaques, thus becoming fools called 'into a circle'.

53 **An if** if

55 **Greek** unintelligible gibberish. Compare *Caesar* 1.2.284: 'it was Greek to me'. Proverbial (Tilley G439, though neither Tilley nor Dent notes this instance). Jaques is perhaps mocking pretentious learning as well as his fellow-courtiers.

invocation . . . circle Witches and wizards inscribed circles to conjure spirits and for other magical purposes, as Prospero does in *Tempest* 5.1.57.5.

57 **firstborn of Egypt** When God killed all the firstborn of Egypt there was a great cry and Pharaoh and the remaining Egyptians rose up in the night (Exodus 12: 29–30); Jaques does not want a similar disturbance to wake him. There may also be a cantankerous reference to Duke Senior, who has led his courtiers into the wilderness, as the Israelites were led from Egypt.

59 **banquet** a light meal, with fruit and wine. Amiens says the Duke 'will drink' (l. 28) and Orlando refers to 'fruit' (2.7.98). (In Oscar Asche's production (His Majesty's, 1907), the exiles munched apples, continuing a still-persistent tradition.) The food and drink have probably been set at the side and to the front of the stage. In the next scene Adam and Orlando enter through one of the stage doors at the back and do not see it. There is a nice visual irony in Adam's almost fainting for lack of food within a few paces of it.

2.6 This brief scene, which in its humanity contrasts vividly with 3.1, further establishes the initial hostility of the forest to strangers, the chilliness of the weather, and Orlando's natural goodness. The

Here lie I down and measure out my grave. Farewell, kind master.

ORLANDO Why, how now, Adam? No greater heart in thee? Live a little, comfort a little, cheer thyself a little. If this uncouth forest yield anything savage I will either be food for it or bring it for food to thee. Thy conceit is nearer death than thy powers. For my sake be comfortable. Hold death awhile at the arm's end. I will here be with thee presently, and if I bring thee not something to eat, I will give thee leave to die. But if thou diest before I come, thou art a mocker of my labour. Well said. Thou lookest cheerly, and I'll be with thee quickly. Yet thou liest in the bleak air. Come, I will bear thee to some shelter, and thou shalt not die for lack of a dinner if there live anything in this desert. Cheerly, good Adam.

Orlando carries Adam off

2.7 *Enter Duke Senior, Amiens and other Lords dressed as outlaws*

DUKE SENIOR

I think he be transformed into a beast,

2.6.16 *Orlando . . . off*] *Exeunt* F 2.7.0.1–2 *Enter . . . outlaws*] *Enter Duke Sen. & Lord, like Outlawes.* F

whole text was set as blank verse by F Compositor B, probably to spread his copy (as he had done to a certain extent in 2.5, on the same page) to avoid beginning the next scene at the bottom of the page. Pope, who first printed the lines as prose, has been followed by all editors since.

5 **thee** Here the familiar, not the formal, pronoun.

comfort comfort thyself. In Lodge, Rosader also becomes faint; he is comforted by Adam, who offers to open his veins to give his young master sustenance (like the pelican who, it was believed, succours her young with her blood rather than let them die). Fortunately the thought is enough to revive Rosader, who goes off in search of more solid, uncannibalistic, food.

6 **uncouth** unfamiliar, strange

7 **conceit** imagination

9 **Hold . . . arm's end** Proverbial (Tilley A317).

10 **presently** quickly, speedily

12 **Well said** well done

2.7 Jaques's big scene, even though his pessimism is countered in words by Duke Senior and in action by Orlando. All the main characters except Oliver and Duke Frederick are now in the forest.

0.1 *Lords* has been accepted since Rowe first emended F's *Lord*, although only '1. *Lord*' appears as a speech prefix during the scene; Amiens, who presumably sings 'Blow, blow, thou winter wind', was first included in the block entry by Capell.

F's *like Out-lawes* links the exiles with Robin Hood and his merry men, who were consistently so described in the ballads, and indicates that they should wear green. In 'A Gest of Robin Hood', King Edward and his knights dress in Lincoln green and ride with Robin and his men into Nottingham, 'Outlaws as they were' (Child, 'A Gest of Robyn Hode', 423), deceiving the townsfolk.

1 **beast** Duke Senior jokingly refers to the belief by some extremely melancholy

For I can nowhere find him like a man.

FIRST LORD

My lord, he is but even now gone hence.
Here was he merry, hearing of a song.

DUKE SENIOR

If he, compact of jars, grow musical
We shall have shortly discord in the spheres.
Go seek him. Tell him I would speak with him.

Enter Jaques

FIRST LORD

He saves my labour by his own approach.

DUKE SENIOR

Why, how now, monsieur, what a life is this,
That your poor friends must woo your company!
What, you look merrily.

JAQUES

A fool, a fool, I met a fool i'th' forest,
A motley fool—a miserable world!—
As I do live by food, I met a fool,
Who laid him down and basked him in the sun,
And railed on Lady Fortune in good terms,

persons that they are birds or animals. The wolf-madness (lycanthropia) of Duke Ferdinand in Webster's *Duchess of Malfi* is a famous dramatic example.

5 **compact of jars** made up of discords

6 **discord in the spheres** Duke Senior is alluding to the theory, attributed to Pythagoras and widely current in the Renaissance, that the earth is surrounded by eight concentric crystalline spheres in which are placed the five then-known planets, the sun, the moon and the fixed stars; the orderly rotation of these spheres produces an ineffable harmony, usually inaudible to humans owing to mortal imperfections; dislocation of the spheres, reflecting conflict on earth, results in discordant sound. These ideas are given delightful expression in *The Merchant of Venice* 5.1.60 ff., and the music itself accompanies the waking of the hero to normality in *Pericles* 21.215. For Jaques to 'grow musical' would need a chaotic reversal of the natural order such as Ulysses describes in *Troilus and Cressida* 1.3.94–126.

9 **what a life is this** A variation on the proverbial 'What a world is this' (Dent W889.1), picked up by Jaques four lines later.

13 **motley** the parti-coloured dress of the professional fool. Leslie Hotson's view that all Shakespeare's fools wore long gowns of woven mixed colour (*Shakespeare's Motley* (1952)) has been disputed by several scholars, most convincingly by David Wiles (1987), who maintain that *motley* is a costume made from segments of different coloured cloth.

a miserable world As Jaques 'looks merrily', he says this joyfully: meeting a fool in so desolate a place as Arden confirms his belief that the world is full of them, according to the proverb, 'The world is full of fools' (Tilley W 896). Hilda Hulme suggests 'world' = 'word', in which case Jaques is lamenting the poverty of the word 'fool' to describe Touchstone (*Explorations in Shakespeare's Language* (1962), p. 208), but see the note to l. 9 above.

In good set terms, and yet a motley fool.
'Good morrow, fool,' quoth I. 'No, sir,' quoth he,
'Call me not fool till heaven hath sent me fortune.'
And then he drew a dial from his poke,
And looking on it with lack-lustre eye
Says very wisely 'It is ten o'clock.'
'Thus we may see', quoth he, 'how the world wags.
'Tis but an hour ago since it was nine,
And after one hour more 'twill be eleven.
And so from hour to hour we ripe and ripe,
And then from hour to hour we rot and rot;
And thereby hangs a tale.' When I did hear
The motley fool thus moral on the time
My lungs began to crow like chanticleer,

17 **set terms** 'roundly', 'with outspoken severity' (*OED, set, ppl. a.* 3b): earliest instance of the phrase in this sense cited by *OED*

19 **fortune** A reference to the proverb 'God sends fortune to fools' (Tilley F220).

20 **dial** a watch or pocket sun-dial. This is an intimation of bawdy to come, since *dial* also had various sexual connotations—it was current slang for male and female sexual organs, Falstaff associates dials with brothels (*1 Henry IV* 1.2.8–9), and, for example, Mercutio claims that 'the bawdy hand of the dial is now upon the prick of noon' (*Romeo* 2.3.104–5).
poke pocket worn on the person (*OED, poke, sb.*[1] 1c. *Obs.* or *arch.*), the earliest instance of this sense cited by *OED*. Here it contains a pun on 'codpiece'. Wiles (p. 187) believes it to be the bagged sleeve at the elbow of Touchstone's gown. The word is still current in Glasgow dialect for 'bag', e.g. 'a poke of chips'.

23 **wags** goes on. 'Let the world wag' is proverbial (Tilley W879). Since 'wagtail' = 'prostitute', a sexual innuendo is implied. Compare Tourneur (Middleton?), *Revenger's Tragedy* 1.3.131–2: 'the wagging of her hair . . . shall put you in'.

25 **eleven** If 'noon' implies erection, as it apparently does in Sidney's 'But lo, while I do speak, it groweth noon with me' (*Astrophil and Stella* 76.9), then 'eleven' indicates tumescence, as in Barnabe Barnes's imitation of Sidney in *Parthenophil and Parthenophe* 23, which ends 'Still smiling at my dial, next eleven!' (See Thomas Roche Jr., '*Astrophil and Stella*: A Radical Reading', in Dennis Kay, ed., *Sir Philip Sidney. An Anthology of Modern Criticism* (Oxford, (1987), p. 200). Compare l. 20n. above.

26–8 **hour . . . tale** The idea of moving from ripe to rotten was proverbial (Tilley R133, though neither Tilley nor Dent notes this example); Touchstone says, again proverbially (Tilley T48), there is more to tell than the simple words suggest. His bawdy depends on pronouncing *hour* as 'whore', as suggested by Kökeritz (pp. 107, 117) but doubted by Cercignani (p. 194), of taking *ripe* to mean 'search into' (*OED, ripe, v.* [2] 4, and compare 2.4.41: 'searching'), and punning on *rot*/'rut', and *tale*/'tail' = 'penis' (*OED, tail, sb.* [1] 5c): the passage then becomes, 'we go into whore after whore and so we grow diseased and impotent', a reading adopted in Terry Hands's 1980 RSC production. This pessimistic view of life would appeal to Jaques.

29 **moral** possibly an adjective, but probably a verb: 'To make a moral application' (*OED, moral, v.* a), the earliest instance of this sense cited by *OED*

30 **chanticleer** cock. If this is an attempt by Jaques at bawdy punning it is extremely clumsy, but '*deep*-contemplative' suggests that it is.

That fools should be so deep-contemplative,
And I did laugh sans intermission
An hour by his dial. O noble fool,
A worthy fool—motley's the only wear.

DUKE SENIOR What fool is this?

JAQUES
O worthy fool!—One that hath been a courtier,
And says 'If ladies be but young and fair
They have the gift to know it.' And in his brain,
Which is as dry as the remainder biscuit
After a voyage, he hath strange places crammed
With observation, the which he vents
In mangled forms. O that I were a fool,
I am ambitious for a motley coat.

DUKE SENIOR
Thou shalt have one.

JAQUES It is my only suit,
Provided that you weed your better judgements

31 **deep-contemplative** (a) philosophical (b) engrossed in sexual matters. For a similar bawdy innuendo on 'deep' compare Middleton, *A Chaste Maid in Cheapside* 4.1.75: 'I see you are a deep scholar', *Romeo* 2.3.91: 'the whole depth of my tale', and the proverb 'The deeper the sweeter' (Tilley D188).

32 **sans** without (French). An affectation, indicative of Jaques's character. Rosaline mocks Biron's use of the word in *L.L.L.*: 'Sans "sans", I pray you' (5.2.416).

34 **motley's the only wear** More bawdy? As well as saying that the fool's garb is just the fashion, Jaques is possibly continuing Touchstone's sexual imagery, using *motley* in the sense of 'variously coloured' (owing to disease) and *wear* as a homonym of 'ware' in its sense 'genitals' (*OED*, *ware*, *sb.*[3] 4†c).

37–8 **'If ladies . . . know it'** Said with a leer, this becomes a sexual phrase, in keeping with the rest of Jaques's report on Touchstone.

39 **dry . . . biscuit** Sea-biscuits, used in place of bread, were excessively dry, and at the end of a voyage would have been even drier; in Elizabethan physiological theory, idiots' brains were supposed to be dry and hard, but very retentive. The joke is partly on Jaques himself: in Jonson's *Every Man Out Of His Humour* Asper describes a gallant 'Who (to be thought one of the judicious) | Sits with his arms thus wreath'd, his hat pull'd here [i.e. over his brow—the recognized pose of the melancholic] . . . And now and then breaks a dry biscuit jest' (Induction, 160–5). 'As dry as a biscuit' was proverbial (Tilley B404).

40 **places** Either or both of 'subjects of discourse' or 'holes and corners'.

41 **vents** utters (*OED*, *vent*, *v.*[2] 5a, first usage cited 1602); but another current meaning, 'to evacuate (urine, etc.)' (*OED*, *vent*, *v.*[2] †2†b, first usage cited 1607) links Jaques's description of Touchstone with his own wish to purge the world (2.7.60).

43 **coat** here in the special sense of a garment indicating a profession (*OED*, *coat*, *sb.* †6)

44 **Thou** The Duke's displeasure is beginning to show; on Jaques's appearance he had used a welcoming 'you', *thou* relegates the courtier to being a servant.

suit (a) clothes (b) petition. This pun leads to another on 'weed' in l. 45. Whiter (pp. 72–82) denies a deliberate quibble, arguing for associative thought instead, as similar connected images occur elsewhere in Shakespeare. Kökeritz, more extremely, sees a pun on 'suit'/'shoot', leading to 'weed' and 'rank'.

Of all opinion that grows rank in them
That I am wise. I must have liberty
Withal, as large a charter as the wind,
To blow on whom I please, for so fools have;
And they that are most gallèd with my folly,
They most must laugh. And why, sir, must they so?
The why is plain as way to parish church:
He that a fool doth very wisely hit
Doth very foolishly, although he smart,
Not to seem senseless of the bob. If not,
The wise man's folly is anatomized
Even by the squandering glances of the fool.
Invest me in my motley. Give me leave
To speak my mind, and I will through and through
Cleanse the foul body of th'infected world,
If they will patiently receive my medicine.

DUKE SENIOR

Fie on thee, I can tell what thou wouldst do.

JAQUES

What, for a counter, would I do but good?

55 Not to] THEOBALD (*conj.* Warburton); *not in* F

48–9 **wind . . . please** 'freedom to criticize whom I will'; Jaques egregiously compares himself to the Holy Spirit, characterized in John 3: 8 as the wind which 'bloweth where it listeth' (Geneva Bible). Latham quotes a description of Malevole, the satirist of Marston's *Malcontent*: 'He is as free as air; he blows over every man' (1.3.2). 'As free as the air' was proverbial (Tilley A88), 'wind' appears to be a Shakespearian variation.

52 **The why . . . parish church** A comparison arising, perhaps, from the biblical allusion of l. 48. As heavy penalties for non-attendance at church were imposed under the third Act of Uniformity (1559), the path to church was well marked; *way* was probably pronounced 'why' for the sake of the pun.

53–7 F's reading has been defended by Whiter and others, and Oxford emends 'Seem aught but senseless', but Theobald's emendation both completes the metre of the line (with an inverted first foot, like l. 60 below) and makes good sense of the passage so that it means 'Someone taunted for good reasons by a fool is silly, even if hurt, not to seem unmoved. If one reacts outwardly then one's foolishness is shown up in all its parts, even by random satirical shafts.'

55 **bob** taunt, scoff, jibe

57 **squandering** straying, straggling; spreading abroad (*OED, squandering, ppl. a.* 2): earliest instance of *squandering* in this sense cited in *OED*

glances satirical hits

58–61 **Invest . . . Cleanse . . . medicine** Jaques is saying that if he is given a fool's licence he will administer a purge to cure the world of its follies. This is the language of John Marston, Joseph Hall, Ben Jonson and other satirists and has led some to believe that Jaques was based on one or other of these.

63 **counter** a token representing real coin, hence, 'the type of a thing of no intrinsic value' (*OED, counter, sb.*[3] 2c): earliest instance of *counter* in this sense cited by *OED*. Jaques is insultingly saying the Duke's opinion is worthless.

DUKE SENIOR
Most mischievous foul sin, in chiding sin;
For thou thyself hast been a libertine,
As sensual as the brutish sting itself,
And all th'embossèd sores and headed evils
That thou with licence of free foot hast caught
Wouldst thou disgorge into the general world.

JAQUES Why, who cries out on pride
That can therein tax any private party?
Doth it not flow as hugely as the sea,
Till that the weary very means do ebb?
What woman in the city do I name
When that I say the city-woman bears
The cost of princes on unworthy shoulders?
Who can come in and say that I mean her
When such a one as she, such is her neighbour?
Or what is he of basest function,

64 Compare the proverb 'He finds fault with others and does worse himself' (Tilley F107), an idea Shakespeare uses several times, e.g. *L.L.L.* 4.3.130: 'You chide at him offending twice as much'.

66 **As . . . sting** as lecherous as lust (*brutish sting*, i.e. animal-like itch).

67 **embossèd . . . evils** The sores of veneral disease[s] (*evils*), bulging and swollen (*embossèd*), with scabby tops (*headed*) like boils. The Duke uses the phrase literally, referring to the results of Jaques's unrestrained behaviour, and metaphorically to refer to his foul bitterness.

69 **disgorge** vomit. The primary meaning is the discharging of the pus and matter of the sores, but in the context of 'cleanse', 'medicine' and the name 'Jaques', evacuation of the bowels is an additional likely meaning. Compare Jonathan Swift's Yahoo in *Gulliver's Travels* Pt. IV (Penguin edn. (Harmondsworth, 1978), p. 270).

70–87 Jaques gives the satirist's stock reply, saying he attacks sin in general, not the individual sinner, and if people feel hurt it is because they see themselves as guilty and the guiltless are unharmed. So, Harington: 'if any man find in these my lines any raiment that suits him so fit, as if it were made for him, let him wear it and spare not, & for my part I would he could wear it out' (p. 184). Jaques begins on the sexual level, responding to the Duke's charge against him, but, taking up the usual meaning of 'pride' as 'arrogance', shifts to the less personal ground of dress—a common target for satirists. Orlando's entry saves him from having to defend himself further.

70 **pride** (a) sexual desire (b) arrogance

71 **private party** (a) lecher (b) individual

72–3 **Doth . . . ebb** The primary meaning is 'Does not lust rise as great as the sea, till the means of satisfying it diminish through sheer physical exhaustion?' As Jaques is already turning to the attack on 'extravagant display in dress' (*OED*, *pride*, *sb.*[1] 7) as the indicator of arrogance, the emergent meaning is 'Does not ostentation increase until it exhausts the resources which fed it?'

F's 'wearie verie meanes' was first emended by Pope, to 'very very'; Whiter defended F, saying 'The sense is, "till that the very means being weary do ebb"' (p. 25); among several other proposed emendations Singer's 'wearer's very means' won wide acceptance; but F's text is intelligible.

77 **come in** (as into a court of law)

79–82 **Or . . . suits . . . speech?** 'What low-born fellow, thinking I aim at him, tells me that I did not pay for his finery, but in doing so matches his extravagance to the spirit of what I say (and so proves my

That says his bravery is not on my cost,
Thinking that I mean him, but therein suits
His folly to the mettle of my speech?
There then, how then, what then, let me see wherein
My tongue hath wronged him. If it do him right,
Then he hath wronged himself. If he be free,
Why then my taxing like a wild goose flies,
Unclaimed of any man. But who comes here?
Enter Orlando, with sword drawn

ORLANDO
Forbear, and eat no more!

JAQUES Why, I have eat none yet.

ORLANDO
Nor shalt not, till necessity be served.

JAQUES Of what kind should this cock come of?

DUKE SENIOR
Art thou thus boldened, man, by thy distress?
Or else a rude despiser of good manners,
That in civility thou seem'st so empty?

ORLANDO
You touched my vein at first. The thorny point
Of bare distress hath ta'en from me the show
Of smooth civility. Yet am I inland bred,
And know some nurture. But forbear, I say.
He dies that touches any of this fruit
Till I and my affairs are answerèd.

87 any man. But] F (any. man But) 87 comes] F2; come F1 87.1 *with sword drawn*] THEOBALD; *not in* F

point).' Jaques again puns on *suits* (compare 1.2.230).

80 **bravery** finery, splendid clothes
82 **mettle** spirit
85 **free** guiltless
86 **taxing** censure. Compare 1.2.79.
87.1 Theobald's stage direction may derive from *Love in a Forest*: '*Enter* Orlando, *his sword drawn*', though the text clearly demands this action (see 2.7.119). Although C. L. Barber (*Shakespeare's Festive Comedy* (Princeton, 1959), p. 224) and others have considered it uncharacteristic that the courteous Orlando should enter so aggressively, this is not odd behaviour: he is driven by desperation, as he was when he attacked Oliver in 1.1. (Inspired in a different way, he defeated Charles the wrestler in 1.2.) He offers an excuse in 2.7.106–9.
90 **Of . . . of** Prepositions were frequently repeated when at a distance from the verb with which they were connected (Abbott §407).
91 **thou** used in startled anger by the Duke to this rudely intrusive stranger (Abbott §231 (3))
94 **touched my vein** assessed my present state
96 **inland bred** having refinement, not outlandish

JAQUES An you will not be answered with reason, I must die.

DUKE SENIOR
What would you have? Your gentleness shall force
More than your force move us to gentleness.

ORLANDO
I almost die for food; and let me have it.

DUKE SENIOR
Sit down and feed, and welcome to our table.

ORLANDO
Speak you so gently? Pardon me, I pray you.
I thought that all things had been savage here,
And therefore put I on the countenance
Of stern commandment. But whate'er you are
That in this desert inaccessible,
Under the shade of melancholy boughs,
Lose and neglect the creeping hours of time,
If ever you have looked on better days,
If ever been where bells have knolled to church,
If ever sat at any good man's feast,
If ever from your eyelids wiped a tear,
And know what 'tis to pity, and be pitied,
Let gentleness my strong enforcement be.
In the which hope I blush, and hide my sword.

DUKE SENIOR
True is it that we have seen better days,
And have with holy bell been knolled to church,
And sat at good men's feasts, and wiped our eyes

100 **An** if. Compare 4.1.29, 36, 46, 64.
reason Since Malone, who is cited by Whiter (pp. 113–15), 'reason'/'raisin' (meaning the fresh grape) has been considered a standard pun, most famously in Falstaff's 'If reasons were as plentiful as blackberries' (*1 Henry IV* 2.5.243); 'raisin of the sun' was the name normally used for the dried fruit. Cercignani, however, suggests that while in *1 Henry IV* a pun 'may perhaps be regarded as actually intended', the quibble in Jaques's line 'cannot be accepted as reliable' (p. 235). Whether or not Jaques is eating from a bunch of grapes, as he does in many productions, his remark lightens a tense situation.

104 **and** and I pray you (Abbott §100). Knowles suggests 'and therefore'.

111 **melancholy** sombre, owing to the shadiness of the boughs

112–26 Orlando's list of the influences which can induce humane kindness is responded to by the Duke in an elegant ritual of courtesy. These lines set a tone of formality which is continued by Jaques's speech which soon follows, but their genuineness contrasts with the hollowness of his.

114 **knolled** rung (*OED*, *knoll*, *v.* 2): earliest instance of *knoll* in this sense cited by *OED*. In l. 121 'knolled' = summoned by the sound of a bell (*OED*, *knoll*, *v.* 3), the earliest instance of this sense cited.

Of drops that sacred pity hath engendered.
And therefore sit you down in gentleness,
And take upon command what help we have
That to your wanting may be ministered.

ORLANDO

Then but forbear your food a little while
Whiles, like a doe, I go to find my fawn
And give it food. There is an old poor man
Who after me hath many a weary step
Limped in pure love. Till he be first sufficed,
Oppressed with two weak evils, age and hunger,
I will not touch a bit.

DUKE SENIOR Go find him out,
And we will nothing waste till you return.

ORLANDO

I thank ye; and be blessed for your good comfort! *Exit*

DUKE SENIOR

Thou seest we are not all alone unhappy.
This wide and universal theatre
Presents more woeful pageants than the scene
Wherein we play in.

JAQUES All the world's a stage,

135.1 *Exit*] ROWE; *not in* F

131 **sufficed** satisfied, content

132 **weak evils** evils causing weakness. *Weak* in this sense not in *OED*.

133 **bit** bite (of food)

134 **waste** consume. The Duke is making a kindly joke, saying that they will save everything until Orlando returns with Adam.

135 **ye** Orlando is being especially respectful to the Duke (Abbott §236).

136–9 As in his opening speech, the Duke is here trying to cheer up his exiled followers: other people are more unfortunate (*unhappy*) than they. He again uses a commonplace (Tilley W882), the idea of man as an actor in a theatre being found at least as early as the Stoic Epictetus (AD *c.*60–117): 'Thou must remember that thou art one of the players in an interlude, and must play the part, which the author thereof shall appoint' (*The Manuell of Epictetus*, tr. James Sandford (1567), fol. 11).

138 **pageants** theatrical shows, spectacles

139–66 In this much-discussed speech Jaques develops the theme of the Duke's remark to draw a pessimistic view of humanity. The division of life into ages is ancient; the number varies between four and ten but seven is common and was included by St Augustine in his description of world history as being divided into seven ages, corresponding to the seven days of creation (see *Patrologia Latina*, vol. 34, cols. 190–4). J. E. Hankins suggests a probable source for Jaques's speech in a well-known school text, Marcellus Palingenius' *Zodiacus Vitae*, translated by Barnaby Googe in 1565 and reprinted several times (*Shakespeare's Derived Imagery* (Lawrence, 1953), pp. 15–28 *passim*). Actors have spoken the lines in numerous ways: having advanced to the footlights (18th–19th centuries), sitting at the Duke's table (E. H. Sothern, 1910), seated, then rising (Vezin, 1882), munching an apple (Asche, 1907; Bryant, 1979), miming

And all the men and women merely players.
They have their exits and their entrances,
And one man in his time plays many parts,
His acts being seven ages. At first the infant,
Mewling and puking in the nurse's arms.
Then the whining schoolboy with his satchel
And shining morning face, creeping like snail
Unwillingly to school. And then the lover,
Sighing like furnace, with a woeful ballad
Made to his mistress' eyebrow. Then, a soldier,
Full of strange oaths, and bearded like the pard,
Jealous in honour, sudden, and quick in quarrel,
Seeking the bubble reputation
Even in the cannon's mouth. And then the justice,
In fair round belly with good capon lined,
With eyes severe and beard of formal cut,
Full of wise saws and modern instances;
And so he plays his part. The sixth age shifts
Into the lean and slippered pantaloon,
With spectacles on nose and pouch on side,
His youthful hose, well saved, a world too wide
For his shrunk shank, and his big, manly voice,
Turning again toward childish treble, pipes
And whistles in his sound. Last scene of all,

each of the ages (Alan Rickman, 1985, reviving a long-dead tradition).

140 **merely players** nothing else but actors.

146 **shining** (from being scrubbed)
creeping like snail Proverbial: 'As slow as a snail' (Tilley S579).

148 **ballad** There is an implication of vulgarity here; compare the ballads Autolycus sells in *Winter's Tale* 4.4.

150 **bearded . . . pard** with a beard bristling like a leopard's whiskers. Jonson writes, 'the grace of [a soldier's] face consisteth much in a beard' (*Cynthia's Revels* 2.3.25, cited by Steevens (1785)).

151 **sudden** hasty, impetuous, rash

152 **bubble reputation** brief, worthless glory. Proverbial: 'Honour (reputation) is a bubble' (Dent B691.1).

153 **the justice** 'The *fifth age*, named *Mature Manhood*, hath . . . fifteene yeares of continuance, and therefore makes his progress so far as six and fifty yeares' (*The Treasury of Ancient and Modern Times* (1613), cited by Furness, p. 123).

154 **capon** de-sexed cock bred for the table, so often used as bribes that corrupt judges were known as 'capon-justices'

156 **saws** sayings, moral tags
modern instances commonplace examples

158 **pantaloon** foolish old man. Named from Pantalone, the lean and slippered dotard in *commedia dell'arte*, the popular form of improvised comedy which flourished in Italy from the sixteenth century to the early eighteenth. While not so well-known in England as in Europe, allusions to *commedia* characters and plots are found in several other English plays; see, e.g., *Volpone* 2.1

160 **hose** breeches

163 **his** its (Abbott §228)

That ends this strange, eventful history,
Is second childishness and mere oblivion,
Sans teeth, sans eyes, sans taste, sans everything.

Enter Orlando bearing Adam

DUKE SENIOR
Welcome. Set down your venerable burden,
And let him feed.

ORLANDO I thank you most for him.

ADAM So had you need;
I scarce can speak to thank you for myself.

DUKE SENIOR
Welcome. Fall to. I will not trouble you
As yet to question you about your fortunes.
Give us some music, and, good cousin, sing.

⌈AMIENS⌉ (*sings*)
Blow, blow, thou winter wind,
Thou art not so unkind
As man's ingratitude.
Thy tooth is not so keen,
Because thou art not seen,
Although thy breath be rude.

166.1 *bearing Adam*] *with Adam.* F 167–8 Welcome . . . burden, | And . . . feed.] *as verse,* ROWE 1714; *as prose,* F 175 ⌈AMIENS⌉ (*sings*)] *Amiens sings.* JOHNSON; Song. F 175–80] *as here,* POPE; *4 lines ending . . . winde, | . . . ingratitude | . . . seene, | . . . rude.* F

164 **history** chronicle play; or perhaps simply a tale

165 **second childishness** Another proverbial allusion: 'Old men are twice children' (Tilley M570).
mere oblivion (a) complete forgetfulness (b) being completely forgotten

166.1 The entry of Orlando with Adam is a visually striking denial of Jaques's pessimism: Orlando, though having little or no beard, is now not reckless and is learning to control his impetuosity; Adam, though old, is no dotard, and is being given love and comfort.

Capell, adding to an anecdote (of doubtful authenticity) recorded by William Oldys, reported that an old Stratford relative of Shakespeare's was said to have remembered seeing him brought on stage on another man's back and that from this it was deduced that the playwright played Adam. (See Schoenbaum, p. 149.) Disregarding the method of carriage, Coleridge rhapsodized, 'Think of having had Shakespeare in one's arms! It is worth having died two hundred years ago to have heard Shakespeare deliver a single line' (*Seven Lectures on Shakespeare and Milton* (1856), p. xvii n).

167 **venerable burden** The heroic gallantry of Orlando is emphasized if this phrase is an allusion to Aeneas' bearing his father Anchises away from burning Troy on his back, as Johnson (1765) suggested: 'That good and godly knight | The son of Venus bare away by night upon his back | His aged father and his gods, an honourable pack' (Ovid, 13, 746–8). It is tantalizingly coincidental that the description of an old man carried on a young man's shoulders matches the recollection of Capell's old Stratfordian, whether or not the actor was Shakespeare.

174 **music** The Duke's separate commands indicate that Amiens was accompanied by one or more musicians.

Hey-ho, sing hey-ho, unto the green holly.
Most friendship is feigning, most loving, mere folly.
Then hey-ho, the holly;
This life is most jolly.

Freeze, freeze, thou bitter sky,
That dost not bite so nigh
As benefits forgot.
Though thou the waters warp,
Thy sting is not so sharp
As friend remembered not.
Hey-ho, sing hey-ho, unto the green holly.
Most friendship is feigning, most loving, mere folly.
Then hey-ho, the holly;
This life is most jolly.

DUKE SENIOR (*to Orlando*)
If that you were the good Sir Rowland's son,
As you have whispered faithfully you were,
And as mine eye doth his effigies witness
Most truly limned and living in your face,
Be truly welcome hither. I am the Duke
That loved your father. The residue of your fortune,
Go to my cave and tell me. (*To Adam*) Good old man,
Thou art right welcome, as thy master is.—
(*To Lords*) Support him by the arm. (*To Orlando*) Give me your hand,
And let me all your fortunes understand. *Exeunt*

181 (*etc.*) Hey-ho] F (*Heigh ho*) 183 Then] ROWE; *The* F 191–4 sing . . . jolly] *sing, &c.* F
202 master] F2; masters F1

181 **Hey-ho** This spelling is used to distinguish the word from F's 'heigh ho' which now has connotations of sighing and ennui.
holly evergreen symbol of Christmas mirth and good fellowship

188 **warp** twist, wrinkle, distort, either by the action of the wind or by turning to ice. Jaques uses the word trenchantly at 3.3.80.

196 **faithfully** convincingly

197 **effigies** likeness (*OED*, *effigies*, *arch.*): earliest instance of *effigies* in this sense cited by *OED*. Stressed on the second syllable (Abbott §490).

198 **limned** portrayed in colour

200 This thirteen-syllable line can be regularized by diminishing the stress on the second syllable of 'residue' (Abbott §467).

202 **Thou . . . thy** Used for the servant, Adam, where the familiar 'you' and 'your' are used for Orlando.

3.1 *Enter Duke Frederick, Lords, and Oliver*

DUKE FREDERICK

Not see him since? Sir, sir, that cannot be.
But were I not the better part made mercy,
I should not seek an absent argument
Of my revenge, thou present. But look to it:
Find out thy brother wheresoe'er he is.
Seek him with candle. Bring him, dead or living,
Within this twelvemonth, or turn thou no more
To seek a living in our territory.
Thy lands, and all things that thou dost call thine
Worth seizure, do we seize into our hands
Till thou canst quit thee by thy brother's mouth
Of what we think against thee.

OLIVER

O that your highness knew my heart in this.
I never loved my brother in my life.

DUKE FREDERICK

More villain thou. (*To Lords*) Well, push him out of
doors,
And let my officers of such a nature
Make an extent upon his house and lands.
Do this expediently, and turn him going.

Exeunt severally

3.1.0.1 *Frederick*] MALONE; *not in* F 18.1 *severally*] OXFORD; *not in* F

3.1 Thrust in between the long scenes in Arden, this brief confrontation between the two evil-doers of the play confirms the palace as a place of violent discord, explosive with anger. Although formerly often cut from productions, the scene is dramatically effective in its tonal contrast with 2.7, it shows us the angry parting of the two wicked brothers immediately after the new-found friendship of the brothers they have driven into exile, and it provides the reason for Oliver's later appearance in the forest. Like 1.1, this scene begins in mid-conversation; it can be played with Duke Frederick in a choleric frenzy, so beside himself that he is blind to the self-condemning irony of l. 15. In Michael Elliott's RSC production (1961), by the end he was white-faced, gibbering with near madness.

3 **argument** subject

6 **with candle** Democritus sought an honest man with a candle, and the woman in the parable swept her house and lit a candle to look for a lost piece of money (Luke 15: 8); Frederick's command is particularly ironic in the light of the verses following (Luke 15: 10): 'there is joy in the presence of the angels of God, for one sinner that converteth [i.e. repents]' (Geneva Bible).

7 **turn** return

10 **seize** in the legal sense of taking possession of property

11 **quit . . . mouth** acquit yourself by means of evidence from your brother's own words

17 **of such a nature** whose job it is

18 **Make an extent** begin legal action, such as taking out a writ, to seize property

19 **expediently** speedily, expeditiously
turn him going send him packing

3.2 *Enter Orlando with a paper*

ORLANDO

Hang there, my verse, in witness of my love;
  And thou thrice-crownèd queen of night, survey
With thy chaste eye, from thy pale sphere above,
  Thy huntress' name that my full life doth sway.
O Rosalind, these trees shall be my books,
  And in their barks my thoughts I'll character
That every eye which in this forest looks
  Shall see thy virtue witnessed everywhere.
Run, run, Orlando; carve on every tree
The fair, the chaste, and unexpressive she. *Exit*

Enter Corin and Touchstone the clown

CORIN And how like you this shepherd's life, Master Touchstone?

3.2.0.1 *with a paper*] CAPELL; *not in* F

3.2 This great central scene, twice as long as any other in the play, is especially concerned with the game of love, but it also plays with time, with affectation, and with the argument between court and country. In Macready's production of 1842 sheep-bells were heard occasionally throughout, and realistic settings reached their peak with Flanagan in 1908 (see Introduction, p. 61) — realism very far from the suspended strips of clear plastic designed by Ralph Koltai for Clifford Williams in 1967 (Old Vic).

1 **Hang there** In Greene's *Orlando Furioso* (c. 1591; printed 1594, 1599), the wicked Sacrepant hangs up roundelays 'on the trees' (2.1.536.2) falsely proclaiming the love of Orlando's sweetheart Angelica for Medor (an incident not found in Ariosto); he succeeds in his purpose of driving Orlando mad. Greene's Sacrepant and Shakespeare's Orlando could have hung their verses on a stage post, or on a property tree.

2 **thrice-crownèd queen of night** The moon goddess Diana (Artemis), on earth the huntress, protector of chastity, was identified with Proserpina (Hecate, Lucina) in the underworld and Luna (Phoebe, Cynthia) in the sky. Although Macready set the scene on a summer evening with the moon seen faintly in the sky, and Wilson maintained that Orlando was speaking at night, he could as easily pray to Diana in the daytime.

4 **huntress' name** Orlando considers Rosalind a follower of Diana because she is chaste, but his reference also links her with the hunt of love and its imagery throughout the play—e.g. he is 'furnished like a hunter' and 'comes to kill [her] heart' (ll. 237–8 below), with its common pun on 'hart'. The aftermath of a hunt proper is brought on stage in 4.2.

sway rule

6 **in their barks** Pastoral lovers habitually carved their sweethearts' names on trees (and the practice persists); in Lodge, Montanus carves whole poems. As Rensselaer W. Lee shows in *Names on Trees: Ariosto into Art*, the motif 'occurs in Greek literature as early as Aristophanes . . . But it was in the richer and more sophisticated amatory context of Roman pastoral and elegiac poetry of the first century B.C. that Renaissance poets naturally found their inspiration to revive the topos' ((Princeton, 1977), p. 9), beginning with Virgil's tenth Eclogue. The main Renaissance example is in Ariosto's *Orlando Furioso* Canto 19.28, where Angelica and Medoro carve their names on stones and trees 'with bodkin, knife or pin' (tr. Harington (1591)).

TOUCHSTONE Truly, shepherd, in respect of itself, it is a good life; but in respect that it is a shepherd's life, it is naught. In respect that it is solitary, I like it very well; but in respect that it is private, it is a very vile life. Now in respect it is in the fields, it pleaseth me well; but in respect it is not in the court, it is tedious. As it is a spare life, look you, it fits my humour well; but as there is no more plenty in it, it goes much against my stomach. Hast any philosophy in thee, shepherd?

CORIN No more but that I know the more one sickens, the worse at ease he is, and that he that wants money, means, and content is without three good friends; that the property of rain is to wet, and fire to burn; that good pasture makes fat sheep; and that a great cause of the night is lack of the sun; that he that hath learned no wit by nature nor art may complain of good breeding or comes of a very dull kindred.

TOUCHSTONE Such a one is a natural philosopher. Wast ever in court, shepherd?

CORIN No, truly.

TOUCHSTONE Then thou art damned.

CORIN Nay, I hope.

TOUCHSTONE Truly thou art damned, like an ill-roasted egg, all on one side.

13–21 Vickers remarks that with this 'remarkable series of paired, symmetrical, antithetical, and finally tautological clauses', Touchstone shows himself to be 'obviously the master of rhetoric as well as logic' (p. 205).

13 **in respect of** with regard to

14 **in respect that** considering, seeing

15 **naught** worthless

15–16 **solitary . . . private** As both words have the similar meaning of being secluded from public haunt, the contrast between them is not immediately clear, but Touchstone is making a bawdy joke, being mockingly moral about things that are private, i.e. referring to the genitals. Compare 2.7.71: 'private party'.

18 **spare** frugal

20 **stomach** Proverbial: 'To go against one's stomach' (Tilley S874, although this instance is not noted).

28 **complain of good breeding** complain of not having been born, or brought up, well

30 **natural philosopher** (a) a philosopher who reaches a standpoint from observations of nature (b) a foolish philosopher. Latham suggests the reference is 'not to Corin but to the ninny he has just described', but Touchstone could easily make this an aside to the audience at Corin's expense.

36 **all on one side** Steevens remarked that 'a fool is the best roaster of an egg, because he is always turning it' was proverbial, but neither Tilley nor Dent records it. Tilley (F504) and F. P. Wilson, however, list 'Set a fool to roast eggs, and a wise man to eat them', so Touchstone's analogy may be derived from long experience; he may simply be saying that Corin is so completely rustic that he has no hope of salvation.

CORIN For not being at court? Your reason?

TOUCHSTONE Why, if thou never wast at court thou never sawest good manners. If thou never sawest good manners, then thy manners must be wicked, and wickedness is sin, and sin is damnation. Thou art in a parlous state, shepherd.

CORIN Not a whit, Touchstone. Those that are good manners at the court are as ridiculous in the country as the behaviour of the country is most mockable at the court. You told me you salute not at the court but you kiss your hands. That courtesy would be uncleanly if courtiers were shepherds.

TOUCHSTONE Instance, briefly; come, instance.

CORIN Why, we are still handling our ewes, and their fells, you know, are greasy.

TOUCHSTONE Why, do not your courtier's hands sweat? And is not the grease of a mutton as wholesome as the sweat of a man? Shallow, shallow. A better instance, I say. Come.

CORIN Besides, our hands are hard.

TOUCHSTONE Your lips will feel them the sooner. Shallow again. A more sounder instance. Come.

CORIN And they are often tarred over with the surgery of our sheep; and would you have us kiss tar? The court-

39 **manners** (a) polite behaviour (b) moral character (*OED* 4†a); the quibble allows Touchstone to make his deduction.

42 **parlous** A corruption of 'perilous'.

46–7 **salute . . . hands** you do not greet at court without you kiss one another's hands

49 **Instance** either a noun 'proof' or a verb 'provide proof'

50 **still** continually

fells fleeces (*OED*, *fell*, *sb.* 3): earliest instance of *fell* in this sense cited by *OED*

52 **your** 'Used with no definite meaning, or vaguely implying "that you know of"' (*OED*, *your*, poss. pron. 5b; and Abbott §221).

53 **grease of a mutton** sweat of a sheep (?). Although the use 'fat' = sweat/sweaty is not attested, there is some support for the view that perspiration was commonly believed to be fat emerging through the pores, as Harold Jenkins shows in his long note to Gertrude's description of Hamlet as 'fat and scant of breath' in the Arden *Hamlet* ((1982), pp. 568–9). As well, *OED*, *swelt*, *v.* †4. 'To exude with heat. *Obs.*' cites 'as mylke swelteth & sweteth oute of the koowes body into the vdder' as an example of 1530, to swelter is 'to sweat profusely' (*OED* *v.* 1), and lanolin, the cholesterin-fatty matter extracted from sheep's wool, is known as 'wool-fat'.

58 **more sounder** Double comparatives were used for emphasis (Abbott §11).

59 **tarred** Until proprietary wound-dressing preparations were introduced in the 1960s, tar was used to stop sheep bleeding from cuts made in shearing; in Australia these modern styptic remedies are now commonly called 'tar'.

ier's hands are perfumed with civet.

TOUCHSTONE Most shallow man. Thou worms' meat in respect of a good piece of flesh indeed, learn of the wise, and perpend: civet is of a baser birth than tar, the very uncleanly flux of a cat. Mend the instance, shepherd.

CORIN You have too courtly a wit for me. I'll rest.

TOUCHSTONE Wilt thou rest damned? God help thee, shallow man. God make incision in thee, thou art raw.

CORIN Sir, I am a true labourer. I earn that I eat, get that I wear; owe no man hate, envy no man's happiness; glad of other men's good, content with my harm; and the greatest of my pride is to see my ewes graze and my lambs suck.

TOUCHSTONE That is another simple sin in you, to bring the ewes and the rams together, and to offer to get your living by the copulation of cattle; to be bawd to a bell-wether, and to betray a she-lamb of a twelve-month to

61 **civet** unctuous substance with a strong musky smell, used in making perfume, and obtained, as Touchstone knows, 'from sacs or glands in the anal pouch of several animals of the Civet genus' (*OED*, *civet*, *sb.*[1] 2)

62 **shallow man** Rowe inserted a comma after *shallow*, but the next sentence indicates that Touchstone has turned from criticizing the argument to criticizing the arguer himself.

worms' meat Gibson suggests 'piece of magotty flesh' rather than the usual meaning, 'corpse'. The point of the withering comparison is that Corin is inferior to Touchstone himself, the 'good piece of flesh indeed'. 'A man is nothing but worms' meat' was proverbial (Tilley M253).

62–3 **in respect of** in comparison with

64 **perpend** consider, weigh. A pomposity used also by Pistol (*Merry Wives* 2.1.110 and *Henry V* 4.4.8), Feste (*Twelfth Night* 5.1.296) and Polonius (Hamlet 2.2.106). Shakespeare evidently enjoyed this word during the years around 1600. G. R. Hibbard suggests that he 'may well have picked it up from *Cambyses* (l. 1018), where it occurs shortly before the passage he parodies in *1 Henry IV* (2.4.379–83)' (*Hamlet* (Oxford, 1987), p. 208).

65 **flux of a cat** Compare Harington: 'God dislikes sluttishness, and every cat gives us an example to cover all our filthiness, & if you will not disdain to use that which cometh from the musk cat, to make your self, your gloves, and your clothes the more sweet, refuse not to follow the example of the cat of the house, to make your entries, your stairs, your chambers, & your whole house, the less sour' (pp. 175–6).

68 **God make incision . . . raw** may you (a) be let blood to cure your dullness (b) have something grafted on to you, like a plant, to remedy your inexperience, or (c) be let blood like meat made ready for roasting; 'simple sin' in l. 74 makes (a) the most likely meaning.

69 **get** earn

71 **content . . . harm** resigned to any misfortune; patient in tribulation

74–81 A passage frequently cut in performance, either partly or completely, owing to its plain-speaking bawdiness or, more recently, for its obscurity. For evidence of such deletions, see for example acting versions or prompt-books for productions by Macready (1842), Marie Litton (1880), Asche (1907), Shaw (1952) and Noble (1985), and others listed in William P. Halstead, *Shakespeare as Spoken*, 12 vols. (Ann Arbor, 1977–9), vol. iii (1978).

76–7 **bell-wether** The leading sheep of the flock, around whose neck a bell is hung; here a ram, not a castrated male (the modern meaning of *wether*).

a crooked pated old cuckoldly ram, out of all reasonable match. If thou beest not damned for this, the devil himself will have no shepherds. I cannot see else how thou shouldst scape.

CORIN Here comes young Master Ganymede, my new mistress's brother.

Enter Rosalind as Ganymede

ROSALIND (*reads*)

'From the east to western Ind
No jewel is like Rosalind.
Her worth being mounted on the wind
Through all the world bears Rosalind.
All the pictures fairest lined
Are but black to Rosalind.
Let no face be kept in mind
But the fair of Rosalind.'

TOUCHSTONE I'll rhyme you so eight years together, dinners, and suppers, and sleeping-hours excepted. It is the right butter-women's rank to market.

ROSALIND Out, fool.

TOUCHSTONE For a taste:

If a hart do lack a hind,

83.1 *as Ganymede*] *not in* F

78 **cuckoldly** Horns, the signs of a man whose wife committed adultery, were a source of constant joking.

83.1 Many acting versions have followed the stage direction in *Love in a Forest*, 'Ros. *takes the paper* Orlando *had hung on the Tree*', but Rosalind already has the verses when she enters; she tells Touchstone, who has watched her approach (l. 82), that she 'found them on a tree' (l. 109), something she would not need to say if he had seen her finding them.

83–106 The rhymes in the verses of both Orlando and Touchstone indicate the pronunciation of 'Rosalind' with a long *i*, in these instances at least.

84 **From . . . western** Proverbial: 'As far as (from) the east from (to) the west' (Dent E43.1).

88 **lined** sketched (*OED*, *line* v.[2] 4): earliest instance of *line* in this sense cited by *OED*

93 **sleeping-hours** time spent in (a) sleeping (b) in whoring. Compare 2.7.26.

94 **right** true, real. Compare l. 113: 'right virtue'.

butter-women's . . . market The general sense of insult here is plain, the detailed meaning obscure, and a bawdy innuendo inescapable. To Touchstone, Orlando's love poem is nothing but jig-jogging doggerel, easily imitated; however *butter-women* (who were notoriously garrulous), *rank* and *market* could all be associated with prostitution. 'Butter quean' and 'butter-whore' were both current usage. Gary Taylor suggests that, according to Touchstone, the poetry is 'like crowding lines of voluble, foul-mouthed, lascivious, repetitive, ignorant market-women trotting to market on horseback or in carts' ('Touchstone's Butterwomen', *Review of English Studies*, NS 32 (1981), 193).

97–108 Touchstone's scurrilous parody was often bowdlerized in performance; Marie Litton's production (1880), for

Let him seek out Rosalind.
If the cat will after kind,
So, be sure, will Rosalind.
Wintered garments must be lined,
So must slender Rosalind.
They that reap must sheaf and bind,
Then to cart with Rosalind.
'Sweetest nut hath sourest rind',
Such a nut is Rosalind.
He that sweetest rose will find
Must find love's prick, and Rosalind.

This is the very false gallop of verses. Why do you infect yourself with them?

ROSALIND Peace, you dull fool, I found them on a tree.

TOUCHSTONE Truly, the tree yields bad fruit.

instance, omitted several lines and altered l. 108 to 'Ti-tum ti-tum Rosalind'.

99 **cat . . . kind** Proverbial (Tilley C135): a cat will do what is natural to it. Touchstone takes up the sexual sense of 'to do the act of kind' = 'to copulate' to initiate a series of *doubles entendres*. Latham remarks, 'His extempore verses are a series of indecent equivocations. Tarlton and Armin were famous for such performances.'

101 **Wintered** worn in winter
lined The bawdy reference is to the copulation of dogs and bitches; 'slender' in the next line glances at Rosalind's shape, which will change with pregnancy.

103–4 **reap . . . cart** 'Reap' is probably a sexual pun (compare 2.7.26), 'cart' certainly is: whores and bawds were carried on and whipped behind carts as public punishment in the streets. The general sense is that those who meddle with Rosalind must take the consequences.

105 **Sweetest . . . rind** Proverbial (Tilley N360). The sexual pun here is on 'nut'/'knot' = 'virginity'; compare *Tempest* 4.1.15: 'If thou dost break her virgin-knot'. The 'rind' is probably Rosalind's male disguise.

107–8 **He . . . Rosalind** The verse and the bawdy come to their climax in this final couplet, which contains at least three strands of meaning: (a) an allusion to the proverb 'No rose without its thorn (prickle)' (Tilley R182) (b) 'He who wants to find the sweetest maiden must find Cupid's arrow and then Rosalind' (c) 'He who wants to take a virginity will have to be sexually aroused and seek out Rosalind', the implication being that she will satisfy him.

109 **false gallop** canter. Touchstone continues with the image of horse-riding implied in l. 94 above. The use of 'infect' in l. 109 suggests that Shakespeare was remembering Nashe's attacking Gabriel Harvey in *Strange News* (1592): 'I would trot a false gallop through the rest of his ragged verses, but that if I should retort his rime doggerel aright, I must make my verse (as he doth his) run hobbling like a brewer's cart upon the stones, and observe no length in their feet, which were *absurdum per absurdius* [clumsy by way of the clumsier] to infect my vein with his imitation' (Nashe, i. 275). To run a 'false gallop' was proverbial (Dent G14.1). In asserting she speaks the truth, Margaret in *Much Ado* says her tongue does not go at a 'false gallop' (3.4.88).

111–16 Rosalind replies with both a surprisingly mild rebuke and some brilliant bawdy punning.

112 **the . . . fruit** Compare Matthew 7: 18, 'A good tree cannot bring forth bad fruit', and 3.2.228–9.

ROSALIND I'll graft it with you, and then I shall graft it with a medlar; then it will be the earliest fruit i'th' country, for you'll be rotten ere you be half-ripe, and that's the right virtue of the medlar.

TOUCHSTONE You have said; but whether wisely or no, let the forest judge.

Enter Celia, as Aliena, with a writing

ROSALIND
Peace, here comes my sister, reading. Stand aside.

CELIA (*reads*)
'Why should this a desert be?
For it is unpeopled? No.
Tongues I'll hang on every tree,
That shall civil sayings show.
Some, how brief the life of man
Runs his erring pilgrimage,
That the stretching of a span
Buckles in his sum of age.

120 a] ROWE; *not in* F   120 be?] ROWE; *bee,* F

113–16 (a) I shall graft it with yew (you) and then I shall be grafting it with a medlar (meddler, since 'every fool will be meddling', Proverbs 20: 3 and Tilley F546; there is also a quibble on 'meddle' = 'engage in sexual activity'); it will then bear the earliest fruit, instead of the latest, as it does normally, because you will go bad before you are halfway to maturity, and medlars are best when decayed (b) I shall graft it first with you and then with a whore and that means you will be diseased before long because disease is the typical quality of the whore. The words also glance back at Touchstone's reported use of 'ripe' and 'rot' (2.7.26–7).

113 **graft** The process of inserting a shoot from one tree or plant into another so that they grow together. For similarly sexual allusions compare e.g. Webster, *The Duchess of Malfi*: 2.1.144–5; ''Tis a pretty art, | This grafting' and *Winter's Tale* 4.4.92–5: 'we marry | A gentler scion to the wildest stock, | And make conceive a bark of baser kind | By bud of nobler race'.

114 **medlar** (a) a tree bearing small brown-skinned apple-like fruit, best eaten when decayed to a soft pulpiness (b) prostitute (slang). Compare Middleton, *Women Beware Women* 4.2.97–9: 'he that marries a whore looks like a fellow bound all his lifetime to a medlar-tree' and *Measure* 4.3.167: 'They would else have married me to the rotten medlar'. In *The School of Salernum* (1607), Harington writes: 'They have one name and fit to be forgotten, | While hard and sound they be, they be not spent, | Good *Medlars* are not ripe, till seeming rotten, | For meddling much with *Medlars* some are shent [i.e., ruined, disgraced]' (repr. 1922, p. 102). 'Medlars are never good till they be rotten' was proverbial (Tilley M863), as well as 'Soon ripe, soon rotten' (Tilley R133).

117 **You have said** Proverbial (Dent S118.1).

125 **erring** wandering (compare 'Life is a pilgrimage', Tilley L249)

126 **stretching of a span** From Psalm 39: 5: 'Thou hast made my days as it were a span long'; compare 'Life is a span' (Tilley L251). A handspan, the distance between the outstretched tips of the little finger and the thumb, is 22.5 cm (9 inches).

127 **Buckles in** encompasses

Some of violated vows
  'Twixt the souls of friend and friend.
But upon the fairest boughs,
  Or at every sentence end,
Will I 'Rosalinda' write,
  Teaching all that read to know
The quintessence of every sprite
  Heaven would in little show.
Therefore heaven nature charged
  That one body should be filled
With all graces wide-enlarged.
  Nature presently distilled
Helen's cheek, but not her heart,
  Cleopatra's majesty,
Atalanta's better part,
  Sad Lucretia's modesty.
Thus Rosalind of many parts
  By heavenly synod was devised
Of many faces, eyes, and hearts

140 *her*] ROWE; *his* F

134–9 **quintessence . . . distilled** Alchemists tried to extract by distillation a fifth essence (beyond the four elements) of which the heavenly bodies were supposed to be composed and which was thought to be latent in all things. Orlando is saying that by the name of Rosalind heaven wanted to show in one person, on a small scale, the essential quality of every spirit (or soul). Heaven therefore directed nature to fill one body with graces from everywhere, and so, Rosalind was composed by astrological conjunction (or by decision of a divine council).

138 **all graces wide-enlarged** The graces found in many will be brought together in Rosalind. She will have the beauty ('cheek') but not the fickleness ('heart') of Helen, the most beautiful woman of the ancient world, whose abduction from her husband Menelaus provoked the Trojan war; the nobility of Cleopatra, the last queen of Egypt, beloved by Julius Caesar and Antony; the beauty but not the cruelty or greed of the huntress Atalanta, whose suitors were executed if they could not outrun her—she was defeated by Melanion (or Hippomenes) who threw three golden apples on to the track and raced past her when she stopped to pick them up; and the modesty of Lucretia, Collatinus' serious ('sad') wife, who was raped by Tarquin and then killed herself—events which became the subject of *The Rape of Lucrece* (1594), Shakespeare's second long poem.

The conceit is similar to that found in the sonneteers, whose mistresses' beauty sometimes results from the gods' and goddesses' bestowing on them their most attractive characteristics. Compare, e.g., Giles Fletcher, *Licia*, 51, and Lodge, *Phillis*, 33, which are both renderings of Ronsard, *Amours*, I, 32.

142 **Atalanta's better part** Her beauty, compared with her swiftness. Compare Ovid, 10, 650–1: 'And hard it is to tell | Thee whether she did in footmanship or beauty more excel.' Since it is her 'footmanship' which leads to the deaths of her suitors, her beauty must be the 'better part'.

145 **synod** (a) a conjunction of heavenly bodies (b) a council of divinities.

To have the touches dearest prized.
Heaven would that she these gifts should have
And I to live and die her slave.'

ROSALIND O most gentle Jupiter! What tedious homily of love have you wearied your parishioners withal, and never cried 'Have patience, good people.'

CELIA How now, back-friends? Shepherd, go off a little. Go with him, sirrah.

TOUCHSTONE Come, shepherd, let us make an honourable retreat, though not with bag and baggage, yet with scrip and scrippage. *Exit with Corin*

CELIA Didst thou hear these verses?

ROSALIND O yes, I heard them all, and more, too, for some of them had in them more feet than the verses would bear.

CELIA That's no matter; the feet might bear the verses.

ROSALIND Ay, but the feet were lame, and could not bear themselves without the verse, and therefore stood lamely in the verse.

CELIA But didst thou hear without wondering how thy name should be hanged and carved upon these trees?

ROSALIND I was seven of the nine days out of the wonder

153 back-friends] THEOBALD, *after* F: backe friends 157 *with Corin*] *Exit* Cor. *and* Clown ROWE; *Exit* F

147 **touches** features. Compare 5.4.27: 'Some lively touches of my daughter's favour'.

150 **Jupiter** Rosalind's entirely appropriate oath was changed to 'pulpiter' in a widely-followed emendation by Spedding (Cambridge).

153 **back-friends** pretended or false friends (*OED, backfriend*, †1 *Obs.*). Theobald's emendation has not been universally accepted, but is defensible because Rosalind's 'Peace . . . Stand aside' (l. 119 above) indicates that she, Corin and Touchstone hide from Celia to hear her reading; when Rosalind speaks and they reveal themselves Celia makes this joking accusation, sending off the clown and the shepherd so that she can tell Rosalind about her discovery of Orlando.

156 **bag and baggage** Though 'honourable retreat' indicates that while Touchstone, still smarting from Rosalind's success over him, is using this phrase in the military sense of 'all the property of an army collectively' (*OED sb.* 20), he is slyly insulting the women as well, since *baggage* also meant 'strumpet' (*OED sb.* 6). The phrase was proverbial (Dent BB1).

157 **scrip and scrippage** Touchstone's nonce phrase to go with 'bag and baggage'. A scrip was a small wallet, bag or satchel carried by shepherds, pilgrims and beggars.

160 **more feet** Line 148 has five feet and fits awkwardly ('lamely', l. 165) with the other lines of Orlando's verse, which have four; the difficulty can, however, be overcome by reading 'Heaven would' as an anapaest (˘˘¯).

168 **seven . . . wonder** As the novelty of an event proverbially lasts nine days (Tilley W728), Rosalind is saying she has been wondering for quite some time already about the verses she has found.

before you came; for look here what I found on a palm-tree; (*showing Celia the verses*) I was never so berhymed since Pythagoras' time that I was an Irish rat, which I can hardly remember.

CELIA Trow you who hath done this?

ROSALIND Is it a man?

CELIA And a chain that you once wore about his neck. Change you colour?

ROSALIND I prithee, who?

CELIA O Lord, Lord, it is a hard matter for friends to meet. But mountains may be removed with earthquakes, and so encounter.

ROSALIND Nay, but who is it?

CELIA Is it possible?

ROSALIND Nay, I prithee now with most petitionary vehemence, tell me who it is.

CELIA O wonderful, wonderful, and most wonderful-wonderful, and yet again wonderful, and after that out of all whooping!

ROSALIND Good my complexion! Dost thou think, though I am caparisoned like a man, I have a doublet and hose

169–70 **palm-tree** The palm is mentioned four times in Lodge, figuratively rather than as a tree growing in Arden (fols. 1^{v}, 8^{v}, 31^{r}, 40^{v}). It may be relevant that the date palm (*Phoenix dactylifera*), native to North Africa and Arabia, was introduced into England in 1597; but the forests of literary romance are rich with a great variety of exotic flora and fauna, and in England branches of willow or other trees were (and still are) substituted for palm in Palm Sunday observances, particularly those of the goat (great round-leaved) willow or sallow, which is called '"palm" in the absence of real palm trees in England' (Ralph Whitlock, 'Memorable Spring', *Guardian Weekly*, 9 April 1990). Edward Armstrong suggests the palm-tree associates Arden with Eden (*Shakespeare's Imagination*, 1946, p. 114n.); Gibson detects a pun on 'poem-tree'. But Rosalind's mind is on matrimony again: palms were 'Best emblem of a peaceful marriage' (Webster, *Duchess of Malfi* 1.1.486) because it was believed they were fruitful only if planted close together.

171 **Pythagoras** Greek philosopher (*fl.* *c.*540–*c.*510 BC) for whom a central belief was the transmigration of souls, 'Removing out of man to beast, and out of beast to man' (Ovid, 15, 186).

that when

Irish rat The Irish were proverbially believed to kill off rats by rhyming incantations (Tilley D158).

173 **Trow you** 'Can you imagine?'

179–80 **mountains . . . encounter** Celia ironically alludes to the proverb 'Friends may meet, but mountains never greet' (Tilley F738).

186–7 **out . . . whooping** beyond all the powers of expression of wonder

188 **Good my complexion** An impatient exclamation (*OED*, *good, adj. 6b*) relating to Rosalind's feminine *disposition* (*OED*, *complexion, sb.* †3).

in my disposition? One inch of delay more is a South Sea of discovery. I prithee tell me who is it quickly, and speak apace. I would thou couldst stammer, that thou mightst pour this concealed man out of thy mouth as wine comes out of a narrow-mouthed bottle—either too much at once, or none at all. I prithee, take the cork out of thy mouth, that I may drink thy tidings.

CELIA So you may put a man in your belly.

ROSALIND Is he of God's making? What manner of man? Is his head worth a hat? Or his chin worth a beard?

CELIA Nay, he hath but a little beard.

ROSALIND Why, God will send more, if the man will be thankful. Let me stay the growth of his beard, if thou delay me not the knowledge of his chin.

CELIA It is young Orlando, that tripped up the wrestler's heels and your heart both in an instant.

ROSALIND Nay, but the devil take mocking. Speak sad brow and true maid.

CELIA I'faith, coz, 'tis he.

ROSALIND Orlando?

CELIA Orlando.

ROSALIND Alas the day, what shall I do with my doublet and hose! What did he when thou sawest him? What said he? How looked he? Wherein went he? What makes he here? Did he ask for me? Where remains he? How parted he with thee? And when shalt thou see him again? Answer me in one word.

190–1 **South Sea of discovery** 'Even the smallest delay is as protracted as an explorer's long voyage across the South Seas'; Rosalind knows already what her *discovery* will be. 'Volumes of sixteenth cent. travel are compressed into Rosalind's metaphor' (Wilson).

197 **so . . . belly** Celia picks up a bawdy meaning of 'drink' = 'have sexual intercourse'; the line was cut from many editions and productions up to the 1950s. (Compare Middleton, *A Chaste Maid in Cheapside* 2.1.15–6: 'Life, every year a child, and some years two; | Besides drinkings abroad, that's never reckon'd'.)

198 **Is . . . God's making?** 'Is he a normal human being?' Proverbial (Tilley M162). Compare 1.1.30–1.

200 **a little beard** Compare Lodge's Rosader: 'casting up his hand he felt hair on his face, and perceiving his beard to bud . . . began to blush' (fol. 5^{r}).

202–3 **Let . . . chin** 'I can wait for his beard, if only you will tell me on whose chin it will grow.'

206–7 **sad . . . maid** with a grave face and on your virgin's honour; seriously and truly

213 **Wherein went he?** What was he wearing?

213–14 **What makes he here?** What is he doing here? Compare 1.1.27.

CELIA You must borrow me Gargantua's mouth first, 'tis a word too great for any mouth of this age's size. To say ay and no to these particulars is more than to answer in a catechism.

ROSALIND But doth he know that I am in this forest, and in man's apparel? Looks he as freshly as he did the day he wrestled?

CELIA It is as easy to count atomies as to resolve the propositions of a lover; but take a taste of my finding him, and relish it with good observance. I found him under a tree, like a dropped acorn—

ROSALIND It may well be called Jove's tree when it drops forth such fruit.

CELIA Give me audience, good madam.

ROSALIND Proceed.

CELIA There lay he, stretched along like a wounded knight—

ROSALIND Though it be pity to see such a sight, it well becomes the ground.

CELIA Cry 'holla' to thy tongue, I prithee: it curvets unseasonably.—He was furnished like a hunter—

ROSALIND O ominous—he comes to kill my heart.

CELIA I would sing my song without a burden; thou bringest me out of tune.

229 forth such] F2; such CAPELL; forth F1 236 thy] ROWE; the F

217 **Gargantua's mouth** A mouth as huge as that of the giant of folk-tale and Rabelais' stories, a character well enough known in sixteenth-century England, though Rabelais was not fully translated until the late seventeenth.

218–19 **say ay and no . . . catechism** to answer 'yes' and 'no' to all these questions is impossible, since it would be beyond all the answers needed for the series of religious questions set down in the Book of Common Prayer.

224 **atomies** specks, motes (e.g. particles of dust discernible in a shaft of sunlight)

226 **observance** attention (*OED*, *observance*, 5): earliest instance of *observance* in this sense cited by *OED*

227–8 **acorn . . . Jove's tree** In the Golden Age, acorns were part of the staple, vegetarian diet when men 'Did live by . . . apples, nuts and pears . . . And by the acorns dropped on ground, from Jove's broad tree' (Ovid, *Metamorphoses*, 1, 119–21). Rosalind is also alluding to Matthew 7: 18 (compare l. 112n.).

232–3 **stretched . . . wounded knight** The melancholy pose (compare 2.1.30n.) indicates Orlando's lovelorn state.

236 **'holla'** 'whoa', a cry to stop a horse. The riding image deriving from 'knight' continues with 'curvet'.

237 **furnished** equipped

238 **heart** A pun on 'hart', strictly, a six-year-old red deer, though if hunted by a king or queen a stag (see 2.1.33) was called a hart.

239 **burden** refrain, or continuous under-song

239–40 **bringest me out** interruptest me

ROSALIND Do you not know I am a woman? When I think, I must speak.—Sweet, say on.

Enter Orlando and Jaques

CELIA You bring me out. Soft, comes he not here?

ROSALIND 'Tis he. Slink by, and note him.

Rosalind and Celia stand aside

JAQUES (*to Orlando*) I thank you for your company, but, good faith, I had as lief have been myself alone.

ORLANDO And so had I. But yet for fashion's sake, I thank you too for your society.

JAQUES Goodbye; let's meet as little as we can.

ORLANDO I do desire we may be better strangers.

JAQUES I pray you mar no more trees with writing love-songs in their barks.

ORLANDO I pray you mar no more of my verses with reading them ill-favouredly.

JAQUES Rosalind is your love's name?

ORLANDO Yes, just.

JAQUES I do not like her name.

ORLANDO There was no thought of pleasing you when she was christened.

JAQUES What stature is she of?

ORLANDO Just as high as my heart.

JAQUES You are full of pretty answers. Have you not been acquainted with goldsmiths' wives, and conned them out of rings?

244.1 *Rosalind . . . aside*] OXFORD; *not in* F 249 Goodbye] F (God buy you); (*also at* 4.1.29, 5.3.45)

241–2 **When ... speak** 'What the heart thinks the tongue speaks' was proverbial (Tilley H334).

243 **Soft** 'Quiet, hush'

247 **fashion's** Since the proverb was 'For fashion's sake (as dogs go to the market [to church])', Orlando is being somewhat insulting. Tilley's example (F76) is from 1721, but Dent cites others from *c.*1598 and 1604.

249 **Goodbye** F's 'God buy you', which became the modern 'goodbye', began as 'God be with you'. 'The substitution of *good-* for *God* may have been due to association with such formulas of leave-taking as *good day*, *goodnight*, etc.' (*OED*).

256 **just** exactly

262 **pretty** clever, ingenious

263–4 Jaques insultingly suggests that Orlando has learned (*conned*) his verses from the trite mottoes inscribed by goldsmiths inside rings. As 'con', 'quaint' (in *acquaint*) and *rings* = 'female sexual organ(s)' he is also making a lewd suggestion about Orlando's behaviour with the goldsmiths' wives, a point underlined in John Dexter's 1979 National Theatre production by Michael Bryant as Jaques giving here a rude gesture.

ORLANDO Not so; but I answer you right painted cloth, from whence you have studied your questions.

JAQUES You have a nimble wit; I think 'twas made of Atalanta's heels. Will you sit down with me, and we two will rail against our mistress the world, and all our misery?

ORLANDO I will chide no breather in the world but myself, against whom I know most faults.

JAQUES The worst fault you have is to be in love.

ORLANDO 'Tis a fault I will not change for your best virtue. I am weary of you.

JAQUES By my troth, I was seeking for a fool when I found you.

ORLANDO He is drowned in the brook. Look but in, and you shall see him.

JAQUES There I shall see mine own figure.

ORLANDO Which I take to be either a fool or a cipher.

JAQUES I'll tarry no longer with you. Farewell, good Signor Love.

ORLANDO I am glad of your departure. Adieu, good Monsieur Melancholy. *Exit Jaques*

ROSALIND (*to Celia*) I will speak to him like a saucy lackey, and under that habit play the knave with him. (*To Orlando*) Do you hear, forester?

ORLANDO Very well. What would you?

ROSALIND I pray you, what is't o'clock?

285 *Exit Jaques*] CAPELL; *not in* F

265–6 **right painted cloth . . . questions** Painted cloths, a substitute for expensive tapestries as wall-hangings, often included moral maxims in their pictures, which were frequently of biblical or mythological incidents. Orlando says he is replying in plain terms, and that Jaques's questions are as unexciting as such clichés.

267–8 **Atalanta's heels** Jaques refers to Atalanta's speed (another reason for thinking that her 'better part' in l. 142 is her beauty).

271 **breather** living person

276 **fool** i.e. Touchstone, but Jaques implies that Orlando is also a fool.

280 **figure** image, likeness (*OED* 9). Jaques is aware of Orlando's implication, and denies it: 'You're wrong—I'll see my own reflection, and I'm no fool'—but Orlando betters him in the next line.

281 **cipher** An arithmetical symbol (0) of no value on its own, hence, a nonentity. Orlando takes up the meaning of 'figure' = 'numerical symbol' (*OED* 19). 'He is a cipher among numbers' was proverbial (Tilley C391).

287 **play the knave** trick him by pretending to be a boy. There is probably an allusion to playing at cards; compare Harington, *Epigrams* (1612): 'A saucy knave, to trump both King and Queen'.

290 **what is't o'clock** A question to engage a stranger in conversation; it may also be intended to suggest the mental superiority of the questioner.

ORLANDO You should ask me what time o' day. There's no clock in the forest.

ROSALIND Then there is no true lover in the forest, else sighing every minute and groaning every hour would detect the lazy foot of time as well as a clock.

ORLANDO And why not the swift foot of time? Had not that been as proper?

ROSALIND By no means, sir. Time travels in divers paces with divers persons. I'll tell you who time ambles withal, who time trots withal, who time gallops withal, and who he stands still withal.

ORLANDO I prithee, who doth he trot withal?

ROSALIND Marry, he trots hard with a young maid between the contract of her marriage and the day it is solemnized. If the interim be but a se'nnight, time's pace is so hard that it seems the length of seven year.

ORLANDO Who ambles time withal?

ROSALIND With a priest that lacks Latin, and a rich man that hath not the gout; for the one sleeps easily because he cannot study, and the other lives merrily because he feels no pain, the one lacking the burden of lean and wasteful learning, the other knowing no burden of heavy tedious penury. These time ambles withal.

ORLANDO Who doth he gallop withal?

ROSALIND With a thief to the gallows; for though he go as softly as foot can fall, he thinks himself too soon there.

ORLANDO Who stays it still withal?

ROSALIND With lawyers in the vacation; for they sleep between term and term, and then they perceive not how time moves.

ORLANDO Where dwell you, pretty youth?

ROSALIND With this shepherdess, my sister, here in the

295 **detect** reveal

296 **swift foot of time** Compare *Sonnets* 19.6: 'And do whate'er thou wilt, swift-footed time'. The idea is proverbial (Tilley T327).

298 **divers** different (kinds of)

299 **ambles** moves at a smooth or easy pace

303 **trots hard** Hard, rapid trotting for any length of time is uncomfortable for the rider.

306 **seven year** Proverbial for a long period (Tilley Y25); *year* is one of the nouns which kept the singular form for the plural after numerals; it still does in some regions. Compare 'fathom' at 4.1.189.

312 **wasteful** causing the body to waste away (*OED, wasteful, a.* 6): earliest instance of *wasteful* in this sense cited by *OED*. It was believed that too much study could cause bodily and mental decay, leading especially to melancholy.

316 **softly** slowly. Proverbial (Tilley F560).

skirts of the forest, like fringe upon a petticoat.

ORLANDO Are you native of this place?

ROSALIND As the coney that you see dwell where she is kindled.

ORLANDO Your accent is something finer than you could purchase in so removed a dwelling.

ROSALIND I have been told so of many; but indeed an old religious uncle of mine taught me to speak, who was in his youth an inland man; one that knew courtship too well, for there he fell in love. I have heard him read many lectures against it, and I thank God I am not a woman, to be touched with so many giddy offences as he hath generally taxed their whole sex withal.

ORLANDO Can you remember any of the principal evils that he laid to the charge of women?

ROSALIND There were none principal; they were all like one another as halfpence are, every one fault seeming monstrous till his fellow-fault came to match it.

ORLANDO I prithee, recount some of them.

ROSALIND No. I will not cast away my physic but on those that are sick. There is a man haunts the forest that abuses our young plants with carving 'Rosalind' on their barks; hangs odes upon hawthorns and elegies on brambles; all, forsooth, deifying the name of Rosalind. If I could meet that fancy-monger, I would give him

346 deifying] F2; defying F1

323 **skirts of the forest** The edge of the forest (*OED, skirt, sb.* 8a *pl.*). Rosalind's irrepressible wit leads to her comparison, giving actresses a chance to express sudden dismay at having betrayed her gender.

325 **coney** rabbit

326 **kindled** born. Used especially for animals such as rabbits which produce numerous progeny. This line was often cut in performance because it was considered indelicate.

328 **removed** remote, secluded (*OED, removed, ppl. a.* 2†a): earliest instance of *removed* in this sense cited by *OED*

331 **inland** And therefore like Orlando, who is 'inland bred, | And know[s] some nurture' (2.7.96–7).

courtship (a) courtly behaviour (b) wooing

332 **there** at court

333 **lectures** admonitory speeches (*OED, lecture, sb.* 6): earliest instance of *lecture* in this sense cited by *OED*

339 **halfpence** Small silver coins of the same design and so noticeably alike among the various coins in circulation.

342–3 **I will ... sick** From Matthew 9: 12: 'The whole need not a physician, but they that are sick', or Mark 2: 17, which is similar. Proverbial (Tilley P271).

345 **elegies** love poems, rather than lamentations; any poems written in the elegaic metres used by the Roman poets (*OED, elegy,* 2): earliest instance of *elegy* in this sense cited by *OED*

347 **fancy-monger** dealer in love

some good counsel, for he seems to have the quotidian of love upon him.

ORLANDO I am he that is so love-shaked. I pray you, tell me your remedy.

ROSALIND There is none of my uncle's marks upon you. He taught me how to know a man in love, in which cage of rushes I am sure you are not prisoner.

ORLANDO What were his marks?

ROSALIND A lean cheek, which you have not; a blue eye and sunken, which you have not; an unquestionable spirit, which you have not; a beard neglected, which you have not—but I pardon you for that, for simply your having in beard is a younger brother's revenue. Then your hose should be ungartered, your bonnet unbanded, your sleeve unbuttoned, your shoe untied, and everything about you demonstrating a careless desolation. But you are no such man. You are rather point-device in your accoutrements, as loving yourself than seeming the lover of any other.

ORLANDO Fair youth, I would I could make thee believe I love.

ROSALIND Me believe it? You may as soon make her that you love believe it, which I warrant she is apter to do

354 are] F2; art F1

348 **quotidian** fever, recurring every day; one of the diseases said to be ruled over by the planet Venus and therefore a symptom of love. Among diseases related particularly to Venus listed by Robert Greene in his *Planetomachia* are 'lethargies, palsies . . . quotidian fevers, pains in the head' (*Life and Complete Works*, ed. A. B. Grosart, 15 vols. (1881–6), v. 103–4); 'love-shaked' in l. 350 could refer to palsy or to feverish shivering.

354 **cage of rushes** a cage easily broken out of. Latham notes that 'Rings plaited from rushes were exchanged by country sweethearts'.

356 **blue eye** eyes with dark rings under them owing to sleeplessness. Compare Silvius's sighing 'upon a midnight pillow' (2.4.24).

357 **unquestionable** not wishing to submit to questioning

359–60 **simply . . . beard . . . revenue** 'Your beard, being virtually non-existent, is like a younger brother's income.' (See 3.2.200.) The remark is general, but Rosalind is being somewhat daring here: she knows that Orlando is a youngest son, but there's no reason that Ganymede should.

361–4 All signs of the melancholy lover. Compare *Hamlet* 2.1.79–81: 'Lord Hamlet, with his doublet all unbraced, | No hat upon his head, his stockings fouled, | Ungartered, and down-gyvèd to his ankle'.

361–2 **bonnet unbanded** hat lacking a band around the crown. Hatbands were often highly ornamental.

363–4 **careless desolation** despondency past caring

365 **point-device . . . accoutrements** 'dressed with fastidious precision'. Rosalind is mocking him—he is too neat to be a lover.

than to confess she does. That is one of the points in the which women still give the lie to their consciences. But in good sooth, are you he that hangs the verses on the trees wherein Rosalind is so admired?

ORLANDO I swear to thee, youth, by the white hand of Rosalind, I am that he, that unfortunate he.

ROSALIND But are you so much in love as your rhymes speak?

ORLANDO Neither rhyme nor reason can express how much.

ROSALIND Love is merely a madness, and I tell you, deserves as well a dark house and a whip as madmen do; and the reason why they are not so punished and cured is that the lunacy is so ordinary that the whippers are in love too. Yet I profess curing it by counsel.

ORLANDO Did you ever cure any so?

ROSALIND Yes, one; and in this manner. He was to imagine me his love, his mistress; and I set him every day to woo me. At which time would I, being but a moonish youth, grieve, be effeminate, changeable, longing and liking, proud, fantastical, apish, shallow, inconstant, full of tears, full of smiles; for every passion something, and for no passion truly anything, as boys and women are for the most part cattle of this colour—would now like him, now loathe him; then entertain him, then forswear him; now weep for him, then spit at him, that I drave my suitor from his mad humour of love to a

372 **still** always
consciences innermost feelings of their hearts

379 **rhyme nor reason** The first instance of this emphatic phrase cited in *OED* dates from 1664 (*OED, rhyme, sb.* 3b), though it was proverbial, and Tilley's earliest exact example (R98) is dated 1540.

381 **Love . . . madness** A theme dealt with more in *Twelfth Night* than in *As You Like It; merely* = 'absolutely'. Proverbially, 'Love is a madness (lunacy)' (Dent L505.2).

382 **dark house and a whip** A current method of treatment for the insane, as seen in the trick played on Malvolio in *Twelfth Night* 4.2 and in Middleton and Rowley's *The Changeling* (1622) 4.3.61–2: 'we are there with our commanding pizzles [i.e. whips]'. The theory was that whipping drove out the devils causing the madness.

389 **moonish** changeable

394 **cattle** A contemptuous use (*OED, cattle, sb.* 7b). Compare Lodge fol. 15^{r}: 'You may see (quoth Ganymede) what mad cattle you women be, whose hearts sometimes are made of adamant that will touch with no impression; and sometime of wax that is fit for every form.' See Introduction, p. 22.
colour 'A horse of that (another) colour' (Tilley H665) is still proverbial.

living humour of madness, which was to forswear the full stream of the world and to live in a nook merely monastic. And thus I cured him, and this way will I take upon me to wash your liver as clean as a sound sheep's heart, that there shall not be one spot of love in't.

ORLANDO I would not be cured, youth.

ROSALIND I would cure you if you would but call me Rosalind and come every day to my cot, and woo me.

ORLANDO Now by the faith of my love, I will. Tell me where it is.

ROSALIND Go with me to it, and I'll show it you. And by the way you shall tell me where in the forest you live. Will you go?

ORLANDO With all my heart, good youth.

ROSALIND Nay, you must call me Rosalind.—Come, sister. Will you go? *Exeunt*

3.3 *Enter Touchstone the clown and Audrey, followed by Jaques*

TOUCHSTONE Come apace, good Audrey. I will fetch up your goats, Audrey. And how, Audrey, am I the man yet? Doth my simple feature content you?

3.3.0.1–2 *Enter . . . Jaques*] *Enter . . . at a Distance, observing them.* CAPELL; *Enter Clowne, Audrey, & Iaques.* F

398 **living** real, actual, not assumed

401 **liver** the seat of passions. A lover's liver was considered to be diseased. Compare Webster, *The Duchess of Malfi* 1.1.297–9: 'they are most luxurious | Will wed twice . . . | Their livers are more spotted | Than Laban's sheep.' Rosalind takes her simile from her assumed role as a shepherd.

406 **cot** cottage

412 From the 'pretty youth' of l. 321, eyed with some amusement, through the more seriously accepted 'fair youth' of l. 367, Ganymede has now become the 'good youth' taken on equal terms. In many productions Rosalind is startled here by a hearty clap on the shoulder or a slap on the back from Orlando which sends her staggering, but which gives opportunity for added vehemence to her closing demand of him.

3.3 The sophistication of the love game initiated by Rosalind is now thrown into sharp contrast by the earthy vulgarity of Touchstone's wooing of Audrey, who was frequently represented from at least 1825 until well into the twentieth century chewing on a turnip or, failing that, an apple. The scene was much mauled until Macready (1842) restored Jaques and Sir Oliver Martext to the action.

3 **feature** Used in the singular as well as the plural for the outline and form of the parts of the face and/or figure. Since *simple* could mean 'single', a bawdy implication is probable, but if Touchstone is asking if Audrey likes his sexual organ, she is too dim to realize it or too coy to admit it if she does, and asks him to be specific.

AUDREY Your features, Lord warrant us—what features?

TOUCHSTONE I am here with thee and thy goats as the most capricious poet honest Ovid was among the Goths.

JAQUES (*aside*) O knowledge ill-inhabited; worse than Jove in a thatched house.

TOUCHSTONE When a man's verses cannot be understood, nor a man's good wit seconded with the forward child, understanding, it strikes a man more dead than a great reckoning in a little room. Truly, I would the gods had made thee poetical.

AUDREY I do not know what 'poetical' is. Is it honest in deed and word? Is it a true thing?

TOUCHSTONE No, truly; for the truest poetry is the most feigning, and lovers are given to poetry; and what they swear in poetry it may be said, as lovers, they do feign.

AUDREY Do you wish, then, that the gods had made me poetical?

TOUCHSTONE I do, truly; for thou swearest to me thou art honest. Now if thou wert a poet, I might have some hope thou didst feign.

AUDREY Would you not have me honest?

18 it] COLLIER (*conj.* Mason); *not in* F

4 **warrant** protect

5 **thee** While Audrey is somewhat in awe of her suitor and uses the deferential 'you', Touchstone, after beginning with conversational 'you' turns to poetical *thee* and 'thou' (Abbott §231 (4)).

6 **capricious . . . Goths** Touchstone is making learned jokes which are lost on Audrey, but not on the eavesdropping Jaques. The Latin poet Ovid, author of *The Art of Love* and lover of the Emperor's daughter Julia, was considerably more *capricious* (lascivious, derived from Latin *caper* = a male goat) than *honest* (pure); he was exiled among the *Goths* (pronounced 'goats' by Elizabethans) who, he complained, could not appreciate his verse.

7–8 **Jove in a thatched house** Classical learning in Touchstone seems to Jaques as ludicrous as the king of the gods in the thatched house of Baucis and Philemon, who received the disguised Jove and Mercury into their humble cottage, of which the roof 'was thatched all with straw and fennish reed' (Ovid, 8, 806).

10 **a man's good wit . . . child** A *double entendre*: since *wit* = 'sexual organ' (see Appendix A), Touchstone is saying 'to have a man's sexual prowess not followed and so confirmed (*seconded*) by a spirited (*forward*) child'; he continues by turning *child* into *understanding*.

11–12 **great reckoning . . . little room** A bill disproportionately large in relation to the meal or accommodation. Though some have found references to Marlowe's death, allegedly in a quarrel over the reckoning in an inn room on 30 May 1593, and to the line 'infinite riches in a little room' in *The Jew of Malta* (1.1.37), neither the idea, nor the expression of it, is unique to Marlowe. The comic context here does not suggest such an allusion.

14 **honest** respectable

15 **true** honest, virtuous

17 **feigning** imaginative, with a play on the sense 'deceitful'

18 **feign** desire (compare l. 41) with a play on the sense 'pretend'

24 **honest** chaste

TOUCHSTONE No, truly, unless thou wert hard-favoured; for honesty coupled to beauty is to have honey a sauce to sugar.

JAQUES (*aside*) A material fool.

AUDREY Well, I am not fair, and therefore I pray the gods make me honest.

TOUCHSTONE Truly, and to cast away honesty upon a foul slut were to put good meat into an unclean dish.

AUDREY I am not a slut, though I thank the gods I am foul.

TOUCHSTONE Well, praised be the gods for thy foulness. Sluttishness may come hereafter. But be it as it may be, I will marry thee; and to that end I have been with Sir Oliver Martext, the vicar of the next village, who hath promised to meet me in this place of the forest, and to couple us.

JAQUES (*aside*) I would fain see this meeting.

AUDREY Well, the gods give us joy.

TOUCHSTONE Amen.—A man may, if he were of a fearful

25–7 The general tenor of Touchstone's lines suggests a bawdy implication, no longer clear, which hinges on 'sauce', as in 'saucy' = wanton, lascivious (*OED a.*[1] 2b). Compare *Measure* 2.4.45–6, where the word also occurs in relation to sweetness: 'Their saucy sweetness that do coin God's image | In stamps that are forbid.'

25 **hard-favoured** ugly. Audrey is not entirely without good looks.

26 **honesty coupled to beauty** Compare 1.2.36n. Dent compares 'Sweet meat must have sour sauce' (Tilley M839).

28 **material** (a) full of matter, sound information, or sense (*OED, material, adj.* †6) earliest instance of *material* in this sense cited by *OED* (b) unspiritual (*OED a.* 4b)

31 **foul** filthy

32 **good meat . . . dish** Touchstone turns a proverbial saying (Tilley M834) into a bawdy joke.

34 **foul** plain, not beautiful. Stage Audreys are sometimes mud-smirched and ragged, to score a humorously ironic point here. If, as Touchstone alleges, beauty cannot live with chastity, Audrey is grateful for not being beautiful.

37–8 **Sir Oliver Martext** *Sir* was used for priests who were not graduates; *Martext* recalls 'Martin Marprelate', the pamphleteer antagonist of the bishops (1588–9), but Sir Oliver shares only his prefix with the author(s) of the spirited tracts which issued from the secret Martinist press. He is one of the many ill-educated, inefficient and ill-paid Elizabethan country clergy. Stage Martexts often carry a large book which they eventually snap shut with rage, producing a cloud of dust. Knowles notes that after *As You Like It* 'stage characters with descriptive names of which the first element is *Mar-* became common' (p. 7) though the earliest he cites is Marall in *A New Way to Pay Old Debts* (1625).

42 **gods give us joy** Audrey may consider this phrase confirms their agreement to marry, particularly as Touchstone piously follows it with 'Amen'. Furness quotes Lyly, *Mother Bombie* l. 1880: 'God give you joy is a binder.' Compare *Much Ado* 2.1.315, where Beatrice says to the newly-matched Hero and Claudio, 'Cousins, God give you joy.'

43–57 Touchstone convinces himself by saying that cuckoldry is inevitable, since women bring infidelity as a dowry when they marry; cuckoldry is hateful, but inevitable, and affects the high born as well as the lowly. The single man, how-

heart, stagger in this attempt; for here we have no temple but the wood, no assembly but horn-beasts. But what though? Courage. As horns are odious, they are necessary. It is said many a man knows no end of his goods. Right: many a man has good horns, and knows no end of them. Well, that is the dowry of his wife, 'tis none of his own getting. Horns? Even so. Poor men alone? No, no; the noblest deer hath them as huge as the rascal. Is the single man therefore blessed? No. As a walled town is more worthier than a village, so is the forehead of a married man more honourable than the bare brow of a bachelor. And by how much defence is better than no skill, by so much is a horn more precious than to want.

Enter Sir Oliver Martext

Here comes Sir Oliver.—Sir Oliver Martext, you are well met. Will you dispatch us here under this tree, or shall we go with you to your chapel?

SIR OLIVER MARTEXT Is there none here to give the woman?

TOUCHSTONE I will not take her on gift of any man.

SIR OLIVER MARTEXT Truly she must be given, or the marriage is not lawful.

JAQUES (*coming forward*) Proceed, proceed. I'll give her.

TOUCHSTONE Good even, good Monsieur What-ye-call't.

50–1 Horns? Even so. Poor men alone?] GRANT WHITE; horns? even so—poor men alone? THEOBALD; hornes, euen so poore men alone. F

ever, is less honourable than the husband, who bears the cuckold's horns, just as a village is less worthy than a fortified town. The anti-feminism of the passage was standard material for jokes, as well as for more serious attacks, and based on the belief that all women, like Eve, fall easily into sin. Compare Benedick in *Much Ado* 5.4.122–3: 'There is no staff more reverend than one tipped with horn.'

45 **horn-beasts** the deer, goats and sheep of Arden. The allusion, of course, is to cuckold's horns.

46 **what though** what does it matter

47 **necessary** inevitable

47–8 **knows no end of his goods** doesn't know his wealth (because he has so much). Proverbial (Tilley E122).

52 **rascal** poorest deer in the herd

53 **walled town** Although the earliest instance in *OED* of 'hornwork' as a term for fortification is dated 1641, the connection between the cuckold's horns and such fortifications seems evident here.

more worthier The comparative is doubled for emphasis (Abbott §11).

57 **to want** to be lacking. H. J. Oliver sees 'another learned quibble because of "the horn of plenty" '.

66 **What-ye-call't** Touchstone delicately avoids saying 'Jakes' and thereby draws attention to the meaning of the name.

How do you, sir? You are very well met. God'ield you for your last company. I am very glad to see you—even a toy in hand here, sir.

Jaques removes his hat

Nay, pray be covered.

JAQUES Will you be married, motley?

TOUCHSTONE As the ox hath his bow, sir, the horse his curb, and the falcon her bells, so man hath his desires; and as pigeons bill, so wedlock would be nibbling.

JAQUES And will you, being a man of your breeding, be married under a bush, like a beggar? Get you to church, and have a good priest that can tell you what marriage is. This fellow will but join you together as they join wainscot; then one of you will prove a shrunk panel and, like green timber, warp, warp.

TOUCHSTONE I am not in the mind but I were better to be married of him than of another, for he is not like to marry me well, and not being well married, it will be a good excuse for me hereafter to leave my wife.

JAQUES Go thou with me, and let me counsel thee.

TOUCHSTONE

Come, sweet Audrey.
We must be married, or we must live in bawdry.

69.1 *Jaques . . . hat*] OXFORD; *not in* F   86 TOUCHSTONE] F2 (*Clo.*); *Ol⟨iuer⟩.* F1

67 'Thank you for your company when we last met, I am very glad to see you just now (*even*) when this trifling matter (*toy*) is under way.' Since he is holding Audrey by the *hand* Touchstone is also punning on *toy* = 'plaything'.

67 **God'ield you** God yield (= reward) you. A common expression of gratitude.

70 **covered** Expecting the marriage to go forward, Jaques as a mark of respect has removed his hat but Touchstone, taking the respect for himself, gives his condescending command, as to an inferior.

72 **bow** yoke. Knowles traces the idea to Ovid (*Tristia* 4.6.1–2): 'In time the peasant's bull submits to the plough, and bows his neck to the crooked yoke.'

73 **bells** Attached to the legs of a hunting falcon so that she can be found easily after bringing her quarry to ground.

74 **nibbling** (a) taking small bites (b) catching, capturing (*OED v.* 4)

79 **wainscot** panelling of oak or other wood **panel** (a) board, with a pun on (b) whore (*OED* † *parnel*: a harlot)

80 **warp** (a) twist (b) go wrong

81–4 Although many have followed Capell in marking this speech as an aside, it is more likely that Touchstone is replying directly to Jaques, who responds by offering to give further advice.

81 **I am not in the mind but** I am inclined to think that

83 **well . . . well** properly . . . advantageously

85 **thou . . . thee** The change from 'you' signals Jaques's taking on a paternal, advisory, role: 'Fathers almost always address their sons with *thou* in Shakespeare' (Abbott §231).

87 **bawdry** unchastity. Touchstone picks up the rhyme begun by Jaques.

Farewell, good Master Oliver. Not
O, sweet Oliver,
O, brave Oliver,
Leave me not behind thee
but
Wind away,
Begone, I say,
I will not to wedding with thee.

SIR OLIVER MARTEXT (*aside*) 'Tis no matter. Ne'er a fantastical knave of them all shall flout me out of my calling.

Exeunt

3.4 *Enter Rosalind as Ganymede and Celia as Aliena*

ROSALIND Never talk to me. I will weep.

CELIA Do, I prithee, but yet have the grace to consider that tears do not become a man.

ROSALIND But have I not cause to weep?

CELIA As good cause as one would desire; therefore weep.

ROSALIND His very hair is of the dissembling colour.

CELIA Something browner than Judas's. Marry, his kisses

89–90 O . . . thee] *as verse*, CAPELL; *as prose*, F
3.4.0.1 *Enter . . . Aliena*] *Enter Rosalind & Celia.* F

89 **O, sweet Oliver** A ballad 'O sweet Oliver, Leave me not behind thee' was entered in the Stationers' Register on 6 August 1584 and 'The answer of O sweet Oliver' on 20 August. On 1 August 1586 'O sweet Oliver altered to the scriptures' was entered. Touchstone may be saying that he'll not sing the first ballad, with its maiden's plea, but the second, which was probably the man's reply, rejecting the girl. The complete words have not yet been found, but they were sung to the tune known as 'Hunt's Up' or 'Peascod Time', both titles peculiarly appropriate to *As You Like It*, the second especially to Touchstone. (See Appendix B.)

93 **Wind** wend

96–7 **fantastical** odd, irrational, crazy. This is usually made to refer to Touchstone's behaviour, as the scene is often staged to end with his singing and dancing around Sir Oliver, sometimes twirling him round by his clerical gown (frequently ragged and fusty), or indulging in more extreme slapstick. In Glen Byam Shaw's 1952 Stratford production, the hapless Martext fell into a pool placed centre stage.

3.4 As well as showing an amusingly petulant side of Rosalind and her deliberately provoking Celia to talk of Orlando, this brief scene indicates the passing of time (l. 31) and, by its change to verse (l. 42), signals a shift in tone preparatory to the entry of Silvius and Phoebe in 3.5.

1–13 Set as verse in F, presumably because they are the last lines on p. 198 [R3^v] of the 'Comedies' section, at the bottom of the second column, and the compositor wanted to complete the page.

2 **grace** sense of propriety

6 **dissembling colour** The French called reddish hair 'dissembling hair'.

7 **Judas's** The betrayer of Christ (Matthew 26: 48–9) was sometimes depicted with red hair and beard during and after the Middle Ages and the tradition passed on to villains in general, persisting into modern times (e.g. the vindictive Hilarion in Coralli's ballet *Giselle* (1841) and the red-headed traitor among the schoolboys in Peter Weir's film *Dead Poets Society* (1989)).

are Judas's own children.

ROSALIND I'faith, his hair is of a good colour.

CELIA An excellent colour. Your chestnut was ever the only colour.

ROSALIND And his kissing is as full of sanctity as the touch of holy bread.

CELIA He hath bought a pair of cast lips of Diana. A nun of winter's sisterhood kisses not more religiously. The very ice of chastity is in them.

ROSALIND But why did he swear he would come this morning, and comes not?

CELIA Nay, certainly, there is no truth in him.

ROSALIND Do you think so?

CELIA Yes. I think he is not a pick-purse, nor a horse-stealer; but for his verity in love, I do think him as concave as a covered goblet, or a worm-eaten nut.

ROSALIND Not true in love?

CELIA Yes, when he is in. But I think he is not in.

ROSALIND You have heard him swear downright he was.

CELIA 'Was' is not 'is'. Besides, the oath of a lover is no stronger than the word of a tapster. They are both the confirmer of false reckonings. He attends here in the forest on the Duke your father.

ROSALIND I met the Duke yesterday, and had much question with him. He asked me of what parentage I was. I told him, of as good as he, so he laughed and let me go.

27 a] F2; *not in* F1

10 **Your** (not Rosalind's, but anyone's). Compare 3.2.52n.

13 **holy bread** At first, bread that was blessed after the Eucharist and given to those who had not been communicants; after the Reformation, bread used for the Eucharist. In the seventeenth century this line was obliterated by a Catholic priest who prepared a copy of F2 for English students at Valladolid in Spain.

14 **cast** (a) discarded (b) moulded (for a statue of Diana, goddess of chastity)

16 **ice of chastity** Proverbial (Tilley I1).

23 **concave** hollow

28 **tapster** bartender or keeper of a tavern; supposedly prone to overcharging customers when making up *reckonings* (bills)

31–2 **question** conversation. This is the only mention by the women of Rosalind's father, whom they set out to join, until they meet him in 5.4. Hartley Coleridge complains about Rosalind, but then excuses her: 'Rosalind is not a very dutiful daughter, but her neglecting so long to make herself known to her father, though not quite proper, is natural enough' (*Essays and Marginalia*, ed. Derwent Coleridge, 2 vols. (1851), ii. 140). The passage, as well as providing opportunity for a joke, reminds the audience of the continuing lives elsewhere in the forest and the success of Rosalind's disguise.

But what talk we of fathers when there is such a man as Orlando?

CELIA O that's a brave man. He writes brave verses, speaks brave words, swears brave oaths, and breaks them bravely, quite traverse, athwart the heart of his lover, as a puny tilter that spurs his horse but on one side breaks his staff, like a noble goose. But all's brave that youth mounts, and folly guides. Who comes here?

Enter Corin

CORIN
Mistress and master, you have oft enquired
After the shepherd that complained of love
Who you saw sitting by me on the turf,
Praising the proud disdainful shepherdess
That was his mistress.

CELIA Well, and what of him?

CORIN
If you will see a pageant truly played
Between the pale complexion of true love
And the red glow of scorn and proud disdain,
Go hence a little, and I shall conduct you,
If you will mark it.

ROSALIND (*to Celia*) O come, let us remove.
The sight of lovers feedeth those in love.
(*To Corin*) Bring us to this sight, and you shall say
I'll prove a busy actor in their play. *Exeunt*

39 puny] F (puisny)

36–40 **brave** fine, excellent. A general epithet of admiration or praise (*OED, brave, adj.* 3a): earliest instance of *brave* in this sense cited by *OED*.

38 **traverse** In knightly combat to strike with the lance obliquely so that it broke across, not directly against, the opponent's breast was considered unskilful and/or cowardly.

39 **puny** F's 'puisny', followed by most editors, is cited by *OED* under *puisne*: 'A. *adj.* †3. Small, insignificant, petty: now spelt PUNY.' First instance of *puisny* in this sense in *OED*.

tilter . . . one side a combatant in a joust who spurs his horse so that he avoids meeting his opponent head-on (and is thus a coward)

47 **pageant** show. Compare Robin Goodfellow in *Dream* speaking of the lovers, 'Shall we their fond pageant see?' (3.2.114).

48 **pale** The lover's sighs supposedly drained blood from the heart, leading to paleness.

49 **red glow** Scorn and disdain were aspects of choler, the hot, dry humour.

51 **remove** move off

54 Another reminiscence of *Dream*, where Robin Goodfellow, seeing that Bottom and his friends are about to rehearse a play, says: 'I'll be an auditor— | An actor, too, perhaps, if I see cause' (3.1.73–4).

3.5 *Enter Silvius and Phoebe*

SILVIUS

Sweet Phoebe, do not scorn me, do not, Phoebe.
Say that you love me not, but say not so
In bitterness. The common executioner,
Whose heart th'accustomed sight of death makes hard,
Falls not the axe upon the humbled neck
But first begs pardon. Will you sterner be
Than he that dies and lives by bloody drops?

Enter Rosalind as Ganymede, Celia as Aliena, and Corin, and stand aside

PHOEBE (*to Silvius*)

I would not be thy executioner.
I fly thee for I would not injure thee.
Thou tell'st me there is murder in mine eye.
'Tis pretty sure, and very probable,
That eyes, that are the frail'st and softest things,
Who shut their coward gates on atomies,
Should be called tyrants, butchers, murderers.
Now I do frown on thee with all my heart,
And if mine eyes can wound, now let them kill thee.
Now counterfeit to swoon, why now fall down;
Or if thou canst not, O, for shame, for shame,
Lie not, to say mine eyes are murderers.
Now show the wound mine eye hath made in thee.
Scratch thee but with a pin, and there remains
Some scar of it. Lean upon a rush,

3.5.7.1–2 *Enter . . . aside*] *Enter Rosalind, Celia, and Corin.* F

3.5 Touchstone's earthiness, the comical sentimentalism of Rosalind, and Celia's somewhat acerbic views on Orlando are now complemented by the exaggerated passions of Silvius and Phoebe. Shakespeare follows Lodge in the disposition of this scene but makes Phoebe even more heartless: Lodge's shepherdess says she does not scorn Montanus (Silvius) but hates love itself, a view she quickly changes when Ganymede appears.

5 **Falls not** does not let fall

7 **dies and lives** lives and works as an executioner till he dies. Compare Oliver's wish to 'live and die a shepherd' (5.2.12).

9 **for** because

11 **pretty sure** almost certain. Phoebe is launching into a sarcastic attack on the traditional poetic idea that looks can kill, an idea accepted easily enough by Orlando, who says Rosalind's 'frown might kill' him (4.1.100) and, later, that his heart is 'wounded . . . with the eyes of a lady' (5.2.24).

Theobald's emendation 'pretty,' which makes ''tis' refer to Phoebe's eye, has been almost universally accepted, but F's punctuation makes good sense in the context, which is concerned with the lethal properties of eyes rather than just their beauty. Shakespeare also uses 'pretty' as an adverb in *All's Well* 2.3.202–3: 'a pretty wise fellow'.

The cicatrice and capable impressure
Thy palm some moment keeps. But now mine eyes,
Which I have darted at thee, hurt thee not;
Nor I am sure there is no force in eyes
That can do hurt.

SILVIUS O dear Phoebe,
If ever—as that ever may be near—
You meet in some fresh cheek the power of fancy,
Then shall you know the wounds invisible
That love's keen arrows make.

PHOEBE But till that time
Come not thou near me. And when that time comes,
Afflict me with thy mocks, pity me not,
As till that time I shall not pity thee.

ROSALIND (*coming forward*)
And why, I pray you? Who might be your mother,
That you insult, exult, and all at once,
Over the wretched? What though you have no beauty—
As, by my faith, I see no more in you
Than without candle may go dark to bed—
Must you be therefore proud and pitiless?
Why, what means this? Why do you look on me?
I see no more in you than in the ordinary
Of nature's sale-work.—'Od's my little life,
I think she means to tangle my eyes, too.
No, faith, proud mistress, hope not after it.
'Tis not your inky brows, your black silk hair,

23 **cicatrice** a scar-like impression on the skin. This is the only example of the usage in *OED*.
capable impressure the impression the skin has been capable of receiving

30 **fancy** love. The prophetic irony of Silvius's lines gains immensely from Rosalind's presence on stage, seen by the audience, unseen by him and Phoebe.

36 **mother** (who must have lacked typical feminine gentleness to have such a cruel daughter)

38 **What though** even though

40 **go dark to bed** go to bed in the dark (so her bedfellow won't see how plain she is). It was (and is) proverbial that 'all cats are grey in the dark' (compare Tilley C50, J57); Rosalind is being even more sarcastically harsh to the attractive Phoebe than the shepherdess has earlier been to Silvius.

43–4 **ordinary . . . sale-work** the ordinary run of ready-made goods

44 **'Od's** God save

47 **inky . . . black** Since black hair and eyes were not the Petrarchan ideal of beauty, Rosalind is being sarcastic at the expense of Phoebe's fair beauty. Compare Sonnet 130.4: 'If hair be wires, black wires grow on her head'. Lodge's Phoebe has 'locks more whiter' than the wool of her sheep.

Your bugle eyeballs, nor your cheek of cream,
That can entame my spirits to your worship.
(*To Silvius*) You, foolish shepherd, wherefore do you follow her
Like foggy south, puffing with wind and rain?
You are a thousand times a properer man
Than she a woman. 'Tis such fools as you
That makes the world full of ill-favoured children.
'Tis not her glass but you that flatters her,
And out of you she sees herself more proper
Than any of her lineaments can show her.
(*To Phoebe*) But, mistress, know yourself; down on your knees
And thank heaven, fasting, for a good man's love;
For I must tell you friendly in your ear,
Sell when you can. You are not for all markets.
Cry the man mercy, love him, take his offer;
Foul is most foul, being foul to be a scoffer.—
So, take her to thee, shepherd. Fare you well.

PHOEBE
Sweet youth, I pray you chide a year together.
I had rather hear you chide than this man woo.

ROSALIND (*to Phoebe*) He's fallen in love with your foulness, (*to Silvius*) and she'll fall in love with my anger. If it be so, as fast as she answers thee with frowning looks, I'll sauce her with bitter words.
(*To Phoebe*) Why look you so upon me?

67–71] *as prose*, POPE; He's . . . she'll | Fall . . . fast | As . . . sauce | Her . . . me? F

48 **bugle** Bugles were tube-shaped beads, frequently black.

50 **wherefore** why

51 **south** south wind. Rosalind ridicules Silvius's sighs and tears.
puffing like the representation of a wind on a map

52 **properer** more handsome. Compare ll. 56 and 116.

55 **glass . . . flatters** The mirror's flattery was proverbial (Dent G132.1).

58 **know yourself** Proverbial (Tilley K175).

59 **fasting** Abstinence from all or specific kinds of food and drink is common to most known forms of religion; here Rosalind makes it an accompaniment to prayers of thanksgiving.

61 **markets** For Rosalind's crude advice, Shakespeare takes a proverbial image (Tilley M670) used by Lodge's Phoebe, who tells Montanus, 'if your market may be made no where else, home again' (fol. 48[v]).

63 **Foul . . . scoffer** ugliness is at its most ugly when it lies in being scornful

70 **sauce** rebuke smartly (*OED, sauce, v.* 4c): earliest instance of *sauce* in this sense cited by *OED*

PHOEBE

For no ill will I bear you.

ROSALIND

I pray you do not fall in love with me,
For I am falser than vows made in wine.
Besides, I like you not. If you will know my house,
'Tis at the tuft of olives, here hard by.
(*To Celia*) Will you go, sister? (*To Silvius*) Shepherd, ply
her hard.—
Come sister. (*To Phoebe*) Shepherdess, look on him
better,
And be not proud. Though all the world could see,
None could be so abused in sight as he.—
Come, to our flock. *Exeunt Rosalind, Celia, and Corin*

PHOEBE (*aside*)

Dead shepherd, now I find thy saw of might:
'Who ever loved that loved not at first sight?'

SILVIUS

Sweet Phoebe—

PHOEBE Ha, what sayst thou, Silvius?

SILVIUS Sweet Phoebe, pity me.

PHOEBE

Why, I am sorry for thee, gentle Silvius.

SILVIUS

Wherever sorrow is, relief would be.
If you do sorrow at my grief in love,
By giving love your sorrow and my grief
Were both extermined.

PHOEBE

Thou hast my love, is not that neighbourly?

74 **in wine** i.e. when drunk

75 **If . . . house** As Silvius already knows where Rosalind lives (ll. 108–9), she must be deliberately teasing Phoebe, perhaps hoping the shepherdess will be lured and so receive more scolding.

79 **see** see you

80 **abused** deceived

82 **Dead shepherd** Christopher Marlowe, who died 1 June 1593 after being stabbed in a Deptford tavern; l. 83 is a quotation from his 'Hero and Leander', published in 1598, and he is called a shepherd here perhaps owing to his lyric 'Come live with me and be my love' ('The Passionate Shepherd to his Love') published in 1599; but many elegies for dead poets were in the pastoral mode.

I find . . . might I understand the virtue of your saying

83 **Who ever . . . sight** Marlowe's phrasing of a proverbial idea (Tilley L426).

90 **extermined** exterminated, ended

91 **neighbourly** Matthew 19: 19: 'love thy neighbour as thyself'.

SILVIUS
I would have you.
PHOEBE Why, that were covetousness.
Silvius, the time was that I hated thee;
And yet it is not that I bear thee love.
But since that thou canst talk of love so well,
Thy company, which erst was irksome to me,
I will endure; and I'll employ thee, too.
But do not look for further recompense
Than thine own gladness that thou art employed.
SILVIUS
So holy and so perfect is my love,
And I in such a poverty of grace,
That I shall think it a most plenteous crop
To glean the broken ears after the man
That the main harvest reaps. Loose now and then
A scattered smile, and that I'll live upon.
PHOEBE
Know'st thou the youth that spoke to me erewhile?
SILVIUS
Not very well, but I have met him oft,
And he hath bought the cottage and the bounds
That the old Carlot once was master of.
PHOEBE
Think not I love him, though I ask for him.
'Tis but a peevish boy. Yet he talks well.
But what care I for words? Yet words do well
When he that speaks them pleases those that hear.
It is a pretty youth—not very pretty—
But sure he's proud; and yet his pride becomes him.
He'll make a proper man. The best thing in him
Is his complexion; and faster than his tongue

92 **covetousness** Phoebe continues to be biblical by accusing Silvius of breaking the tenth commandment. Mere neighbourly love is not enough for him.

94 **it is not that** the time has not yet arrived

96 **erst was** used to be

99 **thine** Knowles notes that this is the 'only adjectival use of this form of the pronoun in the play'. It is indicative of the deliberately self-conscious poeticism of dialogue between Phoebe and Silvius.

104 **broken ears** Silvius likens himself to the poor man in the Bible for whom the rich man leaves some ears of grain in the field after the harvest. See Leviticus 19: 9–10, 23: 22.

109 **Carlot** peasant churl. Perhaps a proper name, as *OED* records this as its only use, and it is in italics in F.

Did make offence, his eye did heal it up.
He is not very tall; yet for his years he's tall.
His leg is but so-so; and yet 'tis well.
There was a pretty redness in his lip,
A little riper and more lusty red
Than that mixed in his cheek. 'Twas just the difference
Betwixt the constant red and mingled damask.
There be some women, Silvius, had they marked him
In parcels as I did, would have gone near
To fall in love with him; but for my part,
I love him not, nor hate him not. And yet
Have I more cause to hate him than to love him,
For what had he to do to chide at me?
He said mine eyes were black, and my hair black,
And now I am remembered, scorned at me.
I marvel why I answered not again.
But that's all one. Omittance is no quittance.
I'll write to him a very taunting letter,
And thou shalt bear it. Wilt thou, Silvius?

SILVIUS
Phoebe, with all my heart.

PHOEBE
I'll write it straight.
The matter's in my head and in my heart.
I will be bitter with him, and passing short.
Go with me, Silvius. *Exeunt*

129 Have I] OXFORD (*conj.* Maxwell); I have F2; Haue F1

122 **lusty** lively, bright

124 **mingled damask** The comparison is between a pure red rose, such as *Rosa gallica* officinalis (the Apothecary's Rose) and *R. damascena* versicolor (York and Lancaster), whose colour varies from deep to very pale pink or some combination of the two. Compare Sonnet 130. 5–6: 'I have seen roses damasked, red and white, | But no such roses see I in her cheeks'.

126 **In parcels** in sections, feature by feature

129 **Have I** This reading is adopted by Wells and Taylor, from J. C. Maxwell's suggestion, as being 'preferable both metrically and on the grounds that omission is more likely within a line than initially' (*Textual Companion*, p. 393).

132 **I am remembered** I remember

134 **Omittance is no quittance** Proverbial (see Tilley F584): failure to do something (here Phoebe's not answering back) at a given time does not mean it will not be done later. Dent notes that the rhyming version, with *omittance* (instead of 'forbearance' or 'sufferance'), is unique to *As You Like It*.

139 **passing short** very curt. Phoebe's purpose is clear enough to the audience, if not to the besotted Silvius.

4.1 *Enter Rosalind as Ganymede, Celia as Aliena, and Jaques*

JAQUES I prithee, pretty youth, let me be better acquainted with thee.

ROSALIND They say you are a melancholy fellow.

JAQUES I am so. I do love it better than laughing.

ROSALIND Those that are in extremity of either are abominable fellows, and betray themselves to every modern censure worse than drunkards.

JAQUES Why, 'tis good to be sad and say nothing.

ROSALIND Why then, 'tis good to be a post.

JAQUES I have neither the scholar's melancholy, which is emulation, nor the musician's, which is fantastical, nor the courtier's, which is proud, nor the soldier's, which is ambitious, nor the lawyer's, which is politic, nor the lady's, which is nice, nor the lover's, which is all these; but it is a melancholy of mine own, compounded of many simples, extracted from many objects, and indeed the sundry contemplation of my travels, in which my often rumination wraps me in a most humorous sadness.

ROSALIND A traveller! By my faith, you have great reason to be sad. I fear you have sold your own lands to see

4.1.0.1–2 *Enter . . . Jaques*] *Enter Rosalind, and Celia, and Iaques.* F 1 be] F2; *not in* F1 7–18 my often] F2; by often F1

4.1 In this climactic scene, Jaques suffers another defeat, the love game reaches its height, along with Rosalind's verbal dexterity, and the rift between the cousins grows wider. Until Macready restored it in 1842, and even then frequently after, Jaques's encounter with Rosalind was omitted in performance and Celia entered only when called on at l. 112. These cuts were intended to heighten the love story.

2 **thee** Jaques's attempted familiarity is immediately rejected by Rosalind's 'you' in the next line.

5–6 **abominable** F's consistent spelling, 'abhominable' (the word occurs 18 times throughout), preserves the false etymology *ab homine* = 'away from man, beastly', so giving a second sense.

betray themselves lay themselves open

modern commonplace. Compare 2.7.156.

9 **post** A post is heavy ('sad') and dumb. Compare Orlando's calling himself 'a mere lifeless block' at 1.2.235.

11 **emulation** dislike of those felt to be superior

12 **proud** (a) haughty (b) lustful

13 **politic** crafty

14 **nice** (a) fastidious (b) wanton

16 **simples** ingredients

17 **sundry** consisting of different elements, of mixed composition

17–18 **my often** The preference of most editors over F's 'by often', which 'may be a simple typographical error since *b* and *m* lie in contiguous compartments of the compositor's case' (Knowles).

18 **often** frequent. Common as an adjective in the sixteenth and seventeenth centuries.

humorous odd; peculiar to Jaques himself

other men's. Then to have seen much and to have nothing is to have rich eyes and poor hands.

JAQUES Yes, I have gained my experience.

Enter Orlando

ROSALIND And your experience makes you sad. I had rather have a fool to make me merry than experience to make me sad—and to travel for it too!

ORLANDO
Good day and happiness, dear Rosalind.

JAQUES Nay then, goodbye an you talk in blank verse.

ROSALIND Farewell, Monsieur Traveller. Look you lisp, and wear strange suits; disable all the benefits of your own country; be out of love with your nativity, and almost chide God for making you that countenance you are, or I will scarce think you have swam in a gondola.

⌈*Exit Jaques*⌉

Why, how now, Orlando? Where have you been all this while? You a lover? An you serve me such another trick, never come in my sight more.

ORLANDO My fair Rosalind, I come within an hour of my promise.

ROSALIND Break an hour's promise in love! He that will divide a minute into a thousand parts and break but a part of the thousand part of a minute in the affairs of love, it may be said of him that Cupid hath clapped him o'th' shoulder, but I'll warrant him heart-whole.

34.1 *Exit Jaques*] DYCE; *after l.* 30 F2; *not in* F1

27 **travel** F's spelling, 'travail' (='work'), provides a pun.

30 To punish Orlando for being late, Rosalind ignores him and continues her derision of Jaques.
lisp speak with an affected foreign accent

31 **strange suits** foreign clothes—a favourite target for satirists
disable disparage

32 **nativity** birth as determining nationality

34 **swam** floated. Venice was believed to be the most licentious of places, and Elizabethan writing is filled with references to its iniquities.

34.1 F has no exit for Jaques, F2 supplies it after 'blank verse', which means that Rosalind speaks to his departing back; directors usually follow Dyce's suggestion, as here.

42 **thousand** thousandth. The form with the *th* ending was not used until the sixteenth century, during which the old form was still current.

43–4 **Cupid . . . shoulder** Although scholars dispute the detailed meaning of this passage, the general sense is that the lover has been touched by love, but not seriously. Cupid has only given him a slap on the shoulder, not driven an arrow into his heart.

44 **heart-whole** having the affections free; with the heart unengaged (*OED, heart-whole, a.* 2); earliest instance of *heart-whole* in this sense cited by *OED*

ORLANDO Pardon me, dear Rosalind.

ROSALIND Nay, an you be so tardy, come no more in my sight. I had as lief be wooed of a snail.

ORLANDO Of a snail?

ROSALIND Ay, of a snail; for though he comes slowly, he carries his house on his head—a better jointure, I think, than you make a woman. Besides, he brings his destiny with him.

ORLANDO What's that?

ROSALIND Why, horns, which such as you are fain to be beholden to your wives for. But he comes armed in his fortune, and prevents the slander of his wife.

ORLANDO Virtue is no hornmaker, and my Rosalind is virtuous.

ROSALIND And I am your Rosalind.

CELIA It pleases him to call you so; but he hath a Rosalind of a better leer than you.

ROSALIND Come, woo me, woo me, for now I am in a holiday humour, and like enough to consent. What would you say to me now an I were your very, very Rosalind?

ORLANDO I would kiss before I spoke.

ROSALIND Nay, you were better speak first, and when you were gravelled for lack of matter you might take occasion to kiss. Very good orators, when they are out, they

55 beholden] F (beholding)

48–56 Some or all of these lines have frequently been omitted in performance, being considered too bawdy, too obscure, or both.

49 **snail** The references are proverbial (Tilley S579, S580).

50 **jointure** property held for the joint use of husband and wife and, by extension, for the life of the wife after the husband's death. Rosalind here betrays her knowledge that Orlando is a younger brother (see 3.2.360).

51 **destiny** 'Cuckolds come by destiny' was proverbial (Tilley C889). Compare 3.3.46–7.

54 **fain** glad under the circumstances

56 **prevents** forestalls or anticipates. Because, even before he marries, the snail has horns, the sign of the cuckold, no one will be able to say, when he does marry, that his wife has been unfaithful.

60–1 Sometimes taken by actresses as a warning that Rosalind is letting her disguise slip.

60 **It pleases . . . so** Dent suggests a proverbial allusion (P407.1).

61 **leer** Celia is making a complex pun, since *leer* could mean (a) features, or complexion—referring to Rosalind's disguising tan (b) the brown colour of sheep or cattle—appropriate for a shepherd boy (c) flank or loin—alluding to Ganymede's true sex. The last meaning is picked up by Rosalind in l. 77.

64 **an** if

68 **gravelled** stuck, like a boat run aground; unable to think of something to say

69 **out** at a loss for words

will spit; and for lovers, lacking—God warr'nt us—matter, the cleanliest shift is to kiss.

ORLANDO How if the kiss be denied?

ROSALIND Then she puts you to entreaty, and there begins new matter.

ORLANDO Who could be out, being before his beloved mistress?

ROSALIND Marry, that should you if I were your mistress, or I should think my honesty ranker than my wit.

ORLANDO What, of my suit?

ROSALIND Not out of your apparel, and yet out of your suit. Am not I your Rosalind?

ORLANDO I take some joy to say you are because I would be talking of her.

ROSALIND Well, in her person I say I will not have you.

ORLANDO Then in mine own person I die.

ROSALIND No, faith; die by attorney. The poor world is almost six thousand years old, and in all this time there was not any man died in his own person, videlicet, in a

70 warr'nt] F (warne)

70 **warr'nt** save, defend. Wilson suggests F's 'warne' is a misreading of 'warn'd', which is a dialect pronunciation of 'warrant'. 'God defend that lovers should run out of things to say to each other.'

71 **cleanliest** cleverest, smartest
shift expedient, best thing to do

78 **honesty ranker . . . wit** Rosalind naughtily plays on 'out' = 'uncovered, exposed', following on from Celia's use of 'leer' in l. 61, and leads Orlando to a trap into which he falls at l. 79. The overt meaning of ll. 77–8 is: 'You would be at a loss if I were your mistress, otherwise I would consider my plain dealing (*honesty*) greater (*ranker*) than my cleverness (*wit*)'; the secondary meaning, which Orlando perceives, is: 'If I were your mistress you would be out of your clothes and ready for love-making, or else I would think my chastity (*honesty*) more erotically inclined (see *OED, rank, a.* †13) than my sexual organ (*wit*).' (See Appendix A.) These lines were cut from this otherwise fairly intact scene in *Love in a Forest*, and have been cut from many productions of *As You Like It* since.

79, 81 **suit** Rosalind scores off Orlando by playing on *suit* = (a) clothes (b) a petition. In F the second *suit* begins a new line and is followed by a colon, then 'Am' begins the next line. The intervening blank may indicate a deliberate deletion.

86 **by attorney** by proxy

87 **almost six thousand** Rosalind's figure comes from biblical chronology, by which it was calculated that about 4,000 years elapsed between the creation of the world and the birth of Christ. St Augustine, for example, says in *The City Of God* (1497), 'less than 6,000 years, according to scriptural evidence, have passed since [man] first came into existence' (tr. Henry Bettenson (Harmondsworth, 1972), p. 486). (The calculations of Archbishop Ussher (published 1650–4) giving 4004 BC as the date of the creation of the world, became standard.) The related belief, that world history was divided into seven ages, was first stated by Augustine in *De Genesi contra Manicheos* (I, 23) and became the accepted way of seeing history. Compare 2.7.139–66n.

88 **videlicet** that is to say, namely

love-cause. Troilus had his brains dashed out with a Grecian club, yet he did what he could to die before, and he is one of the patterns of love. Leander, he would have lived many a fair year though Hero had turned nun if it had not been for a hot midsummer night, for, good youth, he went but forth to wash him in the Hellespont and, being taken with the cramp, was drowned; and the foolish chroniclers of that age found it was Hero of Sestos. But these are all lies. Men have died from time to time, and worms have eaten them, but not for love.

ORLANDO I would not have my right Rosalind of this mind, for I protest her frown might kill me.

ROSALIND By this hand, it will not kill a fly. But come, now I will be your Rosalind in a more coming-on disposition; and ask me what you will, I will grant it.

ORLANDO Then love me, Rosalind.

ROSALIND Yes, faith, will I, Fridays and Saturdays and all.

ORLANDO And wilt thou have me?

ROSALIND Ay, and twenty such.

ORLANDO What sayst thou?

ROSALIND Are you not good?

ORLANDO I hope so.

ROSALIND Why then, can one desire too much of a good thing? (*To Celia*) Come, sister, you shall be the priest and marry us.—Give me your hand, Orlando.—What do you say, sister?

89 **Troilus** The son of King Priam of Troy who loved and was betrayed by Cressida; he was killed by Achilles with a spear or a sword, not by a club.

91 **Leander** Drowned while on his regular nightly swim across the Hellespont to be with Hero of Sestos. His cramp is as much Rosalind's invention as the club which killed Troilus. These doomed classical lovers were well-known literary subjects. Marlowe's *Hero and Leander* was completed by George Chapman and published in 1598; their story was burlesqued by Nashe in *Lenten Stuff* (1599) and again by Jonson in *Bartholomew Fair* (1614).

96 **found** discovered (and declared his drowning was because of). Used in the legal sense, 'To determine and declare (an offence) to have been committed (*obs.*)' (*OED, find, v.* 17†b).

105 **Fridays and Saturdays** fast days. Rosalind will make no exceptions, will take no time off from loving him, even for fast days: by law no flesh was to be partaken of on Fridays, Saturdays, ember days, vigils or in Lent (2 & 3 Edward VI, c. 19 (1548)), so she implies that she will not abstain from love-making, either.

111–12 Dent points out that while a misinterpretation of the proverb 'The more common a good thing is the better' (Tilley T142) supports Rosalind, a correct interpretation of a commoner proverb, 'Too much of one thing is good for nothing' (Tilley T158) refutes her.

113 **marry** In Lodge it is Alinda (Celia) who suggests the mock marriage. Shakespeare's change typically strengthens Rosalind's role and further complicates her relationships with Celia.

ORLANDO (*to Celia*) Pray thee, marry us.

CELIA I cannot say the words.

ROSALIND You must begin, 'Will you, Orlando'—

CELIA Go to. Will you, Orlando, have to wife this Rosalind?

ORLANDO I will.

ROSALIND Ay, but when?

ORLANDO Why now, as fast as she can marry us.

ROSALIND Then you must say, 'I take thee, Rosalind, for wife.'

ORLANDO I take thee, Rosalind, for wife.

ROSALIND I might ask you for your commission; but I do take thee, Orlando, for my husband. There's a girl goes before the priest; and certainly a woman's thought runs before her actions.

ORLANDO So do all thoughts; they are winged.

ROSALIND Now tell me how long you would have her after you have possessed her?

ORLANDO For ever and a day.

ROSALIND Say a day without the ever. No, no, Orlando; men are April when they woo, December when they wed. Maids are May when they are maids, but the sky changes when they are wives. I will be more jealous of thee than a Barbary cock-pigeon over his hen, more

116 **words** Celia is stalling because she knows, as Rosalind does, that a declaration of an intent to marry by two people before a third constituted a binding contract, *per verba de praesenti*; compare *The Duchess of Malfi* 1.1.475–94, where the Duchess marries Antonio in this way. In his *Treatise of Spousals* (1686 but written before 1623), Henry Swinburne wrote, 'that woman, and that man, which have contracted spousals *de praesenti* ... cannot by any Agreement dissolve those Spousals, but are reported for very Husband and Wife in respect of the Substance, and indissoluble Knot of Matrimony' (p. 13). Ann Jennalie Cook has a somewhat contradictory discussion of spousals and of this scene in *Making a Match* (Princeton, 1991), pp. 154–5, 222–3.

118 **Go to** An expression of exasperation, and, in this case, resignation. Celia gives up and begins to paraphrase the marriage service.

119–24 'That Rosalind knows precisely what she is doing is plain when she rejects the grammatically ambiguous "I will" and insists upon the vital present tense' (Latham, p. 135).

121 **fast** (a) quickly (b) bindingly

125 **commission** authority (in taking me for your wife). Even though Orlando is unaware that he is dealing with the real Rosalind, she knows she has the real Orlando by the hand. Helen Faucit's reactions when playing this scene are discussed in the Introduction, p. 59.

126–7 **goes ... priest** answers the question before the priest has asked it

129 **they are winged** 'As swift as thought' was proverbial (Tilley T240).

132 **For ... day** Proverbial (Tilley D74).

137 **Barbary cock-pigeon** Barb pigeons were thought to have been introduced from Barbary (northern Africa) and their place of origin suggested Muslim watchfulness over wives. In *The Illustrated Book of Pigeons* (ed. L. Wright, 1874–6), Robert

clamorous than a parrot against rain, more new-fangled than an ape, more giddy in my desires than a monkey. I will weep for nothing, like Diana in the fountain, and I will do that when you are disposed to be merry. I will laugh like a hyena, and that when thou art inclined to sleep.

ORLANDO But will my Rosalind do so?

ROSALIND By my life, she will do as I do.

ORLANDO O, but she is wise.

ROSALIND Or else she could not have the wit to do this. The wiser, the waywarder. Make the doors upon a woman's wit, and it will out at the casement. Shut that, and 'twill out at the key-hole. Stop that, 'twill fly with the smoke out at the chimney.

ORLANDO A man that had a wife with such a wit, he might

142 hyena] F (Hyen)

Fulton remarks, 'It is difficult to avoid the conclusion that [Shakespeare] was at heart, if not in practice, a fancier, his intimate knowledge of them [i.e. pigeons], comes out in so many ways' (p. 7), causing Furness to expostulate, 'Is there left in the world any human trade, profession or pursuit wherein Shakespeare is not claimed as a fellow-craftsman? Did any of us ever think we should live to see him hailed as a "pigeon-fancier"?'

138 **against** before, and usually, in expectation of. In the Adelaide Hills region of South Australia, black cockatoos flying overhead screeching are said to presage rain.

new-fangled easily taken by novelty

139 **giddy** frivolous, fickle

140–1 **weep . . . merry** 'When the husband is sad (merry) the wife will be merry (sad)' was proverbial (Tilley H839).

140 **Diana** A not uncommon figure in fountains, appropriate here as goddess of the chase and, as Lucina, of marriage and childbirth. Fountains were said to weep, as in Dowland's song, 'Weep you no more, sad fountains'; a fountain erected in Cheapside in 1576 had a Diana with water springing from her breasts, not her eyes, and there is no need to think Shakespeare had this, or any other, particular fountain in mind, as Malone asserted he did.

142 **hyena** Proverbial (Tilley H844). A hyena's bark resembles a laugh. Onions claims that F's *hyen* is a 'late instance of this form, otherwise only 14th cent.' (*A Shakespeare Glossary* (Oxford, 2nd edn., 1919; repr. 1975)); if this is so, then *hyen* could be either a mistake or a printer's dodge to justify a tight line by dropping a letter. However Shakespeare may be recalling Golding's translation of Ovid, 15, 450–2, where the word not only has the disyllabic form, but is used in a particularly relevant context: 'Much rather may we wonder at the *Hyën*, if we please, | To see how interchangeably it one while doth remain | A female, and another while becometh male again.' Rosalind herself is the *hyena* and is even now laughing at Orlando, who is 'inclined to sleep' and, being so, is unaware of her disguise.

148 **Make** shut, close

152–61 Many acting versions omit these lines. Kitty Clive, acting Celia at Drury Lane, first sang the Cuckoo Song from *L.L.L.* at this point (after l. 151), probably on 20 December 1740. It was later taken over by actresses playing Rosalind, who continued to sing it into the twentieth century, although Macready (1842) cut it, and was praised for doing so. Nineteenth-century critics deplored the practice as being quite out of place (though Hazlitt could enjoy an actress playing Rosalind singing it), but it is probable that

say 'Wit, whither wilt?'

ROSALIND Nay, you might keep that check for it till you met your wife's wit going to your neighbour's bed.

ORLANDO And what wit could wit have to excuse that?

ROSALIND Marry, to say she came to seek you there. You shall never take her without her answer unless you take her without her tongue. O, that woman that cannot make her fault her husband's occasion, let her never nurse her child herself, for she will breed it like a fool.

ORLANDO For these two hours, Rosalind, I will leave thee.

ROSALIND Alas, dear love, I cannot lack thee two hours.

ORLANDO I must attend the Duke at dinner. By two o'clock I will be with thee again.

ROSALIND Ay, go your ways, go your ways. I knew what you would prove; my friends told me as much, and I thought no less. That flattering tongue of yours won

the eighteenth century recognized the bawdy of the lines and replaced them with a song about the same subject, cuckoldry. Dora (Dorothy) Jordan, who played Rosalind from 1787 to 1814, held up two fingers, representing cuckold's horns, over Orlando's head while singing 'Cuckoo' in his ear with a gleeful smile.

153 **'Wit . . . wilt?'** Phrase addressed to a person whose tongue is running away with him (*OED, wit, sb.* 2e): earliest instance of *wit* in this sense cited by *OED*, though Wilson cites an example of 1575. Compare 1.2.52–3.

154–5 **you . . . bed** 'You should keep that rebuke until you meet your wife on her way to sleep with your neighbour.' (Compare 4.1.87n. and Appendix A.) Through its sound, *neighbour* is linked with adultery; compare Jeremiah 5: 7–8: 'yet they committed adultery . . . They rose up in the morning like fed horses: for every man neighed after his neighbour's wife' (Geneva Bible).

156 **And . . . that?** And what wisdom could a man have to pardon such infidelity?

157–9 Rosalind turns the tables by changing the sex of the hypothetical neighbour: the clever wife on the way to her neighbour's bed will tell her suspicious husband that she is out looking for *him* because she suspects him of adultery with the neighbour's wife.

157–8 **seek . . . answer** 'A woman's answer is never to seek' was proverbial (Tilley W670).

159–61 **that woman . . . fool** 'If a woman isn't clever enough to turn her errors into an excuse for attacking her husband, then she shouldn't be allowed to suckle her own child, because it will imbibe foolishness with its mother's milk and grow up a fool like herself.' Rosalind's mind is running on maternal lines again. There is also a sexual pun on 'fault' = 'crack': 'The woman who cannot make her sexual availability essential to her husband (so that he does not need to look elsewhere) is a fool.'

160 **occasion** *OED* cites this as its last example for 'The action of causing or occasioning. Also *transf.* That which is caused or occasioned' (*sb*[1]3†d); however it seems rather to exemplify 'That which one has need to do; necessary business; a matter, piece of business, business engagement' (*sb.*[1] †6), with a pun on 'Opportunity of attacking, of fault-finding, or of giving or taking offence; a "handle" against a person' (*sb.*[1] 1a†. In early use). Some eighteenth-century acting editions emend to 'accusation', which is included in Hanmer's edition (1743).

163 Some actresses play this line as Rosalind's being taken off guard and revealing her emotions.

164 **dinner** The main meal of the day, begun around noon.

me. 'Tis but one cast away, and so, come, death! Two o'clock is your hour?

ORLANDO Ay, sweet Rosalind.

ROSALIND By my troth, and in good earnest, and so God mend me, and by all pretty oaths that are not dangerous, if you break one jot of your promise or come one minute behind your hour, I will think you the most pathetical break-promise, and the most hollow lover, and the most unworthy of her you call Rosalind that may be chosen out of the gross band of the unfaithful. Therefore beware my censure, and keep your promise.

ORLANDO With no less religion than if thou wert indeed my Rosalind. So, adieu.

ROSALIND Well, Time is the old justice that examines all such offenders; and let Time try. Adieu. *Exit Orlando*

CELIA You have simply misused our sex in your love-prate. We must have your doublet and hose plucked over your head, and show the world what the bird hath done to her own nest.

ROSALIND O coz, coz, coz, my pretty little coz, that thou didst know how many fathom deep I am in love. But it cannot be sounded. My affection hath an unknown bottom, like the Bay of Portugal.

183 *Exit Orlando*] ROWE; *Exit* F

169 **but one cast away** 'only one poor girl rejected and abandoned (it's nothing to you, to me it may as well be death)'. If l. 163 above is interpreted as previously described, then here Rosalind can be mock melodramatic to cover up her previous genuine emotional response.

172–3 **God mend me** God make me better than I am. Proverbial (Dent G173.1). Compare 5.3.45.

173–4 **dangerous** Profanity, like blasphemy, was punishable by ecclesiastical courts, being considered an offence against God and religion. It was made a temporal offence in 1623 (21 James I. c. 20), though by an act of 1605 to restrain the abuses of players (3 James I. c. 21), anyone in a play 'jestingly or profanely' speaking the name of God, Christ, the Holy Ghost or the Trinity was liable to a fine of ten pounds.

176 **pathetical** pitiable, wretched. In Lodge, Phoebe measures the passions of Montanus 'with a coy disdain' and triumphs in 'the poor shepherd's pathetical humours' (fol. 47^{v}).

178 **gross** large

183 **let Time try** Proverbial (Dent (T308.2).

184 **misused** abused

186–7 **bird . . . nest** Proverbial (Tilley B377). The passage is discussed in the Introduction, p. 13.

189 **fathom** A measure of six feet (1.83 m.), used in taking marine soundings. *Fathom* is among the nouns of measure that kept the singular form for the plural, like 'year' at 3.2.306, 5.2.58.

191 **Bay of Portugal** That part of the sea off the coast of Portugal between Oporto and the Cape of Cintra; within 40 miles (64 km.) of the shore the water reaches a depth of 1,400 fathoms (2,562 m.).

CELIA Or rather bottomless, that as fast as you pour affection in, it runs out.

ROSALIND No, that same wicked bastard of Venus, that was begot of thought, conceived of spleen, and born of madness, that blind rascally boy that abuses everyone's eyes because his own are out, let him be judge how deep I am in love. I'll tell thee, Aliena, I cannot be out of the sight of Orlando. I'll go find a shadow and sigh till he come.

CELIA And I'll sleep. *Exeunt*

4.2 *Enter Jaques and Lords dressed as foresters*

JAQUES Which is he that killed the deer?

193 it] F2; in F1

4.2.0.1 *Lords dressed as foresters*] *Lords, in the habit of foresters* MALONE; *Lords, Forresters* F

192–3 'You do not retain the affection people give you.' Celia is now charging Rosalind with being fickle.

194 **bastard** Cupid, child of Venus by Mars, Jupiter or Mercury, not by her husband, Vulcan; some classical sources say he was the son of Iris, the rainbow goddess, by the West Wind.

195 **thought** Steevens suggested 'melancholy', but several meanings are possible; 'imagination' is as good as any and better than some.

spleen sudden impulse, caprice

197 **eyes** The winged child with bow and arrows depicted in classical art had full use of his eyes, blindness being added to his attributes in the Middle Ages. Irwin Panofsky quotes from a didactic poem of 1213 in which Love says, 'I am blind and I make blind' (*Studies in Iconology* (New York, 1962), p. 105). In *The Third Part of the Countess of Pembroke's Ivychurch* (1592), Abraham Fraunce moralizes a typical representation: 'Cupido . . . was pictured as a boy: lovers are childish; blind: they see no reason; naked: they cannot conceal their passion; winged: love flieth into our eyes and souls, and lovers are light, as feathers' (p. 46). Shakespeare refers to love's blindness at least seventeen times in his plays and poems, four times in *Two Gentlemen* alone.

199 **shadow** Pastoral landscapes abound in shady spots for lovers, both sad and happy. In Lodge, Montanus tells Coridon of his love for Phoebe in a 'shadowed' arbour (fol. 16^{r}) and Rosader reads Ganymede his sonnet to Rosalynde 'upon a green bank, shadowed with fig trees' (fol. 32^{r}); Sidney's Astrophil and Stella meet 'In a grove most rich with shade' (Eighth Song), and Philon, a shepherd bereft of his love in one of William Byrd's *Songs of Sundry Natures* (1589), plays his pipe 'beside a crystal fountain | In shadow of a great oak tree'.

201 **sleep** Perhaps Celia is disgruntled and wants to escape from the situation.

4.2 The main purpose of this 'noisy scene', as Johnson called it, is to fill the passing of time before Orlando returns to Rosalind. It combines elements of animal rites, such as the horn-dance at Abbot's Bromley in Staffordshire, the triumphal presentation to the lord of the successful hunter, who is given the horns, and (sometimes) other parts of the quarry, and the pervasive allusiveness to cuckoldry, which aptly follows the betrothal and marriage-talk of 4.1.

Hunting scenes were currently popular on the Elizabethan stage, some characters, like Falstaff in *Merry Wives* (1597) and Friar Tuck in Munday's *Death of Robert Earl of Huntingdon* (1598), either being crowned with horns or carrying them. Although included in *Love in a Forest*, the scene was cut from all other eighteenth-century acting versions. Despite Macready's restoring it in 1842, many have since omitted it. When included, it can provide for spectacle, song, and dance. (See Appendix B.)

0.1 There may be foresters as well as lords with Jaques, but as the F direction at 2.1

FIRST LORD Sir, it was I.

JAQUES (*to the others*) Let's present him to the Duke like a Roman conqueror. And it would do well to set the deer's horns upon his head for a branch of victory. Have you no song, forester, for this purpose?

SECOND LORD Yes, sir.

JAQUES Sing it. 'Tis no matter how it be in tune, so it make noise enough.

Music

LORDS (*sing*)

What shall he have that killed the deer?
His leather skin and horns to wear.
Then sing him home; the rest shall bear
  This burden.
Take thou no scorn to wear the horn;
It was a crest ere thou wast born.

2 FIRST LORD] I *Lord* MALONE; *Lord* F   7 SECOND LORD] 2 *Lord* MALONE; *Lord* F   9.1 10 *Music* | LORDS (*sing*)] This edition; Musicke, Song. F   12–13 Then . . . bear | This burden] HALLIWELL (Then . . . bear— | This burden.); *as one line*, F

refers to '*two or three Lords like Forresters*' (in stage terms 'like' = 'dressed as'), and as Jaques addresses a question to a forester when the speech prefix gives the reply to a lord (4.2.7), the distinction seems exiguous, if it exists at all.

5 **branch** In classical times, victors in many kinds of contests were crowned with wreaths made from branches of laurel; Jaques is also punning on the 'branch' of deer antlers, and, inevitably, cuckold's horns.

9.1 ***Music*** F's single word is perhaps, as E. Brennecke suggests, 'a signal to a lutenist . . . to give the proper pitch' (*Musical Times*, 93 (1952), 347) rather than a direction for accompaniment; with minor differences in some words and the omission of ll. 12–13, the song was set to music in *Catch that Catch Can, or A Choice Collection of Catches, Rounds, & Canons* (1652, p. 30), compiled by John Hilton. (See Appendix B.)

11 **skin and horns** Trophies of the chase presented to the successful hunter. In Lodge, Rosalynde, discovering Rosader melancholy, says, 'What news Forester? hast thou wounded some deer and lost him in the fall? Care not man for so small a loss, thy fees was but the skin, the shoulder, and the horns: 'tis hunter's luck, to aim fair and miss' (fol. 27^{v}).

13 **burden** refrain. Theobald, whose emendation has been widely followed, made '*The rest . . . burden*' a stage direction on the grounds that 'Then sing him home' is a refrain sung by all, the remainder by a soloist. This arrangement may derive from *Love in a Forest*, in which 'Then . . . home' is repeated twice at the end, with a stage direction '[the Burthen by all.]'. In *Tempest*, however, 'And, sweet sprites, bear | The Burden' (1.2.382–3) is plainly part of a song, not a stage direction.

Stage practice, which varies widely, has included singing, both accompanied and unaccompanied, by a soloist and chorus, and by the whole group (though it is inappropriate for Jaques, being melancholy, to sing); *burden* has also been taken to be the victorious hunter, borne on his fellows' shoulders, the slain deer, or the horns, the implication of the last being that all men are inevitably cuckolds.

14 **Take . . . scorn** do not disdain. 'He wears the horns' was proverbial (Tilley H625).

Thy father's father wore it,
And thy father bore it.
The horn, the horn, the lusty horn
Is not a thing to laugh to scorn. *Exeunt*

4.3 *Enter Rosalind as Ganymede and Celia as Aliena*

ROSALIND How say you now? Is it not past two o'clock? And here much Orlando.

CELIA I warrant you, with pure love and troubled brain he hath ta'en his bow and arrows and is gone forth to sleep.

⌈*Enter Silvius*⌉

Look who comes here.

SILVIUS (*to Rosalind*)
My errand is to you, fair youth.
My gentle Phoebe did bid me give you this.

He offers Rosalind a letter, which she takes and reads

I know not the contents, but as I guess
By the stern brow and waspish action
Which she did use as she was writing of it,
It bears an angry tenor. Pardon me;
I am but as a guiltless messenger.

ROSALIND
Patience herself would startle at this letter,

4.3.0.1 *Enter Rosalind . . . as Aliena*] *Enter Rosalind and Celia.* F 8.1–2 *He . . . reads*] *not in* F

18 **lusty** (a) flourishing (cuckoldry thrives) (b) licentious (being symbolic of the wife's lust)

4.3 The complications of love are now given new impetus, with Rosalind's scolding of Silvius, Oliver's tale of his salvation through Orlando's redemptive love, and his and Celia's love at first sight. Shakespeare draws on Lodge for the main incidents, while reversing their order, but invents Rosalind's fainting, the comic and dramatic climax of the scene.

1–6 Set as verse in F.

5.1 F places Silvius's entrance awkwardly in mid-sentence, after 'brain,' which ends a line. It is, however consistent with several other entrances which are made two and a half lines before the characters speak, e.g. Oliver (1.1.23.1), Duke Frederick (1.3.33.1), Orlando (4.1.24.1) and William (5.1.9.1). The implication is that they first advance to those already on stage.

4–5 **ta'en his bow . . . sleep** gone off for a nap. A colloquialism, not an indication that Orlando in fact has bow and arrows. Proverbial (Dent B564.1); Wilson gives other examples from Greene and Nashe.

8 F2's regularization of this eleven-syllable line by the deletion of 'did' has been widely followed; l. 11 also has eleven syllables, however, and as there the metre can be accommodated by slurring 'of't', so in l. 8 any difficulty is overcome by giving a very light stress to the final 'e' of 'Phoebe'.

And play the swaggerer. Bear this, bear all.
She says I am not fair, that I lack manners;
She calls me proud, and that she could not love me
Were man as rare as Phoenix. 'Od's my will,
Her love is not the hare that I do hunt.
Why writes she so to me? Well, shepherd, well,
This is a letter of your own device.

SILVIUS
No, I protest; I know not the contents.
Phoebe did write it.

ROSALIND Come, come, you are a fool,
And turned into the extremity of love.
I saw her hand. She has a leathern hand,
A free-stone coloured hand. I verily did think
That her old gloves were on; but 'twas her hands.
She has a housewife's hand—but that's no matter.
I say she never did invent this letter.
This is a man's invention, and his hand.

SILVIUS Sure, it is hers.

ROSALIND
Why, 'tis a boisterous and a cruel style,
A style for challengers. Why, she defies me,
Like Turk to Christian. Women's gentle brain

15 **swaggerer** blusterer, bully
Bear . . . all Proverbial (Tilley A172).

18 **as rare as Phoenix** Proverbial (Tilley P256). The *Phoenix* was a mythical bird, of which there was only one alive at any one time; when it died a new one rose from the ashes of the funeral pyre it had built and then burned itself upon. In Ovid the phoenix dies on a nest it has built and strewn with spices, the new rising from the corpse of the old (15, 441).
'Od's my will 'God save my will.' Compare 3.5.44, where ''Od's' is also used in connection with Phoebe.

19 **hare** Hares, symbolic of lust and fecundity, were sacred to the moon in several mythologies, and the Greeks associated them with both Eros and Hecate. In his *History of Four-Footed Beasts* (1607), Edward Topsell says 'Hares were dedicated to love, because (Xenophon saith) there is no man that seeth a hare but he remembreth what he hath loved' (repr. 1658, p. 214). Shakespeare associates the hare with the goddess of love in *Venus* ll. 679–708. Its supposed quality of bisexuality, discussed by Sir Thomas Browne (*Pseudodoxia Epidemica*, III, 17), makes it an especially apt image for Rosalind to use here.

20 **Well . . . well** 'Well, well is a word of malice' was proverbial (Tilley W269).

24 **turned** brought (*OED*, *turn*, *v.* †41†b)

26 **free-stone coloured** *Free-stone* is any fine-grained sandstone or limestone that can be cut or sawn easily, but as its colour around Stratford and in the Cotswolds is brownish-yellow, this is the usual colour imputed to Phoebe's hand.

28 **housewife's hand** (made hard and coarse by housework)

30 **hand** handwriting. Rosalind cannot resist a chance to pun.

34 **Turk to Christian** In old mumming plays the character of the Turkish knight challenged the Christian with fierce oaths.

Could not drop forth such giant-rude invention,
Such Ethiop words, blacker in their effect
Than in their countenance. Will you hear the letter?

SILVIUS
So please you, for I never heard it yet,
Yet heard too much of Phoebe's cruelty.

ROSALIND
She Phoebes me. Mark how the tyrant writes: (*reads*)
'Art thou god to shepherd turned,
That a maiden's heart hath burned?'
Can a woman rail thus?

SILVIUS Call you this railing?

ROSALIND (*reads*)
'Why, thy godhead laid apart,
Warr'st thou with a woman's heart?'
Did you ever hear such railing?
'Whiles the eye of man did woo me
That could do no vengeance to me.'—
Meaning me a beast.
'If the scorn of your bright eyne
Have power to raise such love in mine,
Alack, in me what strange effect
Would they work in mild aspect?
Whiles you chid me I did love;
How then might your prayers move?
He that brings this love to thee
Little knows this love in me,

40, 45 (*reads*)] ROWE; Read. F

35 **giant-rude** extremely rude. Abbott (§430) lists many examples of such compound words.

36 **Ethiop . . . effect** Being written in ink, the words are black, like an Ethiopian, and terrible, but their meaning is even more terrible.

40 **Phoebes me** 'treats me disdainfully and cruelly (as she does you)'.

49 **vengeance** mischief, harm

50 **Meaning . . . beast** implying that I am not a man: Rosalind ignores, or pretends not to understand, Phoebe's claim that Ganymede is a god who has put aside his godhead.

51 **eyne** A 'poetical' form of 'eyes'. Compare 'crystal eyne', *Venus* 633.

54 **aspect** (a) look, glance (b) in astrology, the relative positions of the heavenly bodies as they appear to an observer on earth at a given time; in popular astrological belief, the way they look upon the earth and the influence they thereby exert. According to John Norden's *Vicissitudo Rerum* (1600), 'minds incline, and manners good and bad, | Proceed (some say) by moving and aspects | Of Heaven's spheres, and planets wherewith clad, | That give and take, and work the sole effects | In men and beasts, and in all earthly sects.'

And by him seal up thy mind
Whether that thy youth and kind
Will the faithful offer take
Of me, and all that I can make,
Or else by him my love deny,
And then I'll study how to die.'

SILVIUS Call you this chiding?

CELIA Alas, poor shepherd.

ROSALIND Do you pity him? No, he deserves no pity. (*To Silvius*) Wilt thou love such a woman? What, to make thee an instrument, and play false strains upon thee?—not to be endured. Well, go your way to her—for I see love hath made thee a tame snake—and say this to her: that if she love me, I charge her to love thee. If she will not, I will never have her unless thou entreat for her. If you be a true lover, hence, and not a word; for here comes more company. *Exit Silvius*

Enter Oliver

OLIVER
Good morrow, fair ones. Pray you, if you know,
Where in the purlieus of this forest stands
A sheepcote fenced about with olive trees?

CELIA
West of this place, down in the neighbour bottom;
The rank of osiers by the murmuring stream
Left on your right hand brings you to the place.

79 bottom;] CAPELL N [1774]; ~∧ F

59 **seal . . . mind** send your decision in a sealed letter

60 **kind** nature

62 **make** Possible meanings include: earn; produce; amount to.

68–9 **thou ... thee** Used to register Rosalind's contemptuous anger towards Silvius.

69 **instrument** (a) tool (b) musical instrument. Latham compares Hamlet's speech to Rosencrantz and Guildenstern: 'You would play upon me . . .' (*Hamlet* 3.2.352–60).

71 **tame snake** spineless wretch; wimp

76 **fair** beautiful, handsome. 'Fair' was used for both men and women; Rosalind pretends to complain that Phoebe says Ganymede is 'not fair' (l. 16).

79 Celia, having been pushed increasingly further out of her closeness with Rosalind by her cousin's absorption in Orlando, is ready and available for love. Oliver, his character reformed by the loving action of his brother, is similarly open to invasion.

neighbour bottom nearby valley-bed. More specifically, *bottom* is the flat, alluvial land on either side of a stream running through a valley.

80 **rank of osiers** line of willows (specifically, of the kind cut to produce long straight twigs for basket-making)

81 **Left** passed

But at this hour the house doth keep itself.
There's none within.

OLIVER
If that an eye may profit by a tongue,
Then should I know you by description.
Such garments, and such years. 'The boy is fair,
Of female favour, and bestows himself
Like a ripe sister. The woman low
And browner than her brother.' Are not you
The owner of the house I did enquire for?

CELIA
It is no boast, being asked, to say we are.

OLIVER
Orlando doth commend him to you both,
And to that youth he calls his Rosalind
He sends this bloody napkin. Are you he?

ROSALIND
I am. What must we understand by this?

OLIVER
Some of my shame, if you will know of me
What man I am, and how, and why, and where
This handkerchief was stained.

CELIA I pray you tell it.

98 handkerchief] F (handkercher) (*and at* 5.2.26)

87 **favour** appearance, countenance
bestows himself behaves, carries himself

88 **ripe sister** older, mature sister. Some editors, alarmed at this close reflection on Ganymede's true sex, unnecessarily emend *sister* to 'forester'. In her edition, which has copious stage directions, Elsie Fogerty, who founded the Central School of Speech and Drama in London in 1906, says Oliver 'is never deceived by Rosalind's male attire' (1900, p. 51). As early as 1849–50 Georg Gervinus had suggested that Oliver penetrates the disguise (but after l. 157.1), and tells Orlando (*Shakespeare Commentaries*, tr. F. E. Bunnètt, 6th edn. (1903), p. 387).

88–9 **low | And browner** short (probably 'shorter') and darker-haired. Although both girls presumably smirched their faces with umber (1.3.111–12) at the beginning of their adventure, Rosalind at any rate seems by now to have reverted to her natural complexion, as she grows observably pale later in the scene (ll. 170–2). Several of Shakespeare's comedies contain one girl tall and fair and another short and dark: in *Dream*, e.g., Hermia is 'tawny' (3.2.264), and 'lower' (3.2.305) than the 'dove'-like (2.2.120) 'maypole' (3.2.297), Helena.

94 **napkin** handkerchief. The bloodstained handkerchief is not in Lodge, but a bloody item of clothing is found in other love stories, including the tale of Pyramus and Thisbe (Ovid, 4, 132; *Dream* 5.1.278) and Lyly's *Woman in the Moon* (4.1.114 ff.).

98 **handkerchief** F's 'handkercher' was 'common in literary use in the sixteenth and seventeenth centuries, and remained the current spoken form for some time after *handkerchief* was commonly written' (*OED*). 'So it may be regarded as an indifferent variant' (*Textual Companion*, p. 393).

OLIVER

When last the young Orlando parted from you,
He left a promise to return again
Within an hour, and pacing through the forest,
Chewing the food of sweet and bitter fancy,
Lo what befell. He threw his eye aside—
And mark what object did present itself:
Under an old oak, whose boughs were mossed with age
And high top bald with dry antiquity,
A wretched, ragged man, o'ergrown with hair,
Lay sleeping on his back. About his neck
A green and gilded snake had wreathed itself,
Who with her head, nimble in threats, approached
The opening of his mouth. But suddenly
Seeing Orlando, it unlinked itself,
And with indented glides did slip away
Into a bush, under which bush's shade
A lioness, with udders all drawn dry,
Lay couching, head on ground, with catlike watch
When that the sleeping man should stir. For 'tis
The royal disposition of that beast
To prey on nothing that doth seem as dead.
This seen, Orlando did approach the man

104 itself:] it self. THEOBALD; it selfe‸ F 106 antiquity,] RANN; antiquitie: F

102 **fancy** love. Compare Saladyne's description of fancy as 'a bitter pleasure wrapped in a sweet prejudice' (fo. 50[v]).

104 **object** Not simply the sleeping Oliver, but the total scene.

105 An eleven-syllable line, which can be regularized by eliding 'Und'r an'; instead, some follow Pope in omitting 'old'. **oak** Compare 3.2.227–8n.

109–15 **snake . . . lioness** These are Christian symbols for the evil sin from which the loving action of Orlando rescues Oliver; the scene emblematizes Psalm 91:13: 'Thou shalt walk upon the lion and the asp: the young lion and the dragon shalt thou tread under feet.' The Geneva Bible glosses this verse, 'Thou shalt not only be preserved from all evil, but overcome it whether it be secret or open.' (See also Richard Knowles, 'Myth and Type in *As You Like It*', *ELH*, 33 (1966), 12.)

113 **indented** zigzagging (see *OED, indented, ppl. a.*[1] 1b): earliest instance of *indented* in this sense cited by *OED*

117–19 **'tis . . . dead** Topsell, whose source was Conrad Gesner's *Historiae Animalium* (1587), says 'There is no beast more vehement than a she or female lion' and, of lions generally, 'whatsoever they leave of their meat, they return not to it again to eat it afterwards, whereof some assigned the cause to be in the meat, because they can endure nothing which is unsweet, stale, or stinking; but in my opinion they do it through the pride of their natures, resembling in all things a princely majesty, and therefore scorn to have one dish twice presented to their own table' (repr. 1658, p. 360). In Lodge it is 'a hungry lion' which lies down and watches to see if the sleeper will stir, 'for that lions hate to prey on dead carcases' (fo. 38[r]).

And found it was his brother, his elder brother.

CELIA
O, I have heard him speak of that same brother,
And he did render him the most unnatural
That lived amongst men.

OLIVER And well he might so do,
For well I know he was unnatural.

ROSALIND
But to Orlando. Did he leave him there,
Food to the sucked and hungry lioness?

OLIVER
Twice did he turn his back, and purposed so.
But kindness, nobler ever than revenge,
And nature, stronger than his just occasion,
Made him give battle to the lioness,
Who quickly fell before him; in which hurtling
From miserable slumber I awaked.

CELIA
Are you his brother?

ROSALIND Was't you he rescued?

CELIA
Was't you that did so oft contrive to kill him?

OLIVER
'Twas I, but 'tis not I. I do not shame
To tell you what I was, since my conversion
So sweetly tastes, being the thing I am.

ROSALIND
But for the bloody napkin?

OLIVER By and by.
When from the first to last betwixt us two

123 **render** describe (*OED v.* †5): earliest instance of *render* in this sense cited by *OED*
unnatural excessively cruel or wicked (*OED a. (sb.)* 3)

125 **unnatural** devoid of natural feelings (*OED a. (sb.)* 3b). Oliver enriches the meaning of the word through his new self-knowledge.

129 **kindness** Both (a) kinship and (b) generosity of a wider nature—Oliver is Orlando's brother, but also a fellow human being.
nobler . . . revenge Perhaps a proverbial allusion: 'To be able to do harm and not to do it is noble' (Tilley H170). Compare Prospero: 'Yet with my nobler reason 'gainst my fury | Do I take part. The rarer action is | In virtue than in vengeance' (*Tempest* 5.1.26–8).

130 **just occasion** legitimate reason

132 **hurtling** conflict. In Lodge the lion is killed with a boar-spear; Orlando apparently uses his bare hands—an allusion to Hercules' slaying of the Nemean lion.

135 **contrive** plot

139–57 Oliver's absorption with Celia, and with the strange new development in

Tears our recountments had most kindly bathed—
As how I came into that desert place—
I' brief, he led me to the gentle Duke,
Who gave me fresh array, and entertainment,
Committing me unto my brother's love,
Who led me instantly unto his cave,
There stripped himself, and here upon his arm
The lioness had torn some flesh away,
Which all this while had bled. And now he fainted,
And cried in fainting upon Rosalind.
Brief, I recovered him, bound up his wound,
And after some small space, being strong at heart,
He sent me hither, stranger as I am,
To tell this story, that you might excuse
His broken promise, and to give this napkin,
Dyed in his blood, unto the shepherd youth
That he in sport doth call his Rosalind.
Rosalind faints

CELIA
Why, how now, Ganymede, sweet Ganymede!

OLIVER
Many will swoon when they do look on blood.

CELIA
There is more in it. Cousin Ganymede!

143 I'] OXFORD; I F1; In F2 156 his] F2; this F1 157.1 *Rosalind faints*] POPE; *not in* F

himself, scarcely admits awareness of Rosalind, or even sympathy for her when she faints. In performance, the seriousness of his insistent story-telling often goes unnoticed because of exaggerated comic business; a subtle balance needs to be maintained.

141 **recountments** tales (of their adventures)

142–4 **desert . . . entertainment** These words link Oliver more closely with Rosalind and Celia, who also sought '*entertainment*' in 'this *desert* place' (2.4.71).

147–9 Whereas in Lodge Rosader is wounded saving Aliena from robbers and is tended by Ganymede, Shakespeare strengthens the plot by using the incident to reinforce Oliver's conversion on the one hand and to provide the comedy of Rosalind's fainting on the other. As well, the saving of Oliver and the shedding of Orlando's blood returns the blood relationship of the brothers to its natural course; compare 'diverted blood' (2.3.38).

151 **Brief** In brief
recovered brought him back to consciousness

156 **his** 'The *this* of F may be dittography' (Knowles). F2's *his* is certainly stronger, and has been adopted by most editors.

160–83 After the verse appropriate for the seriousness of Oliver's tale and his meeting with Celia, the prose of comedy asserts itself, except for Oliver's somewhat formal declaration of responsibility at ll. 180–1.

160 **Cousin Ganymede** On the grounds that Celia, in her fright, forgets both her own and Rosalind's disguise and says *Cousin*, then recollects herself and says *Ganymede*, Johnson punctuated '—cousin—

OLIVER Look, he recovers.

ROSALIND I would I were at home.

CELIA We'll lead you thither.
(*To Oliver*) I pray you, will you take him by the arm?

OLIVER Be of good cheer, youth. You a man? You lack a man's heart.

ROSALIND I do so, I confess it. Ah, sirrah, a body would think this was well counterfeited. I pray you, tell your brother how well I counterfeited. Heigh-ho!

OLIVER This was not counterfeit. There is too great testimony in your complexion that it was a passion of earnest.

ROSALIND Counterfeit, I assure you.

OLIVER Well then, take a good heart, and counterfeit to be a man.

ROSALIND So I do; but, i'faith, I should have been a woman by right.

CELIA Come, you look paler and paler. Pray you, draw homewards. Good sir, go with us.

OLIVER
That will I, for I must bear answer back
How you excuse my brother, Rosalind.

ROSALIND I shall devise something. But I pray you commend my counterfeiting to him. Will you go? *Exeunt*

5.1 *Enter Touchstone the clown and Audrey*

TOUCHSTONE We shall find a time, Audrey. Patience, gentle Audrey.

Ganymed!'; as the word appears to have been rarely used between siblings, he may have been right, and the interpretation can provide an effective moment for the actress playing Celia.

162 Rosalind's whimper, a reversion to childhood's need for comfort in distress, is both humorous and touching.

169 **Heigh-ho!** Sometimes interpreted as a sigh, after an attempted return to bravado, but more likely a continuation of the pretence of nonchalance.

174 **take . . . heart** Proverbial (Dent H328.1).

178–9 These are Celia's last words in the play. Having momentarily resumed her former dominance in her relationship with Rosalind, and having fallen in love with Oliver, she has no further active contribution to make.

181 **Rosalind** If the production wants its Oliver to indicate he sees through Rosalind's disguise, here is the actor's chance for significant irony. F's comma before the name is suggestive.

5.1 The attachment of the play's fourth pair of lovers, Touchstone and Audrey, is confirmed by the defeat of William in this scene, which forms a farcical prelude to the gathering movement towards the denouement. Touchstone and Audrey seem, from their conversation, to have just come from their encounter with

AUDREY Faith, the priest was good enough, for all the old gentleman's saying.

TOUCHSTONE A most wicked Sir Oliver, Audrey, a most vile Martext. But, Audrey, there is a youth here in the forest lays claim to you.

AUDREY Ay, I know who 'tis. He hath no interest in me in the world. Here comes the man you mean.

Enter William

TOUCHSTONE It is meat and drink to me to see a clown. By my troth, we that have good wits have much to answer for. We shall be flouting; we cannot hold.

WILLIAM Good ev'n, Audrey.

AUDREY God ye good ev'n, William.

WILLIAM (*to Touchstone*) And good ev'n to you, sir.

TOUCHSTONE Good ev'n, gentle friend. Cover thy head, cover thy head. Nay, prithee, be covered. How old are you, friend?

WILLIAM Five-and-twenty, sir.

TOUCHSTONE A ripe age. Is thy name William?

WILLIAM William, sir.

TOUCHSTONE A fair name. Wast born i'th' forest here?

WILLIAM Ay, sir, I thank God.

TOUCHSTONE Thank God—a good answer. Art rich?

WILLIAM Faith, sir, so-so.

TOUCHSTONE So-so is good, very good, very excellent good. And yet it is not, it is but so-so. Art thou wise?

WILLIAM Ay, sir, I have a pretty wit.

Jaques and Sir Oliver; a great deal has occurred in other parts of the forest since then, however. Time in Arden is elastic.

3 **old** To Audrey, probably anyone over thirty would be *old*, but some actors, like Hermann Vezin (Gaiety, 1875), have taken this description as a cue for presenting Jaques as an old, or prematurely aged, man.

8 **interest in** legal concern in; right or title (to possession or enjoyment of)

9 **William** It has been a stage tradition for William to carry a single bloom, or a comical bunch of flowers.

10 **meat and drink** Proverbial (Tilley M842).
clown peasant, rustic. The contrast being made is between the boorish yokel and the sophisticated court fool equipped with 'good wits', but the word is fraught with irony, especially when F's speech prefix *Clo[wn]* for Touchstone is taken into account. Compare 2.4.63.

12 **flouting** jeering, mocking
hold refrain. Lack of restraint was a characteristic of fools; compare 1.2.98.

14 **God . . . ev'n** 'Good evening' (used any time after noon)

17 **be covered** A nice echo of Touchstone's similarly patronizing request to Jaques at 3.3.70.

22 **A fair name** And also the playwright's.

24 **good** Perhaps Touchstone is mocking William's rustic accent to pun on 'God' and *good*.

TOUCHSTONE Why, thou sayst well. I do now remember a saying: 'The fool doth think he is wise, but the wise man knows himself to be a fool.' The heathen philosopher, when he had a desire to eat a grape, would open his lips when he put it into his mouth, meaning thereby that grapes were made to eat, and lips to open. You do love this maid?

WILLIAM I do, sir.

TOUCHSTONE Give me your hand. Art thou learned?

WILLIAM No, sir.

TOUCHSTONE Then learn this of me: to have is to have. For it is a figure in rhetoric that drink, being poured out of a cup into a glass, by filling the one doth empty the other. For all your writers do consent that *ipse* is he. Now you are not *ipse*, for I am he.

WILLIAM Which he, sir?

TOUCHSTONE He, sir, that must marry this woman. Therefore, you clown, abandon—which is in the vulgar, leave—the society—which in the boorish is company—

5.1.36 sir] F2; sit F1

30–1 **'The fool . . . fool'** A fairly well-known philosophic idea deriving perhaps from Plato's *Apology of Socrates* 21D: 'it seems that I am wiser than [this man] is to this small extent, that I do not think that I know what I do not know' (*The Last Days of Socrates*, tr. Hugh Tredennick (Harmondsworth, 1969), p. 50). Compare 1 Corinthians 3: 18: 'If any man amongst you seem to be wise in this world, let him be a fool that he may be wise', and *Twelfth Night* 1.5.30–2.

31–2 **heathen philosopher** No particular philosopher has been identified, but that is of small moment; Touchstone's rhetoric is intended to impress his listeners and deride learned pomposity.

33–4 **open . . . grapes** The idea is in Lodge: 'Phoebe is no lettuce for your lips, and her grapes hang so high, that gaze at them you may, but touch them you cannot' (fol. 49[r]); this refers to the punishment of Tantalus (Homer, *Odyssey*, 11 583 ff.) who not only divulged secrets of his father, Zeus, but also served up his own son, Pelops, as a dish at a banquet. He was sent to Hades, to stand up to his chin in water which subsided whenever he stooped to drink while above him hung bunches of grapes and other fruit that whisked away whenever he reached up for them. The scene is often played with William's becoming increasingly bamboozled, his eyes growing wider and his mouth gaping ever more open.

37 **hand** The command may be intended to make William think Touchstone is about to act the priest and marry him to Audrey.

40 **figure** verbal device

rhetoric The art of persuasive or impressive speaking or writing; based on classical models and texts, it was an important element in Renaissance education. In a lengthy analysis, T. W. Baldwin shows how Aristotle, Cicero and Quintilian are among those lying behind Touchstone's bewildering display (*Shakespeare's Small Latine & Lesse Greeke*, 2 vols. (Urbana, 1944), ii. 116–20).

42 ***ipse* is he** 'he himself (Latin) is he'; proverbial (Tilley I88). The phrase was particularly applied to a successful lover. Compare Touchstone's question at 3.3.2: 'Am I the man yet?'

of this female—which in the common is woman; which together is, abandon the society of this female, or, clown, thou perishest; or, to thy better understanding, diest; or, to wit, I kill thee, make thee away, translate thy life into death, thy liberty into bondage. I will deal in poison with thee, or in bastinado, or in steel. I will bandy with thee in faction, I will o'errun thee with policy. I will kill thee a hundred and fifty ways. Therefore tremble, and depart.

AUDREY Do, good William.

WILLIAM God rest you merry, sir. *Exit*

Enter Corin

CORIN Our master and mistress seeks you. Come, away, away.

TOUCHSTONE Trip, Audrey, trip, Audrey. (*To Corin*) I attend, I attend. *Exeunt*

5.2 *Enter Orlando and Oliver*

ORLANDO Is't possible that on so little acquaintance you should like her? That but seeing, you should love her? And loving, woo? And wooing, she should grant? And will you persevere to enjoy her?

OLIVER Neither call the giddiness of it in question, the poverty of her, the small acquaintance, my sudden wooing, nor her sudden consenting; but say with me, 'I love Aliena'; say with her, that she loves me; consent with both that we may enjoy each other. It shall be to your good, for my father's house and all the revenue

55 policy] F2; police F1
5.2.4 persevere] F (perseuer) 7 her] ROWE; *not in* F

53 **bastinado** beating with a stick

54 **bandy . . . faction** contend with you in insults and argument (as opposed to physical combat)

55 **policy** cunning. H. J. Oliver suggests '"Machiavellian" policy (using any means to achieve the desired end)'.

59 **seeks** Verbs often ended in 's' after two single subjects (Abbot §336).

61 **Trip** go, walk, skip or run with a light and lively motion (*OED, trip, v.* 3) but, taken in the sense 'trip over', the word provides for such comedy as Anthony Hopkins's pratfall when he played Audrey in the National Theatre's all-male *As You Like It* (Old Vic, 1967)

5.2 This scene is remarkable for Orlando's seriousness, Rosalind's change from banter to prophecy, and the variation in tone which prepares the audience for the relative solemnity of the marriage ceremony.

4 **persevere** F's spelling, 'persever', indicates current pronunciation which accentuated the second syllable; by *c.*1680 the modern spelling was universal.

that was old Sir Rowland's will I estate upon you, and here live and die a shepherd.

Enter Rosalind as Ganymede

ORLANDO You have my consent. Let your wedding be tomorrow. Thither will I invite the Duke and all's contented followers. Go you, and prepare Aliena; for look you, here comes my Rosalind.

ROSALIND God save you, brother.

OLIVER And you, fair sister. *Exit*

ROSALIND O, my dear Orlando, how it grieves me to see thee wear thy heart in a scarf.

ORLANDO It is my arm.

ROSALIND I thought thy heart had been wounded with the claws of a lion.

ORLANDO Wounded it is, but with the eyes of a lady.

ROSALIND Did your brother tell you how I counterfeited to swoon when he showed me your handkerchief?

ORLANDO Ay, and greater wonders than that.

ROSALIND O, I know where you are. Nay, 'tis true. There was never anything so sudden but the fight of two rams,

12.1 *Enter ... Ganymede*] *Enter Rosalind.* F 18.1 *Exit*] *not in* F

11 **estate** settle. Either Oliver, or Shakespeare, has forgotten that Duke Frederick has confiscated the de Boys estate; or are we to believe that Oliver is so bewitched by love, and Arden, that he can see only good in everything? Or that, having spoken with Celia, he knows who she and Rosalind are, and believes that Duke Senior will soon reclaim his dukedom? At 5.4.163 the Duke includes Oliver among the exiled lords whose lands the repentant Frederick has restored.

18 **sister** Oliver's calling Ganymede *sister* has caused anguish to some editors, who feel it shows he has seen through Rosalind's disguise; others consider it evidence that indeed he has (compare 4.3.88 and note), and that therefore Orlando as well knows who Ganymede is. It is feasible, however, that Oliver does so because Orlando has just called 'him' 'Rosalind', keeping up their pretence, and because Ganymede has just greeted Oliver as 'brother', owing to his match with Aliena, Ganymede's sister. F3's giving this line to Orlando (followed by Rowe (1714) and Halliwell) is 'doubtless ... a compositor's error' (Knowles). The situation is tricky, even alarming, and Rosalind quickly diverts Orlando's attention to himself.

20 **thee** As 'Rosalind', Ganymede uses the affectionate pronoun.

scarf as a sling. Rosalind is mocking, but Orlando is in no mood for it.

25 Rosalind reverts to being Ganymede, and to male comradeship.

28 **O, I know . . . are** 'I know what you mean.' Proverbial (Dent W295.1). Rosalind is momentarily thrown off balance by Orlando's reference to 'greater wonders'; has he penetrated her disguise? With relief she realizes he is referring to Oliver's and Celia's falling in love.

29 **two rams** In her eagerness to reaffirm her rural persona Rosalind turns to a pastoral simile; rams in fact do suddenly turn and charge head-on at one another for no apparent reason.

and Caesar's thrasonical brag of 'I came, saw, and overcame', for your brother and my sister no sooner met but they looked; no sooner looked but they loved; no sooner loved but they sighed; no sooner sighed but they asked one another the reason; no sooner knew the reason but they sought the remedy; and in these degrees have they made a pair of stairs to marriage, which they will climb incontinent, or else be incontinent before marriage. They are in the very wrath of love, and they will together. Clubs cannot part them.

ORLANDO They shall be married tomorrow, and I will bid the Duke to the nuptial. But O, how bitter a thing it is to look into happiness through another man's eyes. By so much the more shall I tomorrow be at the height of heart-heaviness by how much I shall think my brother happy in having what he wishes for.

ROSALIND Why, then, tomorrow I cannot serve your turn for Rosalind?

ORLANDO I can live no longer by thinking.

ROSALIND I will weary you then no longer with idle talking. Know of me then—for now I speak to some purpose—that I know you are a gentleman of good

30–1 overcame] F2; ouercome F1

30 **Caesar's** Proverbial (Tilley C540), derived from Julius Caesar who, according to Plutarch's *Lives* 1.2, announced the victory of Zela which ended the Pontic campaign, with the words '*Veni, vidi, vici*', written in a letter; nowadays usually translated, 'I came, I saw, I conquered'; North's (1579) rendering, 'overcame', was followed by Shakespeare and other contemporaries. (See Bullough, v. 75.)
thrasonical boastful; from the boaster, Thraso, in Terence's comedy *Eunuchus*. The classical reference is appropriate to literary pastoral.

31–7 **no sooner met . . . marriage** Rosalind is here using a rhetorical device called *climax, sorites, gradatio* or the marching figure, wittily referring to the method of the figure itself in *degrees* (a step or stage in a process) and *pair* (flight) *of stairs*. Kökeritz sees a pun on 'stares'.

37 **incontinent . . . incontinent** at once . . . unchaste

38 **wrath** heat of passion

38–9 **they will together** According to Burton, 'the last refuge and surest remedy' of Love-Melancholy 'is . . . to let [the lovers] go together, and enjoy one another' (iii. 228 (Pt. III. Sec. 2. Mem. 5. Subs. 5)).

39 **Clubs** Johnson's gloss, 'Alluding to the way of parting dogs in wrath' is vigorous, if somewhat crude.

46 **serve your turn** (a) act as a substitute (b) satisfy sexually. Rosalind's last piece of bawdy before the Epilogue. Compare *L.L.L.* 1.1.286–7: "KING: This 'maid' will not serve your turn, sir. COSTARD: This maid will serve my turn, sir."

49 The tone now changes as Rosalind's plans for the denouement begin to evolve. The rhythms become more stately, an air of mystery and high seriousness is generated, and there is a growing sense of ritual which acts as a preparation for the antiphon of love (ll. 78–100) which soon follows.

conceit. I speak not this that you should bear a good opinion of my knowledge, insomuch I say I know you are; neither do I labour for a greater esteem than may in some little measure draw a belief from you to do yourself good, and not to grace me. Believe then, if you please, that I can do strange things. I have since I was three year old conversed with a magician, most profound in his art, and yet not damnable. If you do love Rosalind so near the heart as your gesture cries it out, when your brother marries Aliena shall you marry her. I know into what straits of fortune she is driven, and it is not impossible to me, if it appear not inconvenient to you, to set her before your eyes tomorrow, human as she is, and without any danger.

ORLANDO Speakest thou in sober meanings?

ROSALIND By my life, I do, which I tender dearly, though I say I am a magician. Therefore put you in your best array, bid your friends: for if you will be married tomorrow, you shall; and to Rosalind if you will.

Enter Silvius and Phoebe

Look, here comes a lover of mine and a lover of hers.

PHOEBE (*to Rosalind*)

Youth, you have done me much ungentleness,
To show the letter that I writ to you.

ROSALIND

I care not if I have. It is my study
To seem despiteful and ungentle to you.
You are there followed by a faithful shepherd.
Look upon him; love him. He worships you.

PHOEBE (*to Silvius*)

Good shepherd, tell this youth what 'tis to love.

52 **conceit** understanding, ability to apprehend

58 **conversed** associated (perhaps implying apprenticeship)

59 **not damnable** that is, not practising black magic, which would put him in league with the devil. Lodge's Rosalynde says, 'I have a friend [i.e. relative] that is deeply experienced in necromancy and magic, what art can do shall be acted for thine advantage: I will cause him to bring in Rosalynde' (fol. 59[r]).

60 **gesture** bearing, carriage, physical attitude

62 **straits of fortune** difficult circumstances

63–4 **inconvenient** inappropriate, wrong (to be using magic)

65 **human as she is** in the flesh, not as a spirit conjured up by magic

67 **tender dearly** Under Elizabethan law (5 Eliza. cap. 16) witchcraft could be punished by death without benefit of clergy if death ensued from acts of conjuration; imprisonment and other lesser penalties followed smaller crimes of magic.

72 **ungentleness** unkindness

SILVIUS
It is to be all made of sighs and tears,
And so am I for Phoebe.
PHOEBE And I for Ganymede.
ORLANDO And I for Rosalind.
ROSALIND And I for no woman.
SILVIUS
It is to be all made of faith and service,
And so am I for Phoebe.
PHOEBE And I for Ganymede.
ORLANDO And I for Rosalind.
ROSALIND And I for no woman.
SILVIUS
It is to be all made of fantasy,
All made of passion, and all made of wishes,
All adoration, duty, and observance,
All humbleness, all patience and impatience,
All purity, all trial, all obedience,
And so am I for Phoebe.
PHOEBE And so am I for Ganymede.
ORLANDO And so am I for Rosalind.
ROSALIND And so am I for no woman.
PHOEBE (*to Rosalind*)
If this be so, why blame you me to love you?
SILVIUS (*to Phoebe*)
If this be so, why blame you me to love you?
ORLANDO
If this be so, why blame you me to love you?
ROSALIND Why do you speak too, 'Why blame you me to love you?'

93 obedience] COWDEN CLARKE (*conj.* Malone); obseruance F

91 **observance** respect, dutiful service

93 **obedience** Most editors agree that the second use of 'observance' is a copyist's or printer's error; Malone's substitution, which he suggested in a note without emending the text, has been widely adopted over others including 'perseverance', 'obeisance' and 'endurance'. H. J. Oliver comments that 'it is just possible that *all observance* is the best Silvius can do to sum up what he has been saying'.

98 **why blame . . . you?** why do you blame me for loving you?

100 A stage Orlando can give added point to this line by fingering Rosalind's chain, which is around his neck.

101–2 Rosalind's startled question changes the tone back to comedy, and the form back to prose. Rowe emended *why* to 'who', which is reasonable in the light of Orlando's reply, but the lover is off in a reverie and 'Because I am speaking' can be understood before 'to her'.

ORLANDO
To her that is not here nor doth not hear.

ROSALIND Pray you, no more of this, 'tis like the howling of Irish wolves against the moon. (*To Silvius*) I will help you if I can. (*To Phoebe*) I would love you if I could.— Tomorrow meet me all together. (*To Phoebe*) I will marry you if ever I marry woman, and I'll be married tomorrow. (*To Orlando*) I will satisfy you if ever I satisfy man, and you shall be married tomorrow. (*To Silvius*) I will content you if what pleases you contents you, and you shall be married tomorrow. (*To Orlando*) As you love Rosalind, meet. (*To Silvius*) As you love Phoebe, meet. And as I love no woman, I'll meet. So fare you well. I have left you commands.

SILVIUS I'll not fail, if I live.

PHOEBE Nor I.

ORLANDO Nor I. *Exeunt severally*

5.3 *Enter Touchstone the clown and Audrey*

TOUCHSTONE Tomorrow is the joyful day, Audrey, tomorrow will we be married.

AUDREY I do desire it with all my heart; and I hope it is no dishonest desire to desire to be a woman of the world. Here come two of the banished Duke's pages.

Enter two Pages

FIRST PAGE Well met, honest gentleman.

TOUCHSTONE By my troth, well met. Come, sit, sit, and a song.

109 I satisfy] DYCE 1864 (*conj.* Douce); satisfi'd F 118.1 *severally*] OXFORD; *not in* F

105 **Irish wolves** The Irish were popularly supposed to worship the moon, and to turn into wolves, and the howling of wolves at the moon was proverbial (Tilley D449, which has 'bark', not 'howl'). Shakespeare echoes Lodge: 'I tell thee Montanus, in courting Phoebe thou barkest with the wolves of Syria against the moon' (fol. 56[r]).

109 **satisfy** Only Rosalind and the audience can be aware of the sexual sense in her use of this word. F's 'satisfi'd' for the repetition of the word implies a (highly unlikely) non-virginal Rosalind.

5.3 Shakespeare again insists on completing his quartet of couples; marriage has been promised for the other three, and Touchstone and Audrey now follow; the scene is neither gratuitous nor simply an excuse for a delightful song which confirms that the season is now spring, and love its great activity.

4 **woman of the world** a married woman. When *the world* is taken as meaning 'the flesh' (see *OED* 4d), as opposed to 'spirit', however, Audrey's desire can be seen to be indeed 'dishonest' (= unchaste), and her remark becomes innocently ironic.

SECOND PAGE We are for you. Sit i'th' middle.

FIRST PAGE Shall we clap into't roundly, without hawking, or spitting, or saying we are hoarse, which are the only prologues to a bad voice?

SECOND PAGE I'faith, i'faith, and both in a tune, like two gipsies on a horse.

PAGES (*sing*)

It was a lover and his lass,
  With a hey, and a ho, and a hey-nonny-no,
That o'er the green cornfield did pass
  In spring-time, the only pretty ring-time,
When birds do sing, hey ding-a-ding ding,
Sweet lovers love the spring.

Between the acres of the rye,
  With a hey, and a ho, and a hey-nonny-no,

5.3.15 PAGES (*sing*)] Song. F 18 In] KNIGHT (Morley, *First Book of Airs*, 1600); *In the* F ring] RANN (*conj.* Steevens 1778); rang F

10 **clap . . . roundly** begin at once, without preliminaries

hawking clearing the throat noisily, something to be expected in the (vulgar) amateur, who, like Amiens (2.5.14) or Balthasar in *Much Ado* (2.3.43), might be self-deprecating or in fact have a bad voice.

11 **only** usual. The pages, as court choristers, are showing confidence in their abilities.

13–14 **two . . . horse** together in unison, moving with the same rhythm

14 **a** one

15–38 F prints the song with the first verse, the refrain and the last verse all in one, then the second and third verses separately, each concluding '*In spring time, &c.*' The rearrangement, which was first made by Johnson, is justified by the setting in Thomas Morley's *First Booke of Ayres or Little Short Songs, to Sing and Play to the Lute* (1600), of which the unique copy is in the Folger Shakespeare Library. A manuscript of 1639 in the National Library of Scotland (Advocate MS. 5.2.14, fol. 18) contains slight differences in the words but is considered to derive from Morley.

This is a country song with a suggestive refrain, and a reminder of mortality. Poised at the end of the play's main action and on the brink of the denouement, it provides a diverting entertainment and a preparatory breathing-space.

16 **hey-nonny-no** This nonsense phrase can be a euphemism for the female sexual organs, as in *The Wit of a Woman* (1604, C1[v]): 'These dancers sometimes do teach them . . . such lavoltas, they mount so high, that you may see their hey nonny, nonny no.' The lavolta was a dance in which the woman was lifted into the air by her partner as he turned around. In his *Orchesography* ([1588] 1589), 'Thoinot Arbeau' [Jehan Tabouret] warns that the girl should 'hold her petticoat and dress in place, lest the swirling air should catch them and reveal her chemise or bare thigh . . . I leave it to you to judge whether . . . in this lavolta both honour and health are not involved and at stake' (tr. Mary Stewart Evans (New York, 1967), p. 121).

17 **cornfield** wheatfield. Under the open field system of cultivating common land, in any one year a particular strip would be given over to one kind of crop.

18 **ring-time** A time for exchanging (wedding) rings, for wedding bells, for dancing in a ring—a 'carol' (l. 27) was originally a song which people sang as they danced with linked hands.

21 **Between the acres** on the unploughed land between the acre-strips under cultivation

These pretty country folks would lie,
In spring-time, the only pretty ring-time,
When birds do sing, hey ding-a-ding ding,
Sweet lovers love the spring.

This carol they began that hour,
With a hey, and a ho, and a hey-nonny-no,
How that a life was but a flower,
In spring-time, the only pretty ring-time,
When birds do sing, hey ding-a-ding ding,
Sweet lovers love the spring.

And therefore take the present time,
With a hey, and a ho, and a hey-nonny-no,
For love is crownèd with the prime,
In spring time, the only pretty ring-time,
When birds do sing, hey ding-a-ding ding,
Sweet lovers love the spring.

TOUCHSTONE Truly, young gentlemen, though there was no great matter in the ditty, yet the note was very untunable.

FIRST PAGE You are deceived, sir, we kept time, we lost not our time.

TOUCHSTONE By my troth, yes, I count it but time lost to

33–8] JOHNSON (and Morley); *after l. 20* F

23 **folks** Morley reads 'fooles', Advocate MS 'fools'.

29 **flower** The idea of life as a flower that soon withers and therefore must be made the most of—the theme of *carpe diem* [seize the day]—is common in the love poetry of the time. An early source is '*De Rosis Nascentibus*', a poem once thought to be by Ausonius, and also sometimes ascribed to Virgil: 'Fair maids, go gather roses in the prime, | And think that as a flower so goes on time' (ll. 49–50). Among several biblical sources is 1 Peter 1:24: 'For all flesh is as grass, and all the glory of man is as the flower of grass. The grass withereth, and the flower falleth away' (Geneva Bible). Compare *Venus* 129–32: 'Make use of time; let not advantage slip . . . Fair flowers that are not gather'd in their prime | Rot, and consume themselves in little time.' See also Tilley (T312) and Dent (L248.1).

35 **prime** (a) the 'spring time' of life (from about twenty-one to thirty years of age) (b) the spring (c) the height of perfection

40 **ditty** the words of the song

41 **untunable** Whether or not *untunable* means 'out of time' or 'discordant', and there are proponents of both, Touchstone is complaining that he didn't think much of the song.

42 **time** Perhaps the page deliberately misunderstands Touchstone, but *time* may have been used for 'melody' and/or 'harmony': this seems to apply in *Richard II* 5.5.45–8: 'And here have I the daintiness of ear | To check time broke in a disordered string; | But for the concord of my state and time | Had not an ear to hear my true time broke.' In any case, Touchstone takes the opportunity to make a further disparaging comment.

hear such a foolish song. Goodbye, and God mend your voices. Come, Audrey. *Exeunt severally*

5.4 *Enter Duke Senior, Amiens, Jaques, Orlando, Oliver, and Celia as Aliena*

DUKE SENIOR
Dost thou believe, Orlando, that the boy
Can do all this that he hath promisèd?

ORLANDO
I sometimes do believe, and sometimes do not,
As those that fear they hope, and know they fear.

Enter Rosalind as Ganymede, with Silvius and Phoebe

ROSALIND
Patience once more, whiles our compact is urged.
(*To the Duke*) You say if I bring in your Rosalind
You will bestow her on Orlando here?

DUKE SENIOR
That would I, had I kingdoms to give with her.

ROSALIND (*to Orlando*)
And you say you will have her when I bring her?

ORLANDO
That would I, were I of all kingdoms king.

ROSALIND (*to Phoebe*)
You say you'll marry me if I be willing?

PHOEBE
That will I, should I die the hour after.

ROSALIND
But if you do refuse to marry me
You'll give yourself to this most faithful shepherd?

PHOEBE So is the bargain.

ROSALIND (*to Silvius*)
You say that you'll have Phoebe if she will.

5.4.0.2 *and Celia as Aliena*] *Celia* F 4.1 *Rosalind as Ganymede, with*] *Rosalinde, Siluius* F

45 **Goodbye** F's 'God buy you' allows Touchstone to be emphatic through parallelism.
mend improve

5.4 The final scene has been criticized for clumsiness and cut about in performance, with Hymen eliminated from several acting versions. It is, however, a felicitous mixture of the serious, the humorous and the mysterious, gathering together all the main characters, either in person or by report, for the final unravelling and tying up of the ends of plot.

4 **fear . . . fear** are aware of being afraid their hope will remain unfulfilled, but are nevertheless still hopeful

5 **compact is urged** agreement is affirmed and pressed forward; *compact* is accented on the second syllable

SILVIUS

Though to have her and death were both one thing.

ROSALIND

I have promised to make all this matter even.
Keep you your word, O Duke, to give your daughter.
You yours, Orlando, to receive his daughter.
Keep your word, Phoebe, that you'll marry me,
Or else refusing me to wed this shepherd.
Keep your word, Silvius, that you'll marry her
If she refuse me; and from hence I go
To make these doubts all even.

Exeunt Rosalind and Celia

DUKE SENIOR

I do remember in this shepherd boy
Some lively touches of my daughter's favour.

ORLANDO

My lord, the first time that I ever saw him,
Methought he was a brother to your daughter.
But, my good lord, this boy is forest-born,
And hath been tutored in the rudiments
Of many desperate studies by his uncle,
Whom he reports to be a great magician
Obscurèd in the circle of this forest.

⌈*Enter Touchstone the clown and Audrey*⌉

JAQUES There is sure another flood toward, and these

21 your] ROWE 1714; you your F 34.1] *after l. 34* ROWE 1714; *after l. 33* F

18 **make . . . even** smooth things out. Rosalind's speech continues the incantatory magical quality, appropriate to her proclaimed magical powers, which has characterized her lines since her entrance.

21 **your** F's 'you your' makes an awkward unmetrical line in the midst of a highly formalized statement; the extra 'you' is best explained as a printer's error of repetition from the previous two lines.

25 **To make . . . even** This line may be short to allow for an elaborate, formal gesture of farewell to conclude this first, ritualistic appearance of Ganymede, the magician. Rather than being a case of 'clumsy repetition' as Wilson claimed, reiterating the idea and some of the words of l. 18 emphasizes the solemnity of the promise, and of the occasion.

27 **lively touches** life-like details. The image is from painting. Compare *Timon* 1.1.37–8: 'It [a painting] tutors nature. Artificial strife | Lives in these touches livelier than life.'

favour looks

32 **desperate** involving serious risk; very dangerous to undertake (*OED, desperate, a.* 5†b): earliest instance of *desperate* in this sense cited by *OED*

29 The 'old religious uncle' of 3.2.329–30 has now become *a great magician.*

34 **circle** Circles were constantly associated with magic and magicians (compare 2.5.55n.); Orlando's words turn the whole forest of Arden into a place of magic and conjuration.

34.1 The entry of Touchstone changes the tone and the play returns to prose.

35 **toward** approaching

couples are coming to the ark. Here comes a pair of very strange beasts, which in all tongues are called fools.

TOUCHSTONE Salutation and greeting to you all.

JAQUES (*to the Duke*) Good my lord, bid him welcome. This is the motley-minded gentleman that I have so often met in the forest. He hath been a courtier, he swears.

TOUCHSTONE If any man doubt that, let him put me to my purgation. I have trod a measure, I have flattered a lady, I have been politic with my friend, smooth with mine enemy, I have undone three tailors, I have had four quarrels, and like to have fought one.

JAQUES And how was that ta'en up?

TOUCHSTONE Faith, we met, and found the quarrel was upon the seventh cause.

JAQUES How, seventh cause?—Good my lord, like this fellow.

DUKE SENIOR I like him very well.

TOUCHSTONE God'ield you, sir, I desire you of the like. I press in here, sir, amongst the rest of the country copulatives, to swear, and to forswear, according as marriage binds and blood breaks. A poor virgin, sir, an ill-

36 **pair** When the flood was coming God told Noah, 'Of every clean beast thou shalt take to thee by sevens . . . but of unclean beasts by couples, the male and the female' (Genesis 7: 2).

40 **motley-minded** as capable of variety as the differently coloured patches on his costume. Despite his pride in being able to show off Touchstone to Duke Senior, Jaques is being patronizing; in *Twelfth Night* Feste assures Olivia 'I wear not motley in my brain' (1.5.52–3).

42–3 **put . . . purgation** test me so that I can clear myself. There is, predictably, a scatological innuendo.

measure a stately court dance, or part of a dance. Compare 5.4.174n.

44 **politic** crafty, Machiavellian

smooth fair-speaking, flattering

45 **undone three tailors** by not paying them (*undone*, ruined). Courtiers were notorious for extravagant clothes (compare Jaques, 2.7.76); in 1583, when a journeyman earned £5 per year, a hatband of pearls costing £30 was stolen from Sir Walter Ralegh (Robert Lacey, *Sir Walter Ralegh* (1973), p. 52). Among the Earl of Leicester's clothes when he died in 1588 were seven doublets and two cloaks valued at £542; in his will the Earl declared, 'I have not dissembled with the world my estate, but have lived always above any living I had (for which I am heartily sorry) lest that through my many debts, from time to time, some men have taken loss of me' (cited by Alan Haynes, *The White Bear: The Elizabethan Earl of Leicester* (1987), p. 198); he may well have undone many more tailors than Touchstone.

46 **like to have fought** come perilously close to having fought—a jibe at courtiers' not standing by their words

47 **ta'en up** settled

49 **seventh cause** The lie direct (see l. 82), which both disputants would, of course, be eager to avoid.

53 **God'ield** God reward

desire . . . like 'I look forward to your continued liking' or, less plausibly, 'Allow me to return the compliment'.

54–5 **copulatives** couples soon to be joined in marriage (and copulation)

swear . . . forswear Proverbial (Dent S1030.1).

55–6 **marriage binds and blood breaks** The

favoured thing, sir, but mine own. A poor humour of mine, sir, to take that that no man else will. Rich honesty dwells like a miser, sir, in a poor house, as your pearl in your foul oyster.

DUKE SENIOR By my faith, he is very swift and sententious.

TOUCHSTONE According to the fool's bolt, sir, and such dulcet diseases.

JAQUES But for the seventh cause. How did you find the quarrel on the seventh cause?

TOUCHSTONE Upon a lie seven times removed.—Bear your body more seeming, Audrey.—As thus, sir: I did dislike the cut of a certain courtier's beard. He sent me word if I said his beard was not cut well, he was in the mind it was. This is called the Retort Courteous. If I sent him word again it was not well cut, he would send me word he cut it to please himself. This is called the Quip Modest. If again it was not well cut, he disabled my judgement. This is called the Reply Churlish. If again it was not well cut, he would answer I spake not true. This is called the Reproof Valiant. If again it was not well cut, he would say I lie. This is called the Countercheck Quarrelsome.

marriage oath which *binds* is broken when *blood* (=lust) leads a man into adultery and thus makes him forsworn.

57 **thing** 'Every man likes his own thing best' was proverbial (Tilley M131; Dent adds 'Merry it is to look on (one's) own thing' (T141.1)).

62 **fool's bolt** Proverbial (Tilley F515): 'A fool shoots his arrow (i.e. does or says things) quickly, without thinking.' Although Touchstone is replying to the Duke's 'swift', *bolt* could mean simply 'a fool's jest'—Armin refers to his long poem *The Italian Tailor and his Boy*, published 1609 but probably written in the 1590s, as 'this fool's bolt' (H2ᵛ). Touchstone typically takes the opportunity to be bawdy, so that 'a fool's bolt is soon shot' is made to refer to premature ejaculation.

63 **dulcet diseases** sweet disabilities. Taking up the bawdy meaning of 'fool's bolt', Touchstone is saying that 'shooting his bolt' (see previous note) is a nuisance, but an agreeable one (since it relates to copulation); he is also making an appropriate pun on the hunting term 'dulcet(s)' = a deer's testicles (*OED*, *doucet*, 3). The phrase has puzzled commentators from Johnson, who said flatly, 'This I do not understand', to Knowles, who suggests that 'the fool's bolt is thought to cause some distress because it speaks home truths'. Latham sees an allusion to Quintilian's commenting on Seneca's style which, while having many bright thoughts, is a bad model because it abounds in pleasing faults (*quod abundant dulcibus vitiis*) (*Institutes of Oratory*, X. i. 129ff., tr. J. R. Watson, Bohn's Classical Library (1856)). In *Queen Anna's New World of Words* (1611), John Florio gives 'a man's pillicocke' as a meaning for 'Dolcemelle', along with 'a musical instrument called a Dulcemell or Dulcemer. Also honey sweet.' Both bawdy and classicism are in Touchstone's line.

67 **seeming** becomingly

did dislike expressed a dislike for

73 **disabled** disparaged (as at 4.1.31)

And so to the Lie Circumstantial, and the Lie Direct.

JAQUES And how oft did you say his beard was not well cut?

TOUCHSTONE I durst go no further than the Lie Circumstantial, nor he durst not give me the Lie Direct; and so we measured swords, and parted.

JAQUES Can you nominate in order now the degrees of the lie?

TOUCHSTONE O sir, we quarrel in print, by the book, as you have books for good manners. I will name you the degrees. The first, the Retort Courteous; the second, the Quip Modest; the third, the Reply Churlish; the fourth, the Reproof Valiant; the fifth, the Countercheck Quarrelsome; the sixth, the Lie with Circumstance; the seventh, the Lie Direct. All these you may avoid but the Lie Direct; and you may avoid that, too, with an 'if'. I knew when seven justices could not take up a quarrel, but when the parties were met themselves, one of them thought but of an 'if', as 'if you said so, then I said so', and they shook hands and swore brothers. Your 'if' is the only peacemaker; much virtue in 'if'.

78 to the] F2; ro F1

78 **Lie Circumstantial** a contradiction given indirectly by circumstances or details (*OED*, *circumstantial*, A. *adj* 1): earliest instance of *circumstantial* in this sense cited by *OED*

83 **measured swords** to ensure that one combatant did not have a longer sword and therefore have an advantage over the other. Compare *Hamlet* 5.2.212: 'These foils have all a length?'

84–98 Jaques is so proud of his protégé that he asks Touchstone to recapitulate.

86 **in print** (a) with precision (b) having read how to do it. In Jonson's *Alchemist*, Kastril, a young country heir, comes up to London 'to carry quarrels | As gallants do, and manage 'em, by line', i.e. according to the rules (2.6.63–4). 'A man in print' was proverbial (Tilley M239).

by the book formal, according to the rules. Among books on duelling published 1590–1600 were *The Booke of Honor and Armes* (1590), attrib. Sir William Segar, Giacomo di Grassi's *True Arte of Defence* (1594), Vincentio Saviolo's *Saviolo His Practise* (1594–5), which contains a section on 'the giving and receiving of the lie', and George Silver's *Paradoxes of Defence* (1599). In *The Courtier* (tr. 1561), Baldassare Castiglione refers to those who 'pass the matter in arguing and points' (repr. 1928, p. 49) and Touchstone is perhaps satirizing such men as much as those like Tybalt, who is so scornfully derided by Mercutio as 'a villain who fights by the book of arithmetic' (*Romeo* 3.1.102).

87 **books for good manners** of which there were many. Richard Whittinton's *Little Book of Good Manners* (1554), a translation of Erasmus's *De Civilitate Morum Puerilium*, Della Casa's *Galateo* (tr. Robert Peterson, 1576) and Hugh Rhodes's *Book of Nurture or School of Good Manners* (1577) were among them.

91 **Circumstance** circumlocution, beating about the bush

97 **swore brothers** swore a pact of brotherly love. A good phrase for this point in the play, after the reconciliation of Oliver and Orlando.

JAQUES (*to the Duke*) Is not this a rare fellow, my lord? He's as good at anything, and yet a fool.

DUKE SENIOR He uses his folly like a stalking-horse, and under the presentation of that he shoots his wit.

⌈Still Music.⌉ Enter Hymen with Rosalind and Celia as themselves

HYMEN

Then is there mirth in heaven
When earthly things made even
  Atone together.
Good Duke, receive thy daughter;
Hymen from heaven brought her,
  Yea, brought her hither,
That thou mightst join her hand with his
Whose heart within his bosom is.

102.1 *Still Music*] *after l. 102.2* F   102.1–2 *with . . . themselves*] *Rosalind in Woman's Cloth[e]s, and Celia* ROWE; *Rosalind, and Celia* F   109 her] F3 (*hir*); *his* F1

101 **stalking-horse** a real or imitation horse or a screen behind which the hunter hides so as not to alarm the quarry. 'To make one a stalking-horse' was proverbial (Tilley S816).

102 **presentation** theatrical . . . representation; a display, show, exhibition (*OED, presentation*, 5a): first instance of *presentation* in this sense cited by *OED*

102.1 ***Still music*** quiet, serious music. The marriage ceremony in *Kinsmen* is introduced by '*Still music of recorders*' (5.3.0.1), and they would be appropriate here. Hymen's verses have been set to music (e.g. by Thomas Arne, Henry Bishop) but that this was intended is unlikely, as all the songs in the play are clearly indicated. F places the stage direction after the entry, creating some ambiguity, as it could accompany it then continue as Hymen speaks.

Hymen The god of marriage. In Jonson's masque *Hymenaei* (1606) he enters accompanied by attendants and dressed in 'a saffron-coloured robe, his under-vestures white, his socks yellow, a yellow veil of silk on his left arm, his head crowned with roses, and marjoram, in his right hand a torch of pine tree' (ll. 49–52). While several productions of *As You Like It* from the eighteenth century on have omitted the god, others have turned his appearance into a climactic spectacle of song and dance (compare l. 135.1 n.). Macready (Drury Lane, 1842) had shepherds and shepherdesses with garlands and wreaths, boys and girls strewing flowers, a kind of temple erected on stage and one of the pages dressed as Hymen. Trevor Nunn's lavish presentation (RSC, 1977) had much line rearrangement, a great deal of singing, and a descending cloud machine which opened to reveal the god. There is further discussion of Hymen in the Introduction, pp. 19–20.

105 **Atone** unite, come together in harmony

107 **heaven** Compare Orlando's 'heavenly Rosalind!' (1.2.274) and note.

108 **hither** F's spelling, 'hether', provides a stronger rhyme.

109 **her** 'hir' in Elizabethan handwriting could easily be misread as 'his'. F's reading has been defended on the ground that Rosalind is still in boy's clothes, but her father, Orlando and Phoebe clearly indicate that they are seeing her as a woman. Malone also emended 'his' to 'her' in the next line; in performance, there is no room for doubt that Hymen means Rosalind's heart is in Orlando's bosom.

ROSALIND (*to the Duke*)
To you I give myself, for I am yours.
(*To Orlando*) To you I give myself, for I am yours.

DUKE SENIOR
If there be truth in sight, you are my daughter.

ORLANDO
If there be truth in sight, you are my Rosalind.

PHOEBE
If sight and shape be true,
Why then, my love adieu!

ROSALIND (*to the Duke*)
I'll have no father if you be not he.
(*To Orlando*) I'll have no husband if you be not he,
(*To Phoebe*) Nor ne'er wed woman if you be not she.

HYMEN
Peace, ho, I bar confusion.
'Tis I must make conclusion
Of these most strange events.
Here's eight that must take hands
To join in Hymen's bands,
If truth holds true contents.
(*To Orlando and Rosalind*)
You and you no cross shall part.
(*To Oliver and Celia*)
You and you are heart in heart.
(*To Phoebe*)
You to his love must accord,
Or have a woman to your lord.
(*To Touchstone and Audrey*)
You and you are sure together
As the winter to foul weather.—

114 **you** Orlando had consistently used 'thee' and 'thou' to Ganymede-as-Rosalind.

115 **shape** a person's body considered with regard to its appearance (*OED, shape, sb.* 6b): earliest instance of *shape* in this sense cited by *OED* is in 1601

123 **eight** More than at the end of any other Shakespearian comedy. In the Pythagorean theory of number, the tetrad (4) is especially important, as it provides a schema for the cosmos; the double tetrad is the numerical basis of the diapason, the scale of notes made up of eight tones, the highest and lowest of which, sounding together, represented complete consonance and harmony.

125 **If . . . contents** i.e. if the revelation of the true identities of Ganymede and Aliena brings real pleasures.

126 **cross** trouble, misfortune, adversity

128 **accord** consent

130 **sure** (a) certain, secure (b) married *Obs.* (*OED a.* † 7a)

Whiles a wedlock hymn we sing,
Feed yourselves with questioning,
That reason wonder may diminish
How thus we met, and these things finish.

Song

Wedding is great Juno's crown,
O blessèd bond of board and bed.
'Tis Hymen peoples every town.
High wedlock then be honourèd.
Honour, high honour and renown
To Hymen, god of every town.

DUKE SENIOR (*to Celia*)
O my dear niece, welcome thou art to me,
Even-daughter welcome, in no less degree.

PHOEBE (*to Silvius*)
I will not eat my word. Now thou art mine,
Thy faith my fancy to thee doth combine.

Enter Jaques de Boys, the second brother

JAQUES DE BOYS
Let me have audience for a word or two.
I am the second son of old Sir Rowland,
That bring these tidings to this fair assembly.
Duke Frederick, hearing how that every day
Men of great worth resorted to this forest,

143 Even-daughter] This edition (*conj.* Knowles); F (Euen daughter) 145.1 *Jaques . . . brother*] ROWE (Jaques de Boyes); *Second Brother* F 146, 178 JAQUES DE BOYS] ROWE (*Jaq. de B.*); 2. *Bro.* F

134 **reason . . . diminish** Seeking rational answers to recent past events may lessen, but will not dispel, wonder at them. Compare *Much Ado* 5.4.70: 'let wonder seem familiar'.

135.1 ***Song*** Sometimes given as a solo by Amiens, who is included in the block entry but has no lines in the scene, sometimes sung by several or all of the cast (see Appendix B).

136 **Juno's crown** the greatest glory of Juno, protector of women and goddess of marriage

138 **peoples** populates. In *Much Ado* Benedick rationalizes his decision to marry Beatrice by saying 'The world must be peopled' (2.3.229–30).

139 **High** (a) exalted (b) grave, serious

143 **Even-daughter** 'even as if you were my daughter'. A realization in reverse of Charles the wrestler's comment that at Frederick's court Rosalind was 'no less beloved of her uncle than his own daughter' (1.1.105–6). *OED* (Even- †2) gives examples including '*even*-disciple', '-servant', '-worker' with the sense of 'fellow-', Latin *co-*. Compare *Hamlet* 5.1.27–8: 'more than their even-Christian' (ed. G. R. Hibbard (Oxford, 1987)).

144 **eat my word** Proverbial (Tilley W825).

149–50 The news thus brought to Duke Frederick gives some justification to the large numbers of lords dressed as foresters with whom directors like Macready and Asche filled the stage.

Addressed a mighty power, which were on foot,
In his own conduct, purposely to take
His brother here, and put him to the sword.
And to the skirts of this wild wood he came
Where, meeting with an old religious man,
After some question with him was converted
Both from his enterprise and from the world,
His crown bequeathing to his banished brother,
And all their lands restored to them again
That were with him exiled. This to be true
I do engage my life.

DUKE SENIOR Welcome, young man.
Thou offer'st fairly to thy brothers' wedding:
To one his lands withheld, and to the other
A land itself at large, a potent dukedom.
First, in this forest let us do those ends
That here were well begun, and well begot.
And after, every of this happy number
That have endured shrewd days and nights with us
Shall share the good of our returnèd fortune
According to the measure of their states.
Meantime, forget this new-fallen dignity
And fall into our rustic revelry.
Play, music, and you brides and bridegrooms all,

159 them] ROWE; him F

151 **Addressed . . . power** prepared a mighty army

152 **In his own conduct** under his personal command

155 **old religious man** Johnson lamented that 'By hastening the end of this work, Shakespeare suppressed the dialogue between the usurper and the hermit, and lost an opportunity of exhibiting a moral lesson in which he might have found matter worthy of his highest powers.' The omission was rectified in prose and blank verse by Joseph Moser in 1809 with the help of 'Father Lodowick, a Friar of the Franciscan Order' and six other additional characters (*European Magazine*, 55, 345–52). In Lodge, the evil Torismond is slain in battle and his army put to flight by Gerismond, the brothers, and the twelve peers of France (fols. 65[r–v]).

162 **offer'st fairly** bringest a fine gift

163 **lands withheld** Duke Senior is unaware that Oliver has decided to give his lands to Orlando and stay in the forest; perhaps with the latest turn of fortune Oliver might change his mind. See 5.2.11n.

164 **at large** in full size (*OED, large*, C. *sb.* 5†a): first instance of *at large* in this sense cited by *OED*. The implication is that, by marrying Rosalind, Orlando has become Duke Senior's heir.

165 **do those ends** achieve those purposes

168 **shrewd** (a) fraught with evil or misfortune, and possibly (b) sharp, piercing, keen—a reminder of the 'winter wind' and 'bitter sky' of Amiens's song in 2.7. Earliest instance in *OED* in this sense is from 1642 (*shrewd*, *a.* 9b).

170 **According . . . states** in proportion to their rank.

171 **new-fallen** newly bestowed

With measure heaped in joy to th' measures fall.

JAQUES

Sir, by your patience. (*To Jaques de Boys*) If I heard you
rightly
The Duke hath put on a religious life
And thrown into neglect the pompous court.

JAQUES DE BOYS He hath.

JAQUES

To him will I. Out of these convertites
There is much matter to be heard and learned.
(*To the Duke*)
You to your former honour I bequeath;
Your patience and your virtue well deserves it.
(*To Orlando*)
You to a love that your true faith doth merit;
(*To Oliver*)
You to your land, and love, and great allies;
(*To Silvius*)
You to a long and well-deservèd bed;
(*To Touchstone*)
And you to wrangling, for thy loving voyage
Is but for two months victualled.—So, to your
pleasures;
I am for other than for dancing measures.

DUKE SENIOR Stay, Jaques, stay.

JAQUES

To see no pastime, I. What you would have

174 **measures** Dignified court dances, 'full of state and ancientry' as Beatrice says in *Much Ado* (2.1.69), such as pavans; they normally began the revels after a court masque, when the noble actors came down from the performing area to the audience and took out partners. Galliards, corantos and other more lively dances followed. A 'measure' was also a discrete section of a dance. Shakespeare puns on the word in *L.L.L.* (5.2.183–93) and *Romeo* (1.4.9–10) as well as here.

177 **pompous** full of pomp and splendour

179 **convertites** those converted to a religious life. Well-known convertites of the period included Charles V of France, who in 1555 gave up his title to live near the monastery of San Geronimo du Yuste in Spain, and the Duc de Joyeuse, who joined the Capuchin order in 1587, left it, then rejoined it in 1599.

184 **allies** relatives, kinsmen, or kinswomen

188 **I am . . . measures** A predictable remark, since the constitutionally melancholy were averse to dancing and music, being 'compact of jars' (2.7.5); as well, there is no partner for Jaques to lead in this marriage measure.

189 **Stay, Jaques, stay** The identical line occurs as 5.7.99 of Jonson's *The Case is Altered* (c.1597).

190 **What you would have** what you want me for

I'll stay to know at your abandoned cave. *Exit*

DUKE SENIOR

Proceed, proceed. We'll begin these rites
As we do trust they'll end, in true delights.
⌈*They dance; then*⌉ *exeunt all but Rosalind*

Epilogue

ROSALIND (*to the audience*) It is not the fashion to see the lady the epilogue; but it is no more unhandsome than to see the lord the prologue. If it be true that good wine needs no bush, 'tis true that a good play needs no epilogue. Yet to good wine they do use good bushes, and good plays prove the better by the help of good epilogues. What a case am I in then, that am neither a good epilogue nor cannot insinuate with you in the behalf of a good play! I am not furnished like a beggar, therefore to beg will not become me. My way is to conjure you; and I'll begin with the women. I charge you, O women, for the love you bear to men, to like as much of this play as please you. And I charge you, O men, for the love you bear to women—as I perceive

193 trust they'll end] POPE; trust, they'l end F
Epilogue] THEOBALD 1740; *not in* F
193.1 *They . . . Rosalind*] *A Dance* CAPELL; *Exit* F

192 **We'll begin** Most editors follow F2 and read 'we will begin', which completes the line metrically; Oxford reads 'we'll so begin' (*conj.* Maxwell). I take it that Duke Senior's 'Proceed, proceed' is called out after the departing Jaques; the next metrical unstressed beat is silent, as he turns back to the company, and the stress on 'we' emphasizes the difference between Jaques, who is staying in the forest, and the rest, who will take part in the communal rites of the marriage dance and then return to court. F's reading is more theatrically effective. Compare 1.3.136.

193.1 The dance that is plainly called for here should be happy but not too fast, and reflect Elyot's comment that 'In every dance, of a most ancient custom, there danceth together a man and woman, holding each other by the hand or the arm, which betokeneth concord' (p. 94).

F's *Exit* was omitted by F2, which added *Exeunt* after l. 21. Many editors and directors leave the whole company on stage when Rosalind steps forward to speak the Epilogue.

Epilogue Theobald (1740) first added the title 'Epilogue', and he has been followed by most editors since.

1 **not the fashion** As no epilogues spoken by women characters in earlier Elizabethan plays have been found, Rosalind's may well have been the first.

2 **unhandsome** unbecoming, unseemly. The earliest instance in *OED* is dated 1645.

3–4 **good . . . bush** good wine needs no advertisement. Proverbial (Tilley W462). A branch or bush of ivy (perhaps because it was sacred to Bacchus, god of wine) used to be hung up as a vintner's sign; hence *bush* came to mean a tavern-sign.

8 **insinuate with** work subtly on

9 **furnished** dressed. Rosalind is wearing a dress fit for a wedding.

11 **conjure** (a) make a solemn appeal (b) affect you by magic (referring to Ganymede's alleged magical powers)

by your simpering none of you hates them—that between you and the women the play may please. If I were a woman I would kiss as many of you as had beards that pleased me, complexions that liked me, and breaths that I defied not. And I am sure, as many as have good beards, or good faces, or sweet breaths, will for my kind offer, when I make curtsy, bid me farewell.

Exit

16 **the play** (a) *As You Like It* (b) love-making (which may well accord with the title)

16–17 **If . . . woman** Until the theatres in England reopened in 1660 after their suppression in 1642 women's roles were played by male actors, usually boys; here the actor draws attention to himself as a male more openly than in any other of Shakespeare's plays. In the modern theatre, actresses sometimes change the line, for example, to 'If I were among you'. For further discussion see Introduction, p. 20.

18 **liked** pleased

19 **breaths** Bad breath was a constant cause of concern (compare *Sonnets* 130.8: 'the breath that from my mistress reeks'). Della Casa advises, 'When a man talketh with one, it is no good manner to come so near, that he must needs breathe in his face; for there be many that cannot abide to feel the air of another man's breath, albeit there come no ill savour from him' (*Galateo*, tr. Robert Peterson (1576), pp. 14–15). Remedy was at hand, however, as Thomas Hill declares: 'There is nothing that doth like sweeten the mouth, as the fresh and green parsley eaten, so that the herb often eaten of them which have an unsavoury and stinking breath, and sendeth forth an odious smell to be abhorred, doth in short time marvellously recover and amend the same' (*The Gardener's Labyrinth* (1577), ed. Richard Mabey (Oxford, 1987), p. 142). The belief is still current.

defied rejected, disdained

21 **bid me farewell** applaud and so release me. Robin Goodfellow in *Dream* and Prospero in *Tempest* make similar appeals.

APPENDIX A
WIT

'WIT' is given thirteen main headings as a substantive in *OED*, but '†The sexual organs. *Obs.*' is not among them. There is, however, evidence in the plays of Shakespeare and his contemporaries, as well as elsewhere, that this was an accepted meaning of the period, and was used particularly in the context of bawdy jokes. In *Two Gentlemen*, for example, Speed reads out the qualities of Lance's sweetheart, who, like Touchstone's Jane Smile, is a milkmaid, a suggestive occupation in itself if the Jonson quotation below is taken into account. He concludes:

SPEED '*Item*, she hath more hair than wit'—
LANCE 'More hair than wit.' It may be. I'll prove it: the cover of the salt hides the salt, and therefore it is more than the salt. The hair that covers the wit is more than the wit, for the greater hides the less.

(3.1.348–52)

Shakespeare uses 'salt' as an adjective in the sense of 'lecherous' (*OED a.*[2] *Obs.* b) at least five times elsewhere, according to Colman (*The Dramatic Use of Bawdy in Shakespeare*, 1974, p. 212), who does not notice its use in *Two Gentlemen*, where it did however provoke Clifford Leech to remark in his Arden edition, 'In this speech the idea of pubic hair seems not far away.'

Romeo may not at first be in much of a joking mood when he meets his mates, yet he is making a sexual pun, listed by Frankie Rubinstein in *A Dictionary of Shakespeare's Sexual Puns and their Significance* (1984), when he says that the unattainable Rosaline 'hath Dian's wit' (*Romeo* 1.1.206), just as the husband of Juliet's nurse did when he laughed at the three-year-old Juliet who fell over and broke her brow: '"dost thou fall upon thy face? | Thou wilt fall backward when thou hast more wit"' (1.3.43–4). In a later passage 'wit' and 'wits' are used with a variety of meanings in quick succession, mostly in a bawdy context, as Mercutio, Romeo, and Benvolio outdo one another in witticisms (2.3.34–93); for example:

MERCUTIO Thy wit is very bitter sweeting, it is a most sharp sauce.
ROMEO And is it not then well served in to a sweet goose? (ll. 74–6)

Mercutio is saying (a) that Romeo's cleverness is sharp, like an apple used for a sauce (b) he is sexually keen, his penis at the ready; Romeo asks (a) is his cleverness then not a good accompaniment with a goose (i.e. a fool), as apple sauce is with a roast goose (b) is his sexual equipment not then just right for a doxy (*served* in the sexual sense; *goose* = 'prostitute').

In Ben Jonson's *Alchemist* (1607) Face says that the whore Doll Common, who is to seduce the disguised Surly,

> must prepare perfumes, delicate linen,
> The bath in chief, a banquet, and her wit,
> For she must milk his epididimis
>
> (3.3.20–2)

OED, which quotes this passage, defines *epididimis* as 'a long, narrow structure attached to the posterior border of the adjoining outer surface of the testicle, and consisting chiefly of coils of the efferent duct, which emerges from it as the vas deferens'; it carries sperm from the testicle during ejaculation.

Middleton's *More Dissemblers Besides Women* (1623) provides an example cognate with *As You Like It* 4.1.157–60; Dondolo has just been initiated into the gipsy band:

GIPSY CAPTAIN Wit, whither wilt thou?

DONDOLO Marry, to the next pocket I can come at: and if it be a gentleman's, I wish a whole quarter's rent in't. Is this my in dock, out nettle? What's gipsy for her?

GIPSY CAPTAIN Your doxy she. (4.1.230–5)

Here, *wit* means (a) penis (b) cleverness, and *pocket* (a) vulva (b) bag. In his note to the passage, Bullen writes, '"*In dock, out nettle*" was in Chaucer's time a proverb for inconstancy. Cf., *Troylus and Cryseyde*, b. iv. st. 62—

> "But kanstow pleyen raket, to and fro,
> *Nettle in dokke out*, now this, now that, Pandare?"'

Perhaps even more relevant is the beginning of his quotation from John Heywood's *Proverbs*—'*In dock out nettle*; | Now in, now out; ...' (Middleton, *Works*, 8 vols. (1885–6), vi. 444), an allusion presumably to the alleviation of pain from the sting of the nettle by the application of bruised dock leaves.

In a later example from Brome's *The Court Beggar* (1640), the hero, in challenging the villain, who has attempted to gain the hero's beloved, casts a savage slur on his manhood:

> Charissa who was mine in faith and honour
> Till you ignobly (which is damnably)
> By a false promise with intent to whore her
> Diverted her weak father from the match
> To my eternal loss. Now whether you
> Have wit or no wit to deny't, or stand to't,
> ... I'll fight or kill you.
>
> (*Dramatic Works*, 1873, I, 248)

In the context of 'whore' and 'stand', *wit* carries its sexual meaning as well as the meaning 'intelligence', given by 'deny't'.

Further evidence for this sense of 'wit', which informs the wordplay of Touchstone's complaint at 3.3.9–12 and the *badinage* of Orlando and Rosalind at 4.1.152–61, may be found in Cotgrave's *Dictionarie of the French and English Tongues* (1611), which gives '*vit*: m. a man's yard [i.e., penis]; a beasts pizle' and '*vite*: f. a woman's &c'. In his *English Pronunciation 1500–1700* (Oxford, 1968) E. J. Dobson says under 'Wit/vit' that the change [v] > [w] 'had currency in vulgar London English ... the sound change in the South East was from [v] to [w]' (2, 948, §374).

APPENDIX B

THE SONGS

SONGS were part of the pastoral mode. *Rosalynde* contains six, seven if Montanus's sonnet in French is sung, and there are five in *As You Like It*—more than in any previous play by Shakespeare. All of them are related to the mood or thought of the play at the particular point where they occur, but there can be no certainty that, if the play was performed when it was written, the appropriate tunes that survive from the period were used.

When it was produced in 1740 Thomas Arne composed music for 'Under the greenwood tree', 'Blow, blow thou winter wind' and 'When daisies pied', which was introduced from *Love's Labour's Lost*. Several other songs were inserted in subsequent productions, even though those original to the text were omitted. A playbill for the Theatre Royal, York, for example, announced that on 14 May 1789 Celia and Phoebe, as well as Amiens, had songs, and Act 1 ended with 'A Hornpipe, by Mr Lassells', who had no part in the play.[1]

In 1824 Frederick Reynolds produced at Drury Lane an 'operatized' version with words from other Shakespearian plays and poetry, set to music or arranged by Henry Bishop. Reynolds was following a successful precedent he had begun in 1816, with *A Midsummer Night's Dream. Twelfth Night*, *The Tempest*, *Two Gentlemen of Verona* and *The Merry Wives of Windsor* had all received similar treatment, the text cut and altered to accommodate spectacular staging, dances and songs.

In any one play the songs themselves could differ between productions. At Drury Lane on 25 November 1824, for example, the music for *As You Like It* included the following 'Songs from Shakespeare's Poetry, arranged by Mr. H. R. Bishop': 'By the simplicity of Venus' Doves' (*Dream* 1.1.171 ff.), 'Under the Greenwood Tree', 'Blow, thou Winter's wind', 'What shall he have that kill'd the Deer?', 'When that I was a tiny little [*sic*] Boy' (*Twelfth Night* 5.1.385–404), 'Come thou Monarch of the Vine' (*Antony* 2.7.110–15), 'In black mourn I' (*P. Pilgrim*, Sonnet 17.13 ff.), 'When Daisies pied' (*L.L.L.* 5.2.879–96), 'Tell me where is Fancy bred' (*Merchant* 3.2.63–72), 'Lo, hear [*sic*] the gentle Lark' (*Venus* 853–6) and a final glee, 'Oh, happy Fair' (*Dream* 1.1.182 ff.). In the fifth Act 'An Allegorical Dance and Chorus of Aeriel Spirits' was introduced in place of Hymen's song, and the evening finished with a farce, *Children in the Wood*.[2] At the Haymarket on 23 May 1825, when Madame Vestris played

[1] Birmingham Shakespeare Library, Playbills, *As You Like It*, vol. 2, p. 157.
[2] Ibid., vol. 1, p. 248.

Rosalind for the first time,[3] the songs were a duet for Celia and Rosalind, 'Whilst inconstant Fortune smil'd' from Richard Barnfield's 'As it fell upon a day' (formerly attributed to Shakespeare, in *P. Pilgrim*), 'Oh! [*sic*] Time, thou shalt not boast' (*Sonnets* 123) from Celia, a glee and chorus, 'Ee'n [*sic*] as the Sun' (*Venus* 1–6) to open Act 2, and another, 'Lo! in the Orient, when the gracious light' (Sonnet 7) to close it, as well as Amiens's two songs, 'If love had [*sic*] lent you Twenty Thousand tongues' (*Venus* 775 ff.) and 'When daisies pied' for Rosalind in Act 4 and 'Then is there mirth in Heaven' for Hymen in Act 5. After the play came a pastoral ballet, *Love and Madness!*, and a farce, *The Mayor of Garratt*.

The vogue for these kinds of productions lasted until 1833, the last being another *Midsummer Night's Dream*, though Reynolds was not, apparently, implicated. Odell remarks that the developing taste for real opera and the return of 'the genuine plays . . . banished this bastard art to the limbo of forgotten things'.[4] The most 'operatic' modern version was Trevor Nunn's 1977 Stratford production. It did not import additional material, but several parts of the text as well as the songs were set to music by Stephen Oliver. (See Introduction, p. 68.)

The many musical settings for the play's five original songs are listed in the *Shakespeare Music Catalogue*, edited by Bryan Gooch and David Thatcher (Oxford, 1991), where the music relating to *As You Like It* appears under entries 387–2017. The following settings, in which several variations to the wording in F occur, are accepted as the earliest available.

(i) *Under the Greenwood Tree* (2.5.1 ff.)

No contemporary setting has survived, the earliest being Thomas Arne's for the 1740 Drury Lane production, published in his collection *The Songs in the Comedies called As you Like It, and Twelfth Night* (1741).

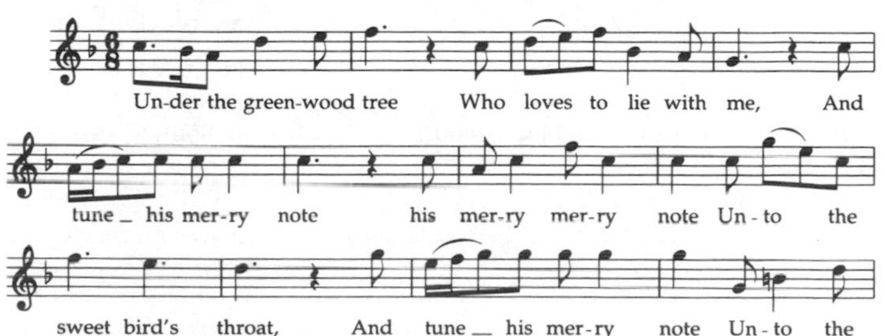

[3] Ibid., vol. 2, p. 2.

[4] George C. D. Odell, *Shakespeare from Betterton to Irving*, 2 vols. (New York, 1920; repr. 1966), ii. 148.

(ii) *Blow, blow, thou winter wind* (2.7.175 ff.)

Arne's setting, which is again the earliest, and also published in *The Songs in the Comedies* . . . (1741), does not include the refrain beginning 'Hey-ho, Sing hey-ho', which was probably not sung on the stage until early in the nineteenth century; only the words set by Arne are included, for instance, in the prompt book edition of the Drury Lane production of the play with Mrs Siddons (R. Butters [1785?]). The first music for the complete song appeared as a four-part setting in R. J. S. Stevens's *Eight Glees Expressly for Ladies* [1793]. The first solo setting of the refrain was added to Arne's music by William Linley, who included it in his *Shakspeare's Dramatic Songs* (2 vols., 1816), the earliest edited collection of songs from the plays. In doing so, Linley himself omitted the word 'sing', and transposed Arne's B♭ setting down to F.

(iii) *O Sweet Oliver* (3.3.89 ff.)

Although the complete words have not survived, a ballad of this title was sung to a tune called both 'The Hunt's Up' and 'Peascod Time', versions of which date from *c.*1570–1666. A version in 4/4 time, from a collection of lute music compiled by Adrian Smout in Leyden

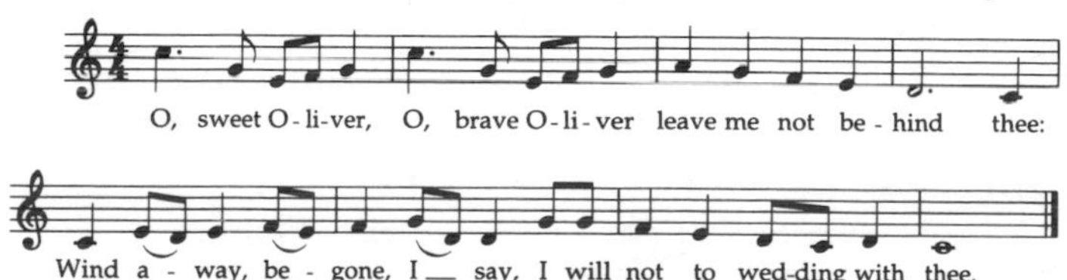

1595–1601 and published as *Het Luitboek van Thysius* (ed. J. P. N. Land, Amsterdam (1882–92)), suits the words better than those in English sources, which are usually in 6/8 or 6/4 time.

(iv) *What shall he have that killed the deer?* (4.2.10 ff.)

The earliest setting for this song is a catch, or round, for four voices in John Hilton's compilation, *Catch as Catch Can: A Choice Collection of Catches, Rounds and Canons* (1652, p. 30). As it does not include the textually puzzling 'Then sing him home; the rest shall bear | This burden', the catch setting could not have been used in any early performances of the play, if there were any, which used the text as printed in the Folio.

During the nineteenth century the song became the excuse for rousing spectacle. At Stratford in 1879, for example, it allowed for a procession with a slain deer, taken from the herd at Charlecote where Shakespeare was, according to myth, believed to have poached a buck; the deer was subsequently stuffed and appeared regularly until Playfair's production (1919). The scene has at times been turned into a bloody pagan rite (e.g. in John Dexter's National Theatre production (1979)) and Adrian Noble made it the occasion of a dream related to growing into adulthood, by Celia, who remained asleep on stage throughout (RSC, 1985).

(v) *It was a lover and his lass* (5.3.15 ff.)

The earliest music for this, perhaps the best-known and most frequently-sung song from Shakespeare's plays, is in Thomas Morley's setting, for voice, lute, and bass-viol, published in his *First Booke of Ayres or Little Short Songs, to Sing and Play for the Lute* (1600). No other setting for a Shakespeare song was printed so close in time to the date of the respective play's composition; but Morley's music could have been written before *As You Like It*. F. W. Sternfeld suggests in a letter (8 Sept. 1990) that the text and the music are 'indebted to popular tradition. . . . The syllabic word-setting, the intertwining between stanzas proper and refrain, the nature of the melodic line . . . all seem to point in that direction.'

(vi) *Wedding is great Juno's crown* (5.4.136 ff.)

Thomas Chilcot, a West Country organist, included this in his *Twelve English Songs* [1743], which also sets words from six other Shakespeare plays.

INDEX

This is a selective guide to significant points in the Introduction and Commentary. Biblical illustrations are grouped together, as are proverbial parallels and instances of punning. Citations from Shakespearian and other texts are listed if the parallels they provide are striking. An asterisk indicates that the note supplements information given in the *OED*.